Winners and Losers

A volume in the series

Cornell Studies in Political Economy

EDITED BY PETER J. KATZENSTEIN

A full list of titles in the series appears at the end of the book.

Winners and Losers

HOW SECTORS SHAPE
THE DEVELOPMENTAL PROSPECTS
OF STATES

D. MICHAEL SHAFER

CORNELL UNIVERSITY PRESS

Ithaca and London

First published 1994 by Cornell University Press.

Printed in the United States of America

♾ The paper in this book meets the minimum requirements of the American National Standard for Information Sciences—Permanence of Paper for Printed Library Materials, ANSI Z39.48-1984.

Library of Congress Cataloging-in-Publication Data

Shafer, D. Michael, 1953–
    Winners and losers : how sectors shape the developmental prospects of states / D. Michael Shafer.
        p.   cm. — (Cornell studies in political economy)
    Includes bibliographical references and index.
    ISBN 0-8014-3000-3 (alk. paper). — ISBN 0-8014-8188-0 (pbk.)
    1. Developing countries—Economic policy—Case studies.   2. Developing countries—Industries—Case studies.   I. Title.   II. Series.
HC59.7.S4462   1994
338.9′1′091724—dc20   94-10383

Dedicated to my children
Moon Hee, Byung Bum, Jeong Deok,
and Jeong Hwan

Contents

Preface

This book began by accident but has become an effort to pull together several widely divergent intellectual and personal, substantive
and theoretical concerns. In 1981, when I should have been starting a
dissertation on military intervention in the Third World, another
member of the Harvard-M.I.T. Research Seminar on Africa suggested that someone ought to investigate the effects of nationalization
in Africa. I was that someone. A study of Zaire and Zambia, two of the
biggest nationalizers, seemed appropriate. I knew next to nothing
about either, and nothing at all about economics, political economy, or
mining. Worse, I came to the project with a head full of unexamined
notions about multinational corporations, nationalization, and Africa's place in the world that I had picked up in college. What I learned
writing "Capturing the Mining Multinationals" (*International Organization* 37 [Winter 1983]) changed all that—and changed my concerns
as a social scientist, too.

Having majored in African history, I saw Africa as special, but by
1981 so did everyone else—for all the wrong reasons. Whenever development was discussed, comments ended with a dismissive "Of
course, this doesn't apply in Africa." Indeed, the belief that failure
was overdetermined in Africa was so entrenched that many *Africanists*
abandoned efforts to explain Africa in general terms, a sad state of
affairs when one considers the preeminence of Africanist scholarship
in the evolution of political science and development economics. Like
the others, I began work assuming that to understand Zaire and Zambia, one had to start there. But the more I learned, the clearer it
became that understanding Zaire and Zambia required understand-

ing the mining industry and metals markets. These—not Humanism, Mobutu's kleptocracy, or the deformations wrought by colonialism— formed the analytic bedrock. And as I looked further, first to other African mining states, then to Latin America and beyond, I realized that Zaire and Zambia were variations on a theme, that much of what seemed special about them was special only if viewed in isolation, that what *did* make them unique could be appreciated only when measured against a more universal metric.

This simple realization sent me off in two directions, one methodological and the other substantive. First, it made me take the comparative method seriously and reject the common practice of "comparative" politics as the study of (one) country that is not the United States. Further, it made me take explanation and causality seriously and reject the common practice of "explanation" by classification into semantic categories. This book embodies my effort to construct a truly comparative, causal theory of the political economy of development, a theory that lives up to the expectations born of my chance encounter with Zaire and Zambia and my frustration with the inadequacy of the tools I found for analyzing them. I offer a single causal logic and, built on it, a parsimonious typology that encourages structured comparisons among cases. The theory provides, I hope, an explanatory common ground for comparison, permitting us to identify what is unique to each case, as well as an explanation of change within and among states, permitting us to make cross-sectional and longitudinal comparisons.

Substantively, the realization that Zaire and Zambia shared much with other mining states *as mining states* led to two questions: If mining structures mining states' domestic political economies in distinctive ways, and international mineral markets structure their engagement in the international economy in distinctive ways, do other industries structure states' domestic and international circumstances as distinctively? And, if so, what shared logic or causal process would permit meaningful comparisons of countries in different categories? A glance at the plantation and peasant cash crop industries of Africa suggested that the answer to the first question was yes; this book offers to the second an answer that meets my self-imposed methodological standards. In fact, it is really my attempt to answer a bigger, more general question: What determines which states, under what conditions, will be able to do how much to further development and improve their standing in the international division of labor?

This question raises the issue of agency and its limits. Whether the context is development writ large, or debt, stabilization, and structural adjustment, or the de-development of Africa, the issue of agency is unavoidable. It is *the* issue in the contest of contending explanations that pits structures and disembodied forces against individuals and self-interest. It is also *the* issue in the nasty North-South battle over who's to blame. I find the first fight sterile and the second offensive, especially in the context of applied policy analysis. Of course structures matter, but structures do not act, people do; of course self-interested individuals make things go, but they do not act in a vacuum, they act in settings largely not of their own making. Put crudely, what either/or analytic permits us to appreciate *both* the corruption of many African leaders, their responsibility for the disaster they have wrought, *and* the overwhelming task they face and the extent to which their behavior is perfectly rational given their circumstances? Which analytic would permit us to appreciate both the quality of East Asian leadership and policy choices *and* the conspiracy of circumstances that makes their task so much easier than that confronting the leaders of Africa?

The problem, therefore, is to offer an explanation *with* and *of* structures *and* agents. Such an explanation must specify the variability across cases of the structures actors confront and act through at a given time (how confining are they? what opportunities do they offer? how flexible are they?), and it must identify the actors and specify the nature and intensity of their interests. It must also specify why, how, and how much structures and actors and their interests change over time. For this project, the problem is to offer an explanation that accounts for the patterned stratification of Third World countries at any given time and that, over time, accounts for the curve of countries' development trajectories and the speed and extent of their divergence. Again, this book is my attempt to sketch one such explanation.

A last note, of a different sort: the historian Jack Hexter somewhere observes that there are two basic types of scholars, lumpers and splitters. I am not a particularly good lumper or splitter, however. This book will offend all of you who know anything about economics, industrial organization, trade unions, tea, any of the countries I study—indeed, anything I touch on, for you surely know more about them than I. No doubt my lumping tendencies have done damage, some of it serious, to subjects and arguments close to your hearts. But then, I've got a synthetic argument to make and, to be fair, should be held blameless unless, having gotten some detail wrong at the margin, I have, in fact, gotten the big argument wrong, too. This book will also offend lumpers. It is too messy, too cluttered. It has too many variables and too much data. It lacks the otherworldly purity of game theory or the elegance of, for example, Ronald Rogowski's extraordinary *Commerce and Coalitions*. But then, with Mies van der Rohe, I think that "God is in the details."

This book is testimony to the intellectual, institutional, and personal debts I have accumulated in the twelve years it took me to write it. The first debt is to three men I have never met or spoken to, but whose work informs every dimension of mine: Jeffrey Paige, Robert Brenner, and Peter Gourevitch. I do not know how to thank them, except to say that but for *Agrarian Revolution*, "The Origins of Capitalist Development," and *Politics in Hard Times*, this book would never have been written. To Alex George, whom I have met only in passing, I also owe thanks. Without his many important contributions to the literature on the comparative method and on social science epistemology more broadly, my work would be much less cogent. To the other members of the Harvard-M.I.T. Research Seminar on Africa—Mary Hildebrand, Masilo Mbeta, Joshua Mvumbu, Dov Ronen, Bob Rotberg, and especially Brian Levy, who introduced me to the intricacies of multinational mining—I owe the project's very inception.

Many other scholars helped shape this book directly, offering comments, criticisms, warnings, and encouragement. In particular, I thank Bob Bates, Richard Bensel, Rick Doner, Jorge Dominguez, Jeff Freiden, Steph Haggard, Terry Karl, David Lake, Charlie Lipson, Joel Migdal, Helen Milner, John Odell, Duncan Snidal, Ray Vernon, Tom Willett, and Ernie Wilson. I owe special thanks to my colleagues Pedro Caban, Ken Finegold, Bob Kaufman, and Ed Rhodes, who have suffered with this project for as long as they have known me. Finally, I owe a great deal to many of my students. Juliet Johnson provided valuable research assistance. Bill Clark and Bill Robinson forced me to modify or fashion new defenses for big chunks of the argument as a result of brutally honest critiques that I hope (I suppose) will appear in print soon. Ken Gilmore and Mehdi Khajenouri are reworking sectoral analysis in dissertations. And then there are the students in my research seminar—Paul Abood, Andrea Bell, Stacy Berger, Bob Berndt, Phil Corbo, Aimee Feldman, Lewis Goldberg, Steve Gordon,

Moon Sook Kim, Trâm Ahn Le, Richard Leavy, Melissa Rosen, Nilofer Shaikh, Liz Smith, Andy Stillufson, Robert Throckmorton, and Lona Valmoro—whose case studies of Chile, Jamaica, the Philippines, and El Salvador gave me so much worry and so much hope.

Equally important are the many men and women in Korea, Sri Lanka, and Zambia who took the time to talk with me—sometimes at risk to themselves. Since many of my informants (especially the many labor and political organizers I interviewed) requested anonymity, I will name no one. But to all of them, those whose words you will read and those whose words merely inform my conclusions, I owe so much.

Lengthy projects also require institutional succor and exposure, and mine was no exception. Without Rutgers University support— and money—this book would have died on the vine. Without the support of Korea University, Colombo University, and the University of Zambia, I could not have completed my fieldwork. In particular, without the invaluable assistance of Park Shin-Il, now consul general of Korea in Boston, I would not have been able to carry out my work in Korea; without the warmth and hospitality of my Korean hosts, Chung Tai Si and Sookchul Shin, my months in Korea would have been far less pleasant. In Sri Lanka, Patrick Panabokke, superintendent of the renowned Geragama Estate, hosted me for weeks and answered all my questions, no matter how ill informed; Dayasiri Warnakulasooriya, restauranteur and founder, owner, and manager of the Midaya Ceramics Company, fed me, housed me, and taught me about entrepreneurialism, Sri Lankan-style. In Zambia, the gentlemanly John Mwanakatwe generously shared his deep personal knowledge of modern Zambian history and politics; James Mtonga explained how the Zambian policy process worked and opened door after door for me; and James Mazyopa took me out to the mining townships to drink with miners and hear their wonderful stories. And without the opportunities I had to try out ideas at the PIPES seminar at the University of Chicago, the international political economy seminars at Columbia University, UCLA, and the University of Southern California, and as a speaker at the Research Program in Development Studies at Princeton University, my argument would be much less nuanced.

Bits and pieces of my argument, some bigger than others, have appeared in various scholarly journals. I would especially like to acknowledge *Comparative Politics* for permission to reprint portions of "Sectors, States, and Social Forces: Korea and Zambia Confront Economic Restructuring" (vol. 22 [January 1990]) and the MIT Press for permission to reprint portions of "Capturing the Mining Multinationals," *International Organization* 37, no. 1 (Winter 1983). I must also acknowledge *Third World Quarterly* for its grudging agreement to allow me to reprint portions of "Undermined: The Implications of Mineral Export Dependence for State Formation in Africa" (vol. 8 [Summer 1986]).

Then there's the hard truth of the academic life: books have to get published. Roger Haydon, now an editor at Cornell, first met me and my project when, hat in hand, I brought Zaire and Zambia to *International Organization.* He had to see to it that the finished version was rather better than the original, and perhaps for that reason it took the best, subtle efforts of my literary agent, Leona Schecter, to get him to buy the book for Cornell. Since that day long ago, he has shown remarkable patience as I have let deadline after deadline slip by. For his part, Peter Katzenstein, the series editor, has offered pages of useful comments, but really endeared himself to me forever at our very first meeting by his response to my hasty and nervous précis of the argument: "Ah, the book Jim Kurth didn't write!"

Finally, and most important, I owe a huge debt to my wife, Evelind Schecter, and my children, Moon Hee, Byung Bum, Jeong Deok, and Jeong Hwan, who have had to suffer the sorrows of this book's writing without tasting any of the rewards. Of course, if I had had fewer dinners to cook, fewer tutoring sessions to drive to, fewer essays to proofread, fewer doctors' appointments to make, fewer squabbles to adjudicate—in short, if I weren't the father of four teenagers—I would have finished a lot sooner. But it wouldn't have been worth the effort.

D. MICHAEL SHAFER

New Brunswick, New Jersey

Winners and Losers

CHAPTER ONE

Old Questions, New Answers

Soon after arriving in America, my daughters, Moon Hee and Jeong Deok, then ages eleven and nine, asked, "If Korea has no gold or oil, how come it's so rich?" Their question captured an intriguing irony: the perverse, inverse relationship between natural resource wealth and economic development in the Third World. How do we explain the success of resource-poor Korea and the stagnation of copper-rich Zambia and tea-infused Sri Lanka? In the extreme, how do we explain OPEC founder Juan Pablo Perez Alfonso's judgment concerning oil and its impact on Venezuela: "It is the devil's excrement. We are drowning in the devil's excrement"?[1]

Hidden in this conundrum is a more general issue. For decades we focused on North-South issues; today we must explain differentiation *within* the Third World. The economic crises of the 1970s and 1980s disclosed sharp differences in states' capacities to implement policies to limit the damage inflicted by exogenous shocks, to promote adjustment and to seize opportunities in international markets. Comparisons of states' past performances and adjustment efforts also reveal patterns, groupings of states with distinct developmental trajectories and abilities to shape their futures.

These differences raise a question that has long stumped political economists: What determines which states, under what conditions, will be able to do how much to further development and improve their standing in the international division of labor? How do external

---

[1] Perez quoted in Terry Lynn Karl, *The Paradox of Plenty* (Berkeley: University of California Press, forthcoming).

1

and internal forces interact to influence the crises states confront and their ability to respond? What explains change over time and whether states can shape its course? And are the answers to these questions unique to each state, or are there patterns from which we might construct a theory of comparative political economy that predicts the development projects different classes of states must undertake, the challenges they face, and their prospects for success?

To answer these questions we need a new approach. It must link the international and domestic arenas with a single logic, and offer a parsimonious typology that encourages structured comparisons among cases—that is, it must provide an explanatory common ground for comparison, permitting us to identify what is unique to each case. It must address the interests of public and private individuals, their prospects for collective action, and the effects of the organizations they form when they can collaborate, as well as the effects of the absence of such organizations when they cannot. It must enable us to categorize states' ties to the international market, and thus specify the economic restructuring project they must undertake and gauge its difficulty. It must also let us judge states' autonomy and capacity to make the needed changes, the resources available to them, and the nature, location, and potency of resistance. Finally, it must permit cross-sectional and longitudinal comparisons by offering an explanation of change (or stasis) within and among states.

This book offers one such approach: sectoral analysis. I argue that a state's capacity to get ahead depends on the attributes of the leading sector through which it is tied to the international economy: light manufacturing, mineral extraction, peasant cash crop production, or industrial plantation crop production. Particular sectoral attributes result in distinct international market structures, each of which rewards different kinds of actors, presents different opportunities and risks, and demands a different strategy. They also influence firms' ability to pursue the required strategies and states' capacity to help. Market structures and the prospects for successful pursuit of the strategies they demand together suggest an outline of the characteristic crises states in a sector face and the restructuring project they must undertake: how they must reallocate resources and reorient economic activity to decrease the risks and increase the gains from international engagement.

States' ability to restructure depends on the tractability of the restructuring project they face and the domestic political economy of the leading sector. Sectoral attributes determine the difficulty of the restructuring project, its implications for the state and sectoral actors, and the location, nature, and intensity of support or opposition. They also result in distinct patterns of state institutional capabilities, and of interest groups with sectorally determined interests and collective-action capabilities. These interact to produce distinct patterns of state autonomy and relative capacity. Sectoral analysis thus explains how different sectors affect the relative autonomy and capacity of the state vis-à-vis leading-sector actors, and the size and political weight of other actors with which the state can ally itself to increase its autonomy and capacity relative to leading-sector elites as it seeks to restructure.

In theory, then, *inter*sectoral differences explain the patterned variation in states' development trajectories and capacity for adjustment. By providing an explanatory common ground, sectoral analysis also highlights the unique features of individual countries that account for *intra*sectoral variation. Further, in a given case and at a given time, sectoral analysis explains the interests of state and societal elites, the relative autonomy of the former from the latter, and their relative capacities. Over time, it allows us to trace the recursive relationship between state action, the changing sectoral composition of the economy, and its implications for future state action.

Most of you probably recognize my argument's genealogy.[2] You may also recognize its ties to other approaches—dependency, neo-classical, statist—and its challenges to them. For now, I shall focus on sectoral analysis, which, after all, is still unstated and unproven. But fear not, I take up comparisons in Chapter 7. Before we start, however, I have questions to answer about states, actors, sectors, and restructuring.

[2] Alexander Gerschenkron, *Economic Backwardness in Historical Perspective* (Cambridge: Harvard University Press, 1962); James Kurth, "The Political Consequences of the Product Cycle," *International Organization* 33 (Winter 1979); Jeffrey Paige, *Agrarian Revolution* (New York: Free Press, 1975); Robert Brenner, "The Origins of Capitalist Development," *New Left Review* (August 1977); Thomas Ferguson, "From Normalcy to New Deal: Industrial Structure, Party Competition, and American Public Policy in the Great Depression," *International Organization* 38 (Winter 1984); Peter Gourevitch, *Politics in Hard Times* (Ithaca: Cornell University Press, 1986); Ronald Rogowski, *Commerce and Coalitions* (Princeton: Princeton University Press, 1989); Jeffry Frieden, *Debt, Development, and Democracy* (Princeton: Princeton University Press, 1991); and Karl, *The Paradox of Plenty*.

STATES AND ACTORS

The first question is, Why the state? In part, the answer is simply because it's there, an obviously important player in daily life. Since the 1800s, publics have increasingly held leaders accountable for their country's economic performance, a tendency exaggerated by the Keynesian revolution and the rise of the welfare state. Since 1945, surging trade and capital flows have added a new urgency to public expectations of the state. And such expectations are highest in the Third World, where many view the state as *the* agent of change. But there are more valid reasons.

Ties to international markets invite domestic disruption, for markets are subject to often violent changes that states cannot control. States try to ameliorate the resulting hurts and manipulate their international market ties to national advantage. But both aims demand a big role for the state in the economy. Where the cost of restructuring to manage market shocks exceeds private means, or where market failure blocks needed investments, states may assume an entrepreneurial role. To promote export-led growth, they may attack vested interests to free resources for more productive uses, encourage new economic actors, and create competitive advantages for national firms. When successful, such actions may alter the international marketplace itself. In short, the state not only mediates between the international and domestic arenas but is a player in both.

Two problems loom, however: the functionalism of assertions about the necessity of the state, and the problematic notion of "the state" as an actor. It may be that state action is critical in successful economic development. But to stop here is to risk falling into the functionalist trap of also assuming that necessity begets reality. It does not, and thus we must define the state and specify what determines states' ability to do what they do.

But defining "the state" is hard. Once when confronted with a particularly reified definition in a conference paper he had been asked to discuss, Robert Bates observed, "When I start a new piece of research, the first thing I ask myself is, 'Who should I take to lunch?' Reading this paper I asked myself, 'How do I take 'the state' to lunch?'"[3] The skeptical reader already has similar questions in mind: What is "the state" as the term is used here? Is it an enduring set of

[3] Comments by Bates on a paper at the Annual Meeting of the American Political Science Association (Washington, D.C., August 30–September 2, 1984).

4

roles and institutions? A specific government? A collection of individuals in office? Indeed, is "it" anything at all, distinct from social or foreign forces and possessing sufficient coherence to be considered an actor? And what does it mean to ascribe agency to it if it is and does?

The argument *against* giving the state explanatory weight is well entrenched.[4] Many theorists reduce states to reflections of international or social forces and view state policies as the result of individual, interest group, or class action. The literature on bureaucratic politics poses additional challenges. After all, the assertion that "the state" acts is an assertion of institutional coherence as well as one of autonomy, and it forces us to "picture the state . . . as making choices on the basis of some *collective* interest or intention."[5] Yet states are complex organizations with many divisions, which may have conflicting aims, compete for resources to meet national and organizational goals, and be staffed by individuals whose actions have organizational and personal as well as state motivations. The state thus may have little coherence, and state policy may be no more than a composite of actions taken by the state's separate parts; whereas *who* the state is, and what their interests and intentions are, may vary dramatically depending on whom one takes to lunch.

But these attacks obscure the task at hand. Their target is a reified definition of the state from which analysis precedes as if the act of definition itself gave substance to the state. Such arguments define the state as some*thing* and not as a *variable*. At issue here, however, is not the state but "stateness": the extent to which, and the conditions under which, it is possible to give explanatory weight to the state. Thus, following Alfred Stepan's definition, the state "is the continuous administrative, legal, bureaucratic and coercive system that *attempts* not only to manage the state apparatus but to structure relations between civil and public power and to structure many crucial relations within civil and political society."[6] Our focus, therefore, is

[4] Hence the splash caused by Peter Evans, Dietrich Rueschemeyer, and Theda Skocpol, eds., *Bringing the State Back In* (New York: Cambridge University Press, 1985). See James March and Johan Olsen, "The New Institutionalism," *American Political Science Review* 78 (September 1984): 734–49; Gabriel Almond, "The Return to the State," and Eric Nordlinger, "Critique of 'Return to the State,'" *American Political Science Review* 82 (September 1988): 853–75 and 875–85.

[5] March and Olsen, "The New Institutionalism," 738–39. Emphasis added.

[6] Alfred Stepan, *Rethinking Military Politics* (Princeton: Princeton University Press, 1988), 4. Emphasis added.

5

fixed on the operative word "attempts," on explaining states' differing degrees of stateness.

In this, two tasks confront us. First, we must identify the essential elements of stateness and offer a general, theoretically grounded explanation for why different states have more or less of them. Second, we must evade the agentless explanation trap, since individuals, not states, desire and act, and patterned variation in their aims and actions explain observed variations among states. We thus also require a general, theoretically grounded explanation of individuals' varying motivations, of how they aggregate, and of how the institutions that result reshape their motivations and capacity for collective action.

THE ELEMENTS OF STATENESS

The answers to three questions define a state's stateness: Can the state formulate policy goals independent of particular groups within its own society? Can the state change the behavior of specific groups? and Can the state directly change the structure of the society in which it operates?[7] Underlying these questions are the three defining elements of stateness, each of which is variable: autonomy, absolute capacity, and relative capacity. Because these terms are so central to the argument—and because they are so often used so promiscuously—it is important to provide explicit, theoretically grounded definitions of each as it will be used here.

Autonomy

Autonomy is the extent to which the state is not merely an arena for conflict but is distinct from nonstate actors. It is the extent to which leaders "are capable of organizationally insulating themselves from societal pressures by controlling channels of interest representation and autonomously defining national tasks."[8] Absent autonomy, it is pointless to discuss the state at all.

[7] Stephen Krasner, "United States Commercial and Monetary Policy," in *Between Power and Plenty,* ed. Peter Katzenstein (Madison: University of Wisconsin Press, 1978), 60.
[8] Stephan Haggard and Chung-In Moon, "The South Korean State in the International Economy," in *The Antimonies of Interdependence,* ed. John Ruggie (New York: Columbia University Press, 1983), 141.

6

Definition, however, is but half the problem. We must also specify under what conditions autonomy is possible, and we must locate state autonomy in "political space" by explaining the identity of the actors from which states must make themselves autonomous, the nature of their demands of the state and of the state's demands of them, the identity and interests of subordinate groups, and states' prospects for turning to them as allies against the dominant societal elites.

Sectoral analysis argues that sectoral attributes are the best starting point for explanations of autonomy. They explain the difficulty leaders have controlling channels of interest representation by defining state-society relations, the depth of sectoral actors' penetration of the state, and whether state agencies are advocates for sectoral interests. By defining the tractability of restructuring, its implications for different actors, their differing capacities for collective action, and the potency of other sectors, sectoral attributes also determine how much societal pressure the state must bear. Finally, sectoral attributes determine whether leaders can define a state interest that is distinct from sectoral interests and that approximates the national interest.

Absolute Capacity and Relative Capacity

Autonomy is not enough; states must be able to act. But whereas autonomy is always relative, it is useful to think of state capacity as both absolute and relative. Absolute capacity is the extent to which the state has the authority and means to extract and deploy resources; a technocratic, meritocratic, and internally cohesive bureaucracy; and effective monitoring and regulatory capabilities. State capacity must also be seen *in relation* to the interests, resources, and capabilities of salient societal actors, however. Thus, at a given time, a state's relative capacity reflects the balance of its resources and institutional capacity, augmented by those of its allies, and the resources and capacity for collective action of the actors it confronts. Over time, a state's relative capacity varies as a function of changes in its absolute capacity in relation to changes in the capacities of its opponents and allies.

Both absolute capacity and relative capacity must be viewed in time. Institutions are "sticky"; indeed, were they not, we would ignore them. We must thus study their origins and histories, for these define present capacity independently of immediate circumstances. As Stephen Jay Gould puts it, "Organisms are not putty before a molding environment. . . . Their inherited forms and behaviors constrain and push back; they cannot be quickly transformed to new optimality every time the environment alters."[9] In politics, too, institutions are hard to establish. Even in crisis, leaders must adapt existing institutions to meet new challenges, though their structures, personnel, and ties to other actors may limit their effectiveness.

Relative capacity is sticky, too, for it reflects stable state-society relations expressing the balance of power between the state and social actors. These relations may be formal corporatist arrangements or simply shared expectations about the rules of the game that "institutionalize" the distribution of power and interest group structure, and ease the management of complex issues when agendas are crowded and time is short. But once established, they take on lives of their own, often extending the longevity of outmoded state-society relations despite changed circumstances.[10] This stickiness, like that of states' absolute capacities, sets the limits within which states can respond to crisis.

Again, the real task is explaining the conditions under which states possess more or less absolute or relative capacity. Case-specific factors ranging from colonial heritage to ethnolinguistic homogeneity influence both. But sectoral analysis offers an explanation that applies across cases and contextualizes the unique features of specific cases. Different sectors generate different levels of resources and distribute them in distinctive, politically salient ways. Extracting resources from different sectors thus poses different challenges, requires different definitions of the state's authority to tax, and demands different institutions. Sectors' differing monitoring and regulatory requirements shape the policy instruments the state needs, and the bureaucracy necessary to apply them. The stickiness of these institutions varies, too, for sectoral differences affect how much and how rapidly they can be altered in crisis. Sectors also generate different patterns of societal actors with sectorally determined interests, resources, and capacities for collective action. States' ability to act, therefore, is the balance of their absolute capacity relative to these sector-specific actors. This balance explains the strategies (corporatist or exclusionary) states pursue, the ties they develop and with whom, and the limits within which they labor in crisis.

[9] Stephen Jay Gould, *The Flamingo's Smile* (New York: Norton, 1985), 53.
[10] Mancur Olson, *The Rise and Decline of Nations* (New Haven: Yale University Press, 1982), 55–56.

8

INDIVIDUALS AND INSTITUTIONS

This discussion of states and societal actors returns us to Bates's question: "Who should I take to lunch?" How do we connect individuals to institutions and ultimately to policy outcomes in a way that permits us to talk about states without pretending that inanimate entities desire and act?

I start by assuming that people are rational and self-interested. I assume that they are rational in a minimal sense: they do not act randomly and do their best to get what they want, given their preferences and the information available to them.[11] By self-interested, I mean simply that people act to get more of what they want, whatever that is. What individuals desire varies, but for my purposes—and without pretense that my list is exhaustive—I focus on such basic motivations as the desires to earn more, work less, and live better; to stay in business and turn a profit; and to stay in office and win peace, prosperity, and glory.

But where do individuals' policy preferences come from? My answer is simple: they derive from individuals' location in the political economy, which is largely determined by sectoral characteristics. Workers' wages, conditions of employment, and opportunities for advancement vary by sector as do, by extension, workers' policy preferences. Similarly, the characteristics of firms and the challenges they face vary by sector as do businesspeople's policy preferences. And if different sectors permit leaders more or less autonomy, generate different levels of resources, distribute them in distinctive, politically salient ways, and mold the very institutions of state, then sectoral attributes also influence politicians' policy preferences.

Still, this book includes little discussion of individuals and their interests; it focuses instead on the organizations and institutions they make—or fail to make. Again, the reason is simple: what matters is not motivation, but like-minded individuals' capacity to combine in taking *collective* action to realize their interests. Or rather, what matters is explaining the conditions under which they can do so. And here I offer familiar collective-action arguments with a sectoral twist, for I contend that sectoral characteristics shape like-minded individuals' capacity for collective action.

[11] Frieden, *Debt, Development, and Democracy*, 15–29; and Edward Rhodes, *Power and MADness* (New York: Columbia University Press, 1989), chap. 2.

In sum, sectoral analysis links individuals and institutions, interests and outcomes in a single argument. It releases us from agentless explanation by founding institutions on individuals with sectorally defined interests, preferences, and capabilities. It permits us to discuss politicians whose interests, autonomy, and absolute capacity reflect sectoral characteristics. Further, it permits us to identify relevant social groups, specify their interests and policy preferences, and explain their capacity for collective action relative to each other and to the state. Thus, it permits us not only to specify what the contest between the state and societal actors is about—the details of the restructuring project—but to explain their relative capacities in the contest and even predict the likely winner.

SECTORS AND RESTRUCTURING

After "the state," the most problematic terms in this book are "sector" and "restructuring." Both are defined in Chapter 2. In brief, *sector* refers to a type of economic activity (mining, industrial plantation crop production, peasant cash crop production, or light manufacturing) that constitutes an enduring, coherent whole defined by a distinctive combination of four variables—capital intensity, economies of scale, production flexibility, and asset/factor flexibility[12]— that produces equally distinctive state structures and capabilities, external and internal distributions of power, and sets of societal actors. More generally, since the economic variables covary across sectors, we can imagine a single continuum between two polar ideal types: high/high sectors (mining, industrial plantation crop production), marked by high capital intensity, high economies of scale, and high production inflexibility and asset/factor inflexibility; and low/low sectors (light manufacturing, peasant cash crop production), marked by the opposite. In the essential argument of this book, I contend that we can also imagine a parallel continuum between polar ideal types of the resulting high/high and low/low *political* economies.

Restructuring refers to deliberate, state-led efforts to reallocate resources and reorient economic activity by altering the sectoral compo-

[12] Production flexibility is the ability to meet short-term market shifts by varying output levels or product mix. Asset/factor flexibility refers to the sector-specificity of facilities, supporting infrastructure, and workforce skills; it determines the long-run difficulty of restructuring.

10

sition of the economy to reduce a country's vulnerability to the risks associated with its current leading export sector, or to seize greater or safer opportunities presented in other sectors, or both. Restructuring thus has both economic and political aspects and involves both firms and the state. For the purposes of clarity, however, it is important to keep all the related pieces separate. *Firms* in different sectors face different competitive pressures, have different growth and exit options, wield different amounts of political clout, and thus have different *adjustment* problems. The different sector-specific adjustment problems facing a country's firms determine the *restructuring* project confronting the *state*. Restructuring, therefore, varies in nature and extent (from state aid to firms in trading up within a sector to efforts by the state to shift the very sectoral base of the economy) and in difficulty (from relatively easy to nigh impossible), depending on the nature of firms' adjustment problems.

Unfortunately, although the difficulty of restructuring varies by sector, it is always hard, for sectors are broadly and deeply institutionalized.[13] They are, on the one hand, tied to distinctive distributions of physical assets (factories, plantations, infrastructures, communities) and distinctive private and public institutional arrangements (financial institutions, regulatory and revenue agencies). On the other hand, they define individuals' political identities and the groups with which they associate, and they influence those groups' collective strength. Some intrasectoral variation is inevitable, but the key point is simple: because they are broadly and deeply institutionalized, sectors have an independent impact and are sticky—that is, hard to restructure.

Still, periodic restructuring is essential if states are to get ahead. As Robert Gilpin argues in another context, the key to economic development and power "is neither the possession of particular monopolies and/or technologies nor economic self-sufficiency, but rather the capacity of the economy to transform itself and to respond to changes in the global economic environment, such as shifts in comparative advantage or price changes."[14] Put differently, when significant, these changes—mediated through the adjustment problems they pose for firms—define the outlines of the restructuring projects countries face. Furthermore, since restructuring inevitably involves state action,

[13] Stephen Krasner, "Sovereignty," *Comparative Political Studies* 21 (April 1988): 74–77.
[14] Robert Gilpin, *The Political Economy of International Relations* (Princeton: Princeton University Press, 1987), 77.

it inevitably prompts investigation of the prospects for successful state intervention. Thus, we must ask: What kinds of crises confront leaders? What do crises require of leaders? Will leaders possess the autonomy to formulate a restructuring program? What institutions do they require to implement it and do they command them? What opposition do they face and what allies can they turn to?

In brief, each sector's international market structure is defined by the sector's distinctive mix of capital intensity, economies of scale, and sector-specific production and product characteristics. These determine the competitiveness of the market, the number and nature of players in it, the opportunities for gain and the degree of risk, the requirements for success, states' capacity to help firms to meet them, and the main outlines of the adjustment problems firms face, as well as the resulting restructuring project states must pursue.

Domestically, different sectors have distinctive patterns of capital intensity, economies of scale, production flexibility, and asset/factor flexibility. These patterns shape the nature and (in)tractability of the restructuring project and its implications for the state, capital, and labor. They also mold states' absolute capacity and the identities, aims, and capacity for collective action of the leading-sector actors they confront, as well as those of the other groups with which they might ally themselves. Sectoral attributes thus define the extent to which state leaders can autonomously formulate restructuring policies and their relative capacity to implement them.

BASIC PROPOSITIONS

Ignoring subtlety for the moment, we can now sketch two polar ideal types: high/high sectors and low/low sectors. The argument for sectoral analysis awaits in Chapter 2; here I state six propositions that incorporate the essentials of sectoral analysis.

International Market Structure and Restructuring

1a. High/high sectors display high barriers to entry, oligopolistic markets prone to boom and bust, and sharp shifts in market power upstream and downstream. They are dominated by multinational corporations (MNCs) able to collude in oligopoly management or to

12

pursue individual risk management strategies or both. National firms are disadvantaged in the pursuit of either strategy, for their governments cannot aid them; thus they and their countries suffer the full violence of market volatility. To escape, states must shift the sectoral base.

1b. Low/low sectors display low barriers to entry and highly competitive markets. MNCs play a minor role at the production stage, and market-conforming strategies are the key to survival. Profit margins are thin, but Third World firms can compete on an equal footing with any player in the market and their governments can aid them. Restructuring thus entails deepening and diversification, not radical change.

The (In)tractability of the Restructuring Project

2a. High/high sector firms' production inflexibility means that they respond ineffectively to market signals. Downturns devastate firms, lead to intense pressure on the state for aid, and gut government revenues. But asset/factor inflexibility born of big investments in sector-specific facilities, infrastructure, and work force training raises barriers to exit, incites leading-sector actors to fight restructuring, and forces the state to build the new structures ex nihilo.

2b. Low/low sector firms' production flexibility means that they can adjust to market downturns. Their capacity for "evasive action" reduces the pressures on the state and the depletion of revenues. Asset/factor flexibility born of the general-purpose nature of public and private investments minimizes barriers to exit, gives leading-sector actors incentives to switch, not fight, and eases the burden on the state.

Absolute Capacity

3a. States with high/high sectors face a few big leading-sector firms. They develop specialized tax authorities to tap the huge, concentrated revenue streams such sectors produce, and specialized agencies to monitor, regulate, and promote the activities of these few critical firms. They do not establish institutions to tax, monitor, regulate, or promote other sectors. This and the stickiness of leading-sector–specific institutions limit their ability to restructure.

3b. States with low/low sectors face a vast number of tiny, geographically dispersed firms. They develop flexible, deeply penetrating tax authorities to extract revenue from this multitude of marginally profitable firms, and flexible, general-purpose agencies to monitor, regulate, and promote the diverse activities of firms throughout the country. These institutions lend themselves readily to restructuring.

Societal Actors' Capacity for Collective Action

4a. High/high sectors comprise a few big firms run by sophisticated, well-connected professionals who are likely to be practiced at collusion. They also provide steady employment for large numbers of workers who labor in large gangs and live in homogeneous communities. Although distributional issues divide them, labor and management have grounds to cooperate. Collective action is easy; thus leading-sector firms and workers are potent political actors.

4b. Low/low sectors comprise a huge number of tiny, geographically dispersed, mutually competitive firms managed by isolated small businesspeople. They draw unskilled workers from mixed communities and employ them in tiny, dispersed sweatshops under the supervision of owners adamantly opposed to labor organization. Collective action by firms or workers is unlikely and neither group packs political clout.

Autonomy

5a. Leaders enjoy little autonomy when facing high/high sectors. The complexity of operations, and of monitoring and regulating them, demand close ties between state agencies, management, and labor, making it hard to control the channels of interest representation. The absence of alternatives outside the leading sector and the concentration of wealth in the state give everyone incentives to penetrate the state. Finally, asset/factor inflexibility and weak state institutions bar leaders from defining a national interest—restructuring—that is autonomous of sectoral interests.

5b. Leaders enjoy great autonomy when facing low/low sectors. Firms can be monitored and regulated by general-purpose agencies without a need for expertise supplied from below. The wide dispersion of economic activity and the state's difficulties in raising revenues kill incentives to pentrate the state. Asset/factor flexibility and the state's institutional capacity permit leaders to define a national interest that is autonomous of sectoral interests.

14

Relative Capacity

6a. States with high/high leading export sectors cannot restructure because they lack what it takes to accomplish the task at hand and defeat the opposition. Production inflexibility and asset/factor inflexibility make the crises they face crushing and the restructuring project daunting. Opposition by leading-sector actors is intense and well organized, and leaders have neither the autonomy to formulate a restructuring program nor the absolute capacity to implement one.

6b. States with low/low leading export sectors have better prospects for handling the restructuring project and the opposition. Production flexibility and asset/factor flexibility moderate the crises they face and make the restructuring project more tractable. Leading-sector opposition is weak, and leaders possess both the autonomy to formulate a restructuring program and the institutional capacity to implement it.

To show all this, I proceed in three steps. First, in Chapter 2, I lay out sectoral analysis. I identify the variables, explain how they combine and why, predict likely outcomes, and state the expected causal connections linking initial conditions to the outcomes. Second, in Chapter 3–6 I present four case studies, one for each of the sectors I treat: mining (Zambia), industrial plantation crop production (Sri Lanka), peasant cash crop production (Costa Rica), and light manufacturing (Korea). These studies test the extent to which real cases exhibit the predicted causal connections between sectoral base and policy outcomes, and establish the bounds of *inter*sectoral variation. Third, in Chapter 7 I analyze *intra*sectoral variation. These steps cannot, however, "prove" sectoral analysis, nor are they intended to. Instead, this book is, in effect, an extended plausibility probe. As you read, therefore, I invite you to ask two equally critical questions: How well do the facts of the cases fit the sectoral model? and Is there an alternative that provides a more *accurate,* more *general,* more *parsimonious* explanation that can account for this breadth of cases and materials?

USE, SELECTION, AND LIMITS OF CASE STUDIES

Case studies are problematic and promising. The problem is obvious: too many variables, too few cases. The benefits are obvious, too, for unlike large-n statistical analyses, case studies let us trace complex processes, test causal connections, and analyze deviant cases.[15] The trick is to capture the benefits and minimize the costs, the key to which is ensuring that the argument does not *derive* from the cases but rather that they *test* it. I begin, therefore, by specifying sectoral analysis in Chapter 2 such that each case is structured identically and tests prestated predictions against the facts. Mere congruence is not enough, however; thus to establish causality, I "process trace," that is, track the "decision process by which initial conditions are translated into outcomes."[16]

Still, the persuasiveness of case study research ultimately depends on the quality of case selection. If it is tendentious, no amount of manipulation will make the "findings" meaningful. It is thus essential to make clear the logic of case selection and to address the cases' limits.

This book's major cases—Korea, Sri Lanka, Zambia, and Costa Rica—were chosen because of the centrality of a single sector in their economies and the importance of the core commodity they produce in international trade. Light manufactures accounted for 24 percent of Korean exports in 1960, 60 percent in 1970, and more than 35 percent in the 1980s; coffee accounted for 54 percent of Costa Rican exports in 1960, 32 percent in 1970, and the same in 1985; tea accounted for 60 percent of Sri Lankan exports in 1960, 55 percent in 1970, and 33 percent in 1985; and copper accounted for 100 percent of Zambian exports in 1960, 95 percent in 1970, and 80 percent in 1985. In 1989, 49 countries exported copper worth $15.8 billion per year; 49 countries exported tea worth $2.2 billion per year; and 50 countries exported coffee worth $14 billion per year; in 1978, the Group of 7 countries alone imported manufactured goods worth $66

[15] Charles Tilly, *Big Structures, Large Processes, Huge Comparisons* (New York: Russell Sage, 1984), 76–77; Bruce Russett, "International Behavior Research," in *Approaches to the Study of Political Science*, ed. Michael Haas and Henry Kariel (Scranton, Pa.: Chandler Publishing, 1970), 428–29.

[16] Alexander George, "Case Studies and Theory Development," in *Diplomacy: New Approaches in History, Theory, and Policy*, ed. Paul Gordon Lauren (New York: Free Press, 1979); George, "The Causal Nexus between Cognitive Beliefs and Decision-Making Behavior," in *Psychological Models in International Politics*, ed. Lawrence Falkowski (Boulder, Colo.: Westview Press, 1979); and George and Timothy McKeown, "Case Studies and Theories of Organizational Decision Making," in *Advances in Information Processing in Organizations*, ed. Lee S. Sproull and Patrick D. Larkey, vol. 2 (Greenwich, Conn.: JAI Press, 1985), 35.

billion from the Third World, the equivalent of 33 percent of their total imports from the Third World.[17]

But "pure" cases pose problems and oblige us to ask: How common are single-sector political economies? and How great is intrasectoral variation? As for the first question, single-sector political economies are the norm. Only 22 of 99 "developing economies" listed in the annual *International Financial Statistics* of the International Monetary Fund (IMF) derive less than 25 percent of their total export earnings from a single *commodity;* 39 derive 26–50 percent, 15 derive 51–75 percent, 23 derive 76–100 percent, and 12 derive 90–100 percent. Even more striking, in only 11 of those economies does a single *sector* generate less than 25 percent of total export earnings; in 35 of them a single sector generates 26–50 percent, in 24 a single sector generates 51–75 percent, in 29 a single sector generates 76–100 percent, and in 15 a single sector generates 90–100 percent.[18] Unfortunately, no answer exists to our second and more important question, without an examination of additional cases. I start that process in Chapter 7, but interested others will have to complete it.

The use of so many cases also raises the question of comparability. They differ, after all, in virtually every dimension, from geopolitical position to the timing of entry into world markets. But sectoral analysis does not seek to explain whole countries, complete with their fortuitous endowments of culture and colonial heritage. Indeed, whatever the merits of parsimony, the obvious complexity of our world should make us skeptical of any theory promising too much. Rather, sectoral analysis simply specifies the common challenges faced by leaders in different states with similar sectoral bases, and how sectors shape their ability to meet them. At a minimum, it provides a badly needed common metric against which the uniqueness of each country can be measured and appreciated. I contend—though the validity of my assertion is for you to judge—that sectoral analysis also explains much of the variance, such that what *is* unique to different countries is, in fact, fortuitous and therefore immaterial to cross-national comparisons.

[17] United Nations, *Yearbook of International Trade Statistics,* vol. 2 (1989); William Cline, *Exports of Manufactures from Developing Countries* (Washington, D.C.: Brookings Institution, 1984), 216.

[18] 1985 figures, excluding three countries in which "reexports" predominate. International Monetary Fund, *International Financial Statistics* (1988 and April 1992). Agricultural commodities categorized according to Paige, *Agrarian Revolution.*

No one can be an expert on so many cases; my aim, however, is not to capture reality but rather to structure and simplify it in a theoretically useful way. Indeed, as Alexander George says, "some loss of information and some simplification is inherent . . . in any effort at theory formulation. The critical question . . . is whether the loss of information and simplification entailed jeopardize the validity of the theory and its utility."[19] After all, the point of theory, according to Brian Berry, is to "help us to interpret and understand some complex social phenomenon by seizing on some crucial aspect of it and enabling us to think more clearly and systematically about it than we would have been able to do without the theory."[20] The question, in sum, is not Do the cases leave stones unturned? but Do they leave out or distort facts that would invalidate the sectoral argument? It is not Is this a total explanation? but Is there an alternative that better accounts for *both* the details of any one case *and* the observed patterns of variation across all the cases?

CAVEATS

Before proceeding, I should perhaps preempt a few attacks. Some readers of early drafts faulted my focus on the Third World and the suggestion that it differs from the First World. It does not. This book focuses on the Third World because it interests me and because the relative simplicity of my cases makes it easier to identify and track sectoral effects than if I were studying the United States. But this is just a practical matter. As my roots in the Eurocentric work of Gerschenkron, Kurth, Gourevitch, and Rogowski should suggest—and as I contend in Chapter 7—sectoral analysis offers a general, if incomplete, answer to the core question: What determines which states, under what conditions, will be able to do how much to further development and improve their standing in the international division of labor?

Other readers disliked the way I seem to treat sectors as if they fell full blown from the sky. And I do. After all, most countries' leading sectors were imposed by a colonial power and were fully developed at the time of independence. Since my focus is on how sectors shape

[19] George "Case Studies and Theory Development," 47.
[20] Brian Berry, "Review Article: *Crisis, Choice, and Change*," *British Journal of Political Science* 7 (1977): 237.

sovereign states, it seems reasonable to start with what existed at independence. But what if preexisting conditions affect how sectors develop? To assess this possibility, in Chapter 7 I contrast Costa Rica and El Salvador, which both produce coffee, but because of different initial conditions do so by different means (peasant production versus commercial hacienda) and with very different political consequences. Analysis shows, however, that El Salvador is an exception that proves the rule—that though local conditions matter, outcomes reflect a common sectoral logic.

Still other readers asked, Why bother with sectors at all? Why not follow Rogowski's lead and start with states' differing factor endowments to argue, as Stephan Haggard so neatly put it, that "endowment is fate"?[21] The problem is that an argument based on factor endowments is both too broad and too narrow for my purposes. Many countries with essentially identical *factor* endowments can grow both tea and coffee—but depending on which crop the colonial power favored, today have high/high or low/low *sectoral* endowments with radically different consequences. Sri Lanka, for example, began as a coffee economy only to undergo a wrenching shift to a tea economy when a leaf rust killed off the coffee bushes, a shift that radically altered its political economy and present circumstances. Conversely, although Zambia and Korea have different *factor* endowments, the fact that they now have increasingly similar *sectoral* types explains why they now confront similar travails in restructuring. Even the notion that "*sectoral* endowment is fate" is problematic. A high/high sectoral endowment may, indeed, be destiny, but a low/low sectoral endowment means that a state has leeway to shape its own future—which, of course, suggests why I think that sectoral endowment answers this book's core question.

But this raises the issue of determinism, which pained still other readers. Leaders act on an existing economy via existing institutions and in the face of existing social actors. The challenge they confront, the structure of the economy, the caliber of the institutions they command, and the interests and capacities of societal actors influence what they attempt and their prospects for success. And insofar as the leading export sector molds all of these, sectoral variables "determine" outcomes. This does not mean, however, that leaders have no choices; it simply means that they must choose under conditions that make some alternatives costly and others alluring. Sectoral charac-

[21] Rogowski, *Commerce and Coalitions;* Haggard, personal communication.

teristics thus serve more as "constraints on the options open to political and socio-economic actors . . . than as straightforward determi-
nants of policy preferences pointing clearly in one and only one direction."[22] Furthermore, the extent to which policy makers actually are
confined may be affected by contingent factors ranging from colonial
heritage to ideology. Still, as a matter of explanation (if not determinism), it is also important to remember that without a common metric
such as that provided by sectoral analysis, reference to contingent
variables is meaningless in any comparative context.

Early readers also attacked me as a "development fascist" because
sectoral analysis suggests that autonomy and capacity are necessary, if
not sufficient, conditions for restructuring. These critics associate
autonomy and capacity with authoritarian governments and a capacity to squeeze peasants and repress labor. But the key to restructuring
is state leaders' autonomy from *elites* with a vested interest in the status
quo and the capacity to force *them* to reallocate resources. Indeed,
authoritarian states' actions show their leaders' *lack* of autonomy from
economically vulnerable elites unable to survive except by recourse to
political repression. Conversely, there is a normative case against
states lacking autonomy and capacity. Zambia's lack of them, for example, has meant that the country's vast resources have been plundered by a parasitic elite, whereas the autonomous, capable (and repressive) Korean state has forced elites to alter their behavior in
nationally productive ways.

We must also resist associating autonomy and capacity with "good"
policy. They do not make leaders omniscient, wise servants of the
nation; policy makers may misunderstand what is needed, or pursue
narrowly statist ends, or just line their own pockets. Autonomy and
capacity do, however, affect the types of policy pursued. The leaders
of states lacking autonomy and capacity eschew many policies pursued by more autonomous and capable states because they recognize
that they cannot implement them, and vice versa. The corporatist
strategies common in mining states, for example, represent an effort
by policy makers acutely aware of their limited autonomy and capacity
to tame powerful sectoral actors. Conversely, the absence of corporatism in light manufacturing states (and policy makers' ability to pursue exclusionary, even repressive strategies) reflects the absence of
societal actors able to resist the state.

[22] Personal communication from Jeffry Frieden.

This, then, is the project, and like any *prise de position,* it is a risky one. The opening theoretical chapter is an easy target and invites the reader to play the game "What generalizations won't stand up?" It is a risk I accept because I believe that this is how social science ought to be done. It would be safer to begin with "exploratory" case studies structured by my invisible hand, and then offer a summary of my "findings" as "revealed" by the cases. That would be a fraud. Without an initial statement of my theory and the assumptions, hypotheses, and expectations that shaped my research, readers cannot judge my conclusions or assess the route by which I arrived at them. This being the case, however, I have one request: read to the end. The book is an invitation to take a journey, to follow my research from temerarious beginning to tempered conclusion. The measure of sectoral analysis is not its crude first approximation in Chapter 2, but its tested—and more timid—final version in Chapter 7. Bear with me.

CHAPTER TWO

Sectoral Analysis:
The Model's Bare Bones

"The nice thing about time," the economist Joan Robinson once said, paraphrasing the philosopher Henri Bergson, "is that it keeps everything from happening at once." "The nice thing about theory," adds Mancur Olson, paraphrasing Robinson, "is that it keeps us from having to think about everything at the same time."[1] In this spirit, I sketch in this chapter the bare bones of sectoral analysis, the skeleton that will structure the mass of facts to follow. It is a purely speculative, fact-free construction and should be taken as such; its aim is to specify the variables, identify the actors, and clarify the hypothesized interactions of sector, international market, state, and society. The case studies that constitute the rest of the book flesh out this dry skeleton and test the imagined musculature of sectoral analysis against reality, sector by sector.

To introduce sectoral analysis, I construct and contrast two polar ideal types, the endpoints anchoring a continuum between high/high and low/low sectors. These are presented pure and full-blown, without historical antecedents or mitigating factors. The chapter presents the strongest possible case for sectoral analysis based, without apology, on its two core—and controversial—contentions: that sectors have an optimal, or at least typical, *economic* organization and pose distinctive economic challenges to all producers and states, and that states with similar sectoral bases face similar *political* constraints when they address these challenges, do so from similar institutional positions, and arrive at similar policy outcomes.

[1] Off-the-cuff comment made at Columbia University International Political Economy Workshop, February 2, 1989.

I proceed in two steps. In the first section I analyze sectors' typical organization and how sectoral characteristics shape international markets. I explore the nature of the competition firms confront in different sectors, the risks and opportunities they face, the strategies they must pursue to avoid the one and seize the other, and their ability to do so. The section concludes with a discussion of the characteristic adjustment problems firms in different sectors confront, the extent to which states can aid them in overcoming these problems, and the restructuring project states must undertake. In the second section I take up the domestic politics of restructuring, analyzing the (in)tractability of the restructuring project and its implications for the state and societal actors; how sectoral characteristics influence the defining elements of stateness, absolute capacity, autonomy, and relative capacity; and the identity and capacity for collective action of societal actors. I then combine assessments of the (in)tractability of different sectoral restructuring projects, the state's interests, autonomy and capacity as regards restructuring, and societal actors' interests and capacity for collective action in defense of those interests to explain the different patterns of policy outcomes observed among states with different sectoral bases.

Sectoral analysis builds on two core variables—capital intensity and the extent of economies of scale—in sectors' production processes, and on two composite variables—production flexibility and asset/factor flexibility—that recombine elements of both. All four variables covary. The result is admittedly inelegant, a state of affairs little improved by lumping the four variables together to describe two polar ideal types or sectoral "syndromes." Although my excuses will not satisfy purists who want to know exactly what variables are doing the theoretical work, my reasons for not streamlining the argument further are simple. First, this book is still a crude first exploration of sectoral analysis, conducted at a far higher level of abstraction than, I suspect, real sectoral analysis will have to be conducted. This being the case, however, it seems inappropriate to demand more precision than my data permit. Second, although the result is inelegant, my broadly defined variables capture and make sense of a wide array of descriptively important material that figures prominently in the concrete cases I examine.

I define both capital intensity and the extent of economies of scale very broadly. Capital intensity refers to the capital costs of start-up, production, research and development, inventory, and distribution, and is a proxy for such other critical characteristics as fixed costs, technical complexity, management professionalism, and work force skill levels. The extent of economies of scale—the extent to which efficiency demands large-scale production—may affect production, research and development, marketing, distribution, and financing, and is also a proxy for the size and geographical concentration of facilities; the size, concentration, and stability of the work force; and the extent of specialized infrastructure required. Capital intensity and the extent of economies of scale account for the "divisibility" of production (its openness to broad participation), the sector-specificity of capital equipment and other assets, and the rigidity of barriers to exit from the sector.

Production flexibility expresses a sector's degree of short-run market vulnerability, and thus the severity of the shocks that market shifts deliver to firms and to the state. It is composed of three elements reflecting the extent of capital intensity and of economies of scale. First is the size of fixed costs, which determines whether production decisions respond to market conditions (if they are low) or are driven by debt service requirements (if they are high). Second is the size of firms' investment in the work force, or rather their interest in retaining workers so as not to lose that investment. Third is the sensitivity of firms' physical plant to shutdown. As a rule, the greater the capital intensity and extent of economies of scale, the more likely facilities will suffer from being shut down—mines will flood, furnace linings will crack as they cool, plantations will go to pot.

Asset/factor flexibility determines the long-term difficulty of reallocating resources, and thus the (in)tractability of restructuring. It reflects five dimensions of sector-specificity, or the extent to which assets and factors can be reused elsewhere. The greater a sector's capital intensity and extent of economies of scale, (1) the larger, more geographically concentrated, and more specialized are its facilities and equipment; (2) the more concentrated and sector-specific are the necessary infrastructures (power grids, railroads, pipelines, ports); and (3) the more specialized the production technology is. On the human side, the greater a sector's capital intensity and extent of economies of scale, (4) the greater the concentration of skilled workers in stable and homogeneous communities that owe their existence and identity to the sector they serve; and (5) the more specialized management is, reflecting the greater need for specialized services within the firm, specialized management organizations, training systems, and corporate cultures. Finally, each element of asset/factor flexibility is

24

reflected—inverted, as in a mirror—in the development of other sectors: the greater a sector's size, concentration, and specialization, the less developed they are.

THE INTERNATIONAL DIMENSION

Market Structure and Sectoral Strategies

High/high and low/low sectors exhibit radically different market structures and pose equally different challenges to firms located in them. Where capital intensity and economies of scale are high, oligopoly prevails; the number of firms is small, and each can influence the market. High capital costs, big economies of scale, technical complexity, and the need for specialized infrastructure, management, and labor pose high barriers to entry; high switching costs for consumers further protect oligopolists' privileged market position. Large sunk investments in sector-specific capital equipment, facilities, infrastructure, management, and skilled labor also guarantee high barriers to *exit,* however. Conversely, where capital intensity and economies of scale are low, competition prevails. The number of firms is large and their size small, there being no barriers to entry or limits to the divisibility of production. Firms are at the mercy of the market. But limited sunk investments, non-sector-specific capital equipment, facilities, infrastructure, and management, and an unskilled work force minimize barriers to exit. These different circumstances require that firms pursue different strategies if they are to succeed in their respective sectors.

Oligopoly has two faces: limited competition and high barriers to entry let oligopolists extract monopoly rents from consumers; but their size and market power make unrestrained competition devastating. The existence of few players and high switching costs also leads to markets characterized by bilateral monopoly between different stages of production. Such markets often fail, as a result shifting market power sharply between buyers and sellers. Both harsh competition and market power shifts mean disaster for firms obliged to produce at full capacity to meet high fixed costs and keep huge operations working efficiently. Oligopoly thus poses two challenges to oligopolists: as a group, they must manage twin threats to profitability—new entrants and price competition; as individual firms, they must manage the risk inherent in high fixed costs and unstable markets. Put differently,

25

oligopolists confront a delicate collective-action problem: how to meet the dictates of individual-competitive and collective-collusive rationality simultaneously.[2]

Oligopolists must pursue three strategies to manage the market and risk: vertical integration, horizontal integration, and joint venturing. Vertical integration permits individual firms to evade the nasty shocks of market failure. Despite organizational costs, it can also cut the transaction costs incurred in arms-length sales, ease conflict resolution, ensure the availability of low-cost information, lessen uncertainty, and facilitate better planning and quicker adjustments to changing conditions.[3] It does not, however, address the problems of oligopoly management resulting from the size of minimum efficient scale (MES) facilities that, when brought on line, may trigger gluts and price wars. Oligopoly management thus requires the horizontal integration of firms to coordinate investment and production, and consequently supply and prices. But continuing competition makes coordination hard. Indeed, the problems are the worst when it is most needed or most successful, because then the interests of each firm are best served by cheating. Firms therefore prefer joint ventures, which, in effect, make their competitors collaborators.

Joint ventures let oligopolies achieve the collective rationality needed to defend monopoly rents, contain competition, and fend off new entrants. By rendering lumpy investments divisible, they let firms and the industry escape the dilemma posed by big economies of scale: how to avoid overexpansion without building less than MES facilities.[4] By reducing the number of independent firms in an industry and requiring information sharing, joint ventures ease collective action by alleviating the problems of coordinating and monitoring firms' actions. They further ease coordination by "homogenizing" firms' cost structures and risk profiles, thus also "homogenizing" their needs, expectations, and outlooks. Finally, joint ventures let oligopoly members coopt new entrants and challengers.

Joint ventures benefit individual firms, too. By making huge projects divisible, they reduce firms' risk exposure in a given project, let firms share in the management of several projects, and help firms

[2] John Stuckey, *Vertical Integration and Joint Ventures in the Aluminum Industry* (Cambridge: Harvard University Press, 1983), 187–88.
[3] Oliver Williamson, "The Vertical Integration of Production," *American Economic Review* 61, no. 2 (1971): 113.
[4] Stuckey, *Vertical Integration*, 154–55.

diversify more than they could alone. They also improve the firms' standing in capital markets, since investors recognize them as "vehicles for efficient vertical integration, improved oligopolistic coordination, and efficient intangible asset exchange." Thus, joint ventures "relieve the capital cost penalties and quantity rationing that the capital market imposes upon projects that are highly risky, require large amounts of capital, or both."[5]

Firms in low/low sectors face entirely different challenges. Argues Michael Porter: "The nature and degree of competition in an industry hinge on five forces: the threat of new entrants, the bargaining power of customers, the bargaining power of suppliers, the threat of substitute products or services, . . . and the jockeying among current contestants."[6] Here all five are at full power. The absence of barriers to entry and the resulting large number of firms mean no monopoly rents and no prospect for managing the market. Small firm size renders each firm a negligible buyer of inputs, reducing bargaining power with suppliers; the lack of proprietary technology and of product differentiation limits switching costs, putting customers on top. There are thus no limits to competition, which is brutal and unceasing.

Intense competition demands that firms pursue very different strategies. In this dog-eat-dog world, collective responses and market control are out of the picture. Instead, firms must pursue individual market-conforming strategies. They must improve their ability to follow the market and adjust quickly to changes in order to lose less than the competition in downturns and get more in upturns. Unable to shape their environment, firms must adapt themselves to its dictates better than their competitors do, or die.

Firms must concentrate on the three keys to competitiveness in low/low sectors: price, on-time delivery, and quality. Since firms employ common technology, the achievement of all three goals turns on management and labor. As for price, labor costs matter, but labor productivity matters more; and since technology is stable, labor productivity and productivity gains reflect better training and shop floor management, materials handling, and job flow and inventory control.[7] These also explain quality control (reflecting the quality of su-

[5] Ibid., 183–84 and 170.
[6] Michael Porter, "How Competitive Forces Shape Strategy," *Harvard Business Review* 57 (April–March 1979): 137.
[7] David Morawetz, *Why the Emperor's New Clothes Are Not Made in Columbia* (New York: Oxford University Press, 1981), 85–86.

pervision, workers' skill, and the organization of production) and on-time delivery (reflecting the quality of management, the efficiency of labor and equipment utilization, and workers' skill). But these are not enough. Such firms do not have the luxury of specialization; they must balance the pursuit of efficiency with flexibility.

Flexibility is the key to risk management in low/low sectors. Firms do not make standardized items with a long production run, but a mix of products that may change seasonally. Thus, firms must have the managerial flexibility to absorb new designs and move them rapidly into production, the technical flexibility to adjust efficiently to the new production requirements, and work force flexibility to meet the labor productivity, quality, and on-time delivery requirements.[8] Flexibility is also critical for damage control. Market volatility demands that firms retain the ability to shrink and that they diversify to reduce their vulnerability to the vagaries of a given market. Staying ahead of the competition demands that firms innovate, cut costs, and trade up to more rapidly growing or higher-value-added segments of the market.

Implications for the State

These sectoral characteristics and strategies have critical implications for states. At issue are the extent of firms' prospects for success in pursuing the required strategies relative to other players in the market—that is, firms' ability to solve adjustment problems—and whether states can help them. Answers to these questions explain the likelihood and nature of the market shocks states experience and define the restructuring project they must undertake.[9]

In high/high sectors, states and firms are disadvantaged relative to their MNC competition, whose very structure reflects adaptation to the sector's challenges. They may reap monopoly rents—but only if they, too, can collectively manage the oligopoly to maintain high and stable profits and individually manage the risk of catastrophe. Put differently, the question is whether they can find alternatives to

[8] Donal Keesing, "Linking Up to Distant Markets," *American Economic Review* 73 (May 1983): 340.

[9] Not all shocks have sectoral origins (for example, oil shocks and world recession). But even these shocks are *experienced* by states via the institutions and institutionalized patterns of international integration defined by sector. States' *responses*, too, are bounded by the sectorally determined difficulty of restructuring, and by their autonomy, absolute capacity, and relative capacity, all of which have sectoral bases.

MNCs' solutions to the problems of oligopoly and risk management. The short answer is no, and thus their prospects are not good.

In part, the problem is MNC retaliation. In the 1970s and 1980s, MNCs slashed investment in many countries, focusing instead on "safe" areas where they did not risk expropriation. This forced many countries to borrow, often at far higher rates than obtained by their MNC competition, and also forced them to depend on expensive international engineering, management, and marketing firms to replace services once provided by the MNCs, or to develop the needed expertise locally. But over time these problems can be overcome.

The same is not true of the problems national firms face because their very existence undercuts the profitability and stability of high/high sectors—and their prospects in them. States and national firms have been hardest hit by the resulting deconcentration of production, for though patterns of ownership in these sectors changed with expropriation,

> they remained highly capital-intensive industries, with high fixed costs and low variable costs, whose enterprises therefore were unusually vulnerable to small variations in output levels. A decline in the degree of vertical integration of these industries increased the exposure of buying and selling firms to such variations. At the same time, although the [firms] were no longer small enough in numbers to allow for effective stabilization schemes, neither were they yet so numerous as to offer the promise of an efficient open market.[10]

Deconcentration hurt the interests of states and MNCs alike by impeding collective rationality, cutting profits, increasing price volatility, and complicating risk management.

But these developments hurt Third World firms more severely than their MNC competition because they are unintegrated. Whereas MNCs can homogenize risks and costs by investing in several areas and even in competing products, national firms cannot. More important, they are exposed to all the risks of an unstable oligopolistic market. Indeed, because MNC vertical integration stabilizes supply and demand in much of the market, the volatility of the thinner, unintegrated portion occupied by national firms is even greater.

Collectively, national firms face the same challenge of oligopoly

---

[10] Raymond Vernon, *Two Hungry Giants* (Cambridge: Harvard University Press, 1983), 50.

management as the MNCs, but they cannot meet it. Their response is the "producer association" intended to achieve market control through production and price coordination. These fail, however, as the unavoidable result of state control of production. Where private oligopolists can "concentrate on the common objective of high and stable profits," state firms bring their governments' concerns to the bargaining table, and these impede oligopoly management.[11] States must consider the leading sector's contribution to employment, revenues, export earnings, and debt service. Since all of these suffer with falling demand, there are strong political pressures to cut prices to maintain production. This kills collusion, however, and efforts to establish joint ventures die in similar battles over who gets the projects and the spin-offs they offer.

In short, despite the prospect of bonanza profits, the implications of integration into the international economy via a high/high sector are not good. Third World firms are disadvantaged vis-à-vis their MNC competitors: in good times their bonanza is meaner; in bad times their losses may be crushing. And there is nothing states can do to help, as none of the critical variables are within their reach. Pursuit of the required strategy is impossible; indeed, the state's own interests dictate policies antithetical to it.

How much worse are states' prospects in the hypercompetitive markets associated with low/low sectors? Here we meet a marvelous irony: however competitive low/low sectors are, the dominance of market-conforming strategies locates the variables critical for success within the reach of local actors and the state, and ensures that they can compete on an equal footing with any player in the marketplace.

States can easily enhance local firms' competitiveness. They can implement exchange rate policies that do not distort price signals and give firms incentives to export, and trade policies that give firms access to inputs at world prices.[12] States can reduce firms' production, transaction, and information costs by regulating wages, or by dissem-

---

[11] Raymond Vernon, "State-Owned Enterprises in Latin American Exports," *Quarterly Review of Economics and Business* 21 (Summer 1981): 106.

[12] Even in the labor-intensive industries of which these sectors are comprised, inputs constitute the biggest proportion of total costs, often twice as large as labor. In the apparel industry, for example, labor generally constitutes 15–25 percent of total costs, but textiles may constitute 35–60 percent. Morawetz, *The Emperor's New Clothes*, 92; and United Nations Industrial Development Organization, *Industrialization of Developing Countries*, UNIDO Monograph on Industrial Development no. 7, 1969.II.B.39(7) (Vienna, 1969), 56.

inating timely information about distant markets that small firms cannot get on their own. More generally, they can invest in the infrastructure needed to move information, inputs, and product rapidly; provide financial services; and establish efficient customs services to cut the time lost clearing exports and imports. Finally, states can help firms by providing subsidized loans, investment tax credits, and access to foreign exchange, and they can help firms innovate, cut costs, improve quality, diversify, and trade up.

In sum, low/low sectors have very different implications for states than do high/high sectors. They offer no bonanza profits, but the risks they present are limited and manageable. Their competitiveness ensures that they do not suffer the boom-bust cycles that plague oligopolistic markets. Further, the flexibility required of firms in low/low sectors lets them absorb market shocks, insulating the state. Finally, low capital intensity and low economies of scale mean that no one is barred from the game and no one has a structural advantage over any other; what matters is firms' competitiveness. And here the state can ensure that national firms compete on an equal footing with all comers.

Put differently, the argument is *not* that big is bad and small is good. High/high sectors are high/high sectors because they *require* huge capital investments and because there are rapidly rising returns to scale. The characteristics of low/low sectors mean that firms often suffer from undercapitalization, inadequate technology, and lack of relevant product and market information. The critical question for us, however, is whether firms can pursue the risk management strategies required to overcome the challenges posed by the different sectors in which they are located and whether their states can help. The answer varies by sector. Third World firms in high/high sectors profit by the same rising returns to scale as MNCs. They are less able to pursue the required risk management strategies, however, and the state cannot help them because none of the critical variables are within its reach. Third World firms in low/low sectors can pursue all the required risk management strategies as well as any of their competition and the state can help.

By extension, sectoral differences in the adjustment problems faced by firms dictate different restructuring projects for leaders. The limited opportunities and huge risks associated with high/high sectors, combined with states' inability to seize the one and contain the other, suggest that leaders must reallocate resources to other sectors having

31

better prospects and fewer risks. Leaders' ability to abet success in low/low sectors, combined with manageable risk and the potential profits of trading up, suggest that they should pursue competitiveness and high-growth, higher-value-added markets within the sector. The measure of the state in high/high sectors is the ability to change the sectoral composition of the economy; the measure of the state in low/low sectors is the ability to deepen it. But here we must shift our focus to explaining different sectors' implications for stateness.

THE DOMESTIC DIMENSION

Taking the measure of states' "stateness" is best done in two steps. First, we must assess the challenge leaders face: how and to what extent do sectoral attributes determine the severity of the crisis that market shocks inflict, the (in)tractability of the restructuring project with which they must respond, and the intensity of societal actors' opposition to it. We can then examine how different sectors shape the elements of stateness and predict likely outcomes.

The (In)tractability of Restructuring

The (in)tractability of restructuring reflects sectors' production flexibility and asset/factor flexibility. These are inversely related to capital intensity and economies of scale: the greater the capital intensity and extent of economies of scale a sector exhibits, the less flexibility it will have. And the less flexibility a sector has, the more severe the crisis, the more intractable the restructuring project, and the more intense the opposition.

Again, we can imagine continua between two poles. At one end of the production flexibility continuum lie high/high sectors, in which firms are saddled with high fixed costs, large skilled work forces they cannot lay off, and facilities they cannot close but are forced to keep producing even at a loss when markets go bad; at the other end lie low/low sectors, in which firms are blessed with low fixed costs, unskilled workers, and facilities that do not suffer from shutdowns, so they are able to vary production as the market dictates. In the case of asset/factor flexibility, firms in sectors at one pole are marked by extreme size, concentration, and specialization. The barriers to exit are high, because nothing lends itself to other uses and no alternative

32

sector exists. At the other pole are sectors in which firms are marked by smallness, deconcentration, and limited specialization. Here the barriers to exit are low, because leading-sector firms' assets and factors are mobile and alternative sectors are already in place.

The Implications of (In)flexibility

Sectoral differences in production flexibility and asset/factor flexibility are most clearly evident in three areas: market behavior; the nature and intensity of the interests of leading-sector capital and labor; and the nature of the short-term crisis and long-term challenge the state faces. Together, these define the context within which leaders must act and set the stage for the analysis of stateness that follows.

In a crisis, firms' market behavior reflects the production (in)flexibility of their respective sectors. Firms in low/low sectors can respond to market downturns with market-conforming behavior—by lowering production, cutting costs, and laying off workers. Firms in high/high sectors cannot. They must keep producing flat out even when glutted markets force prices below production costs. This imposes high costs on firms and states, exaggerates such markets' tendency to boom and bust, kills monopoly rents, increases risks, and erodes collective efforts to manage them.

Firms' (in)ability to follow the market determines the intensity of sectoral actors' interests and the nature of their demands. In the short term, production flexibility lets firms take "evasive action" such that market downturns need not be disastrous. The diversity of activities engaged in by firms in such sectors also means that all firms will not be affected simultaneously or equally but will display a wide range of "impactedness." Shocks thus produce moderate and diffuse upset and the help firms demand, in keeping with the requirements of competitiveness in such sectors, can be economic (market conforming) and easily granted by the state. Production inflexibility means that firms cannot take evasive action when demand falters, and so they face disaster. Their cries for help are unanimous, loud, and anguished. And because the state cannot help firms compete, the demands are for political, market-resisting relief.

These differences in the intensity and nature of sectoral actors' interests are even greater when viewed in the long term. In low/low sectors, little is sector-specific or must be written off with change; this ensures that the costs of reallocating resources are low. Furthermore, because high asset–factor flexibility is also related to the greater development of other sectors, those obliged to leave the leading sector have ready investment and employment opportunities. Thus, leading-sector actors have only limited incentives to oppose restructuring and are more likely to devote their energy to winning state aid to make the jump.

The opposite is true of asset/factor inflexible sectors, for the barriers to exit are insurmountable. Geographic concentration; sector-specific equipment, facilities, and infrastructures; nontransferable skills; and the absence of other sectors to move into mean that restructuring entails writing everything off and total dislocation for individuals and communities. Sectoral actors' backs are to the wall; they have no option but to oppose restructuring tooth and nail. Furthermore, they cannot help themselves, nor are there economic solutions to their problems; they must pursue political strategies aimed at obtaining state protection against the market and change.

Differences in production flexibility and asset/factor flexibility also affect the state directly. In the short term, production-flexible firms' ability to evade shocks insulates the state against rapid, serious losses of revenues and foreign exchange earnings, and the vitality of other sectors means that losses can be replaced. Further, such firms' demands are modest and manageable, and seek more of what the state is already doing to promote competitiveness. Production inflexibility means that market downturns have instantaneous, catastrophic consequences for the state; revenues and foreign exchange earnings plummet, and debt soars. Facing disaster and unable to save themselves, sectoral actors turn to the state. And without other sectors to help in meeting these demands, the state has only nasty, zero-sum allocative choices that involve taking from the weak to sustain the strong.

Again, these differences are exaggerated in the long run. Where asset/factor flexibility prevails, restructuring is less pressing, less difficult, and less costly. Because there are fewer sunk investments and sector-specific assets, less must be written off and the state faces lower demands for new investment capital. Indeed, low barriers to exit mean that leading-sector actors may change sectors on their own. Given firms' geographical dispersion and other sectors' vitality, restructuring does not dislocate leading-sector-dependent communities or regions, and so the state is not confronted by the costs and political travails dislocation entails. Other sectors' dynamism means that the

34

state has the revenues and foreign exchange to restructure and the support of established alternative-sector actors.

Asset/factor inflexibility presents the state with intractable problems. High sector-specificity means that neither the state nor private actors can salvage the huge sums sunk in facilities, equipment, infrastructure, job skills, management know-how, and labor organization. There being no private actors able to invest, the state itself must build the new structure ex nihilo—and in the teeth of bitter opposition. Because of facilities' geographical concentration and size, restructuring destroys communities and dislocates regions, resulting in terrible human, economic, and political costs. In the absence of other sectors, these costs must be incurred while the leading sector hemorrhages, and when new revenues are not yet available. And without other sectors, the state has no allies in restructuring but must create them even as it attacks the once powerful.

The Different Sectors' Domestic Political Economies

But this is only half the story. At issue are not just sectors' implications for the (in)tractability of restructuring in the abstract. More interesting are their implications for autonomy, for absolute capacity and relative capacity, and for leaders' ability to formulate and implement policies for restructuring.

Absolute Capacity

Absolute capacity is the extent to which the state has the authority and means to extract and deploy resources; a technocratic, meritocratic, and internally cohesive bureaucracy; and effective monitoring and regulatory capacities. This section explores how sectors mold state institutional capacities to tax and to monitor, regulate, and direct economic activity—and states' consequent ability to restructure.

Sectors differ in the level of taxable resources they generate, the ease with which such resources can be tapped, the institutions needed to do so, the availability of other revenue sources, and the state's ability to tap them. High/high sectors yield monopoly rents that are easily tapped by the state. High concentration eases the monitoring of production and exports and the extraction of revenues; moreover,

35

such sectors' international market structures let firms shift costs downstream, reducing their resistance to state exactions. Their technical complexity, sophisticated management, and international ties require that the state build sophisticated tax agencies. Although they are highly specialized, these agencies can be small, given such sectors' concentration and the ease of extraction. They can also target just the leading sector, for they can tap vast revenues from it at low cost, whereas the underdevelopment of other sectors means that extraction efforts will produce little revenue at high cost, especially in view of tax authorities' sector-specific specialization.

Taxing low/low sectors poses different challenges and requires different institutions. Such sectors' competitiveness and firms' scant resources limit the revenues the state can extract without damaging the firms. Furthermore, the large number, small size, and wide geographical dispersion of firms makes monitoring and taxing them hard, and their owners' thin profit margins and inability to pass on costs encourage tax evasion. States thus need flexible, deeply penetrating institutions able to monitor and tax even tiny firms throughout the country, so that the smallness of each tax return is made up for by the volume of returns processed. Given limited leading-sector resources and strong extraction capabilities, states have incentives to tax other sectors that, being developed, yield tidy revenues at low cost.

These contrasting patterns of institutional development shape states' ability to restructure in crisis. In high/high sectors, production inflexibility means that market downturns reduce state revenues. But just as asset/factor inflexibility limits firms' ability to adjust, tax authorities' sector-specificity limits their ability to find new resources to replace lost leading-sector revenues. The same is true if the state attempts to restructure, since restructuring cuts revenues from the leading sector. Thus, both market shocks and restructuring threaten the state's ability to fund itself. Indeed, sticky tax institutions establish a high barrier to exit for leaders, giving them statist incentives to defend the status quo. Conversely, low/low sectors' production flexibility limits downturns' impact on state revenues. Moreover, tax agencies' flexibility and ability to tax other sectors mean that the state can replace lost leading-sector revenues, or raise revenues even during restructuring. Flexible tax institutions thus lower the state's barriers to exit from a sector, and mean that leaders need not fear that restructuring will cut revenues.

Sectors also shape states' ability to monitor, regulate, and promote

36

economic activity. Here, too, varying capabilities reflect the same elements that explain asset/factor flexibility. In high/high cases, facilities' size and concentration facilitate monitoring and regulation but require specialized agencies with sector-specific technical and financial expertise. The concentration and specialization of facilities require an ability to provide sector-specific infrastructures ranging from large power grids to roads, railroads, pipelines, ports, and specialized financial, information, and communications systems. The size and concentration of and investment in skilled labor—and labor's potential power—require specialized labor organizations to control what is the core of the national work force, and to serve its specialized needs. The state requires ties to leading-sector firms and to the peak organizations representing them. These sectors' technical complexity requires sector-specific, technology-related services (schools of mining or crop-specific extension services and research units). Their dominant position discourages leaders from developing institutions to address non-leading-sector needs.

In low/low cases, states have incentives to develop very different institutional capabilities. Firms' small size and wide geographical dispersion pose monumental monitoring and regulatory tasks requiring far-flung organizations, and firms' heterogeneity demands that they be staffed by generalists. For the same reasons, states require agencies to provide general-purpose transportation, energy, communications, and information infrastructures to serve very diverse firms. Similarly, firms' small size, dispersion, and heterogeneity require flexible, deeply penetrating institutions to meet the diverse interests, needs, and demands of firms and workers throughout the country. The heterogeneity of leading-sector technologies and the requirements of competitiveness also demand flexible technical service agencies that are able, for example, to promote flexibility, diversification, and trading up. Other sectors' vitality encourages leaders to establish institutions to monitor, regulate, and promote them, too.

These differences mean that states in different sectors face different barriers to exit from the old and have different capacities to promote the new. States in high/high sectors confront towering barriers to exit. They lack institutions geared to new sectors' needs, and the specialized agencies established to monitor, regulate, and service the old are inappropriate. No less important, those who staff existing organizations fear for their own futures in a new world where their specialized skills are worthless, and they will fight from within to

37

preserve their agencies and prevent the growth of new ones that might eclipse them. States in low/low sectors can reorient themselves easily, however. They already have agencies serving the new, and the flexibility of agencies serving the old means there are few sunk organizational investments to be written off. They thus confront limited internal resistance to restructuring and need not engage in an orgy of new institution building.

Finally, sectors may shape other institutions that affect the state's ability to restructure. Here the argument is more problematic. Sectors do not, for example, explain external threats and thus powerful armed forces, a colonial legacy of strong police forces and thus state coercive capabilities, ethnic or regional cleavages and thus payoff politics, or leaders' ideological preferences. But sectors may be critical in explaining how these influence outcomes, and why the conventional wisdom about their role is so often wrong.

Regardless of institutions' origins, states must be able to support and use them. The conventional wisdom is that states facing external threats and possessing powerful security forces can extract resources easily and deploy them at will—to restructure. Being strong, it is argued, they can ignore interest group pressures and "make the tough choices" development requires. But states depending on payoff politics cannot extract resources or restructure. Unable to resist pressures from below, they squander the resources needed to build for tomorrow to buy time today. But without reference to sectors, this picture may be misleading.

The issue is stickiness. States in high/high sectors, for example, can afford to pamper security forces or pay off challengers. But because restructuring threatens state revenues, in a crisis their leaders must preserve the sectoral status quo—those with coercive capabilities will use them to extract resources to maintain the military, and those without such capabilities will borrow against the future to sustain the payoff system. In each case, they deepen dependence on the old and squander the resources needed to build the new. Although it is hard, states in low/low sectors can raise the revenues to fund security forces or payoffs. But leaders are not wedded to the old and can use their coercive capabilities to force restructuring, or use payoffs to ease transition costs and offer incentives for restructuring. In short, neither coercive power nor its opposite explains states' capacity to restructure. Both are meaningful only in light of leaders' interests,

38

which reflect the sector-determined (in)tractability of restructuring and the institutional endowment with which they face it.

The measure of an institution's contribution to state capacity is its ability to do some*thing* desired by leaders either *to* or *for* someone. Here the context in which an institution operates is critical, for context dictates what resources are available, what the institution is supposed to be doing, and to or for whom it is supposed to be doing it. All three may have a sectoral component: the availability of resources is conditioned by sector; what institutions are supposed to do may be affected by sectoral characteristics or the nature of the restructuring project or both; and who institutions are supposed to do it to or for may be determined by which groups different sectors make politically salient.

But as this last point suggests, the idea of "absolute" capacity by itself is silly. States' ability to act must be measured not only against the challenges of restructuring but against sectoral actors' capacity to resist when the state's aims hurt their interests. The next section explores how sectors affect the capacity of capital and labor for collective action. This information in hand, we can put the state in context—analyzing how a sector influences the state's autonomy from societal actors and its relative capacity to manipulate them.

CAPACITY OF CAPITAL AND LABOR FOR COLLECTIVE ACTION

So far we have focused on the state, restructuring, and sectors' implications for firms. These dictate firms' *interests;* they define the challenges the market and the state pose for firms, and suggest what firms *should* do. But interests alone are irrelevant; as the old saying goes, "if wishes were horses, all beggars would ride." What matters is whether firms in a given sector can *realize* their interests. What matters is their capacity for collective action.

Firms' capacity for collective action varies according to the size and number of firms in a sector; the competitive relationship among them; the resources they command; and their owners' sophistication, connections to other groups, and confidence in their ability to act. Thus, firms in high/high sectors face limited collective action problems. Their small numbers make organizing easy, and each firm's contribution has a proportionally large return. As oligopolists, they

39

are practiced at collusion, and they can monitor each other's compliance and sanction cheaters. These capabilities generalize easily to the political sphere, where such firms' size and advantage as concentrations of economic activity give them huge resources. Further, their professional, educated managers can analyze sectoral problems, plan strategies for getting the state to solve them, and use their personal and professional ties to other powerful actors (lawyers, banks, regulators, MNCs) to get help. Not surprisingly, they are confident of success.

In contrast, low/low sectors present firms with daunting collective action problems. The number and dispersion of firms makes organizing hard, and each firm's tiny contribution to success and equally tiny return encourage free riding. Further, dog-eat-dog competition produces pervasive distrust and the fear that others will cheat, not collude. It also leads firms to resist the monitoring and sanctioning mechanisms collective action requires, for fear they will give competitors an advantage or reduce flexibility. Although together, such firms have the wherewithal to confront the state, each one's tiny reserves and the poor prospects for collective action minimize the actual resources available. Such firms tend to be mom-and-pop operations, whose owners have neither the skills and knowledge of the "big picture" necessary to formulate lobbying strategies nor the ties to powerful patrons to help implement them. They therefore lack the confidence to take on the state.

We must also distinguish between workers' interests and their collective capacity to realize them. Here, too, we find a perverse relationship. The well-paid workers in the high/high sectors that are most in need of restructuring can organize to defend their privileges and can collaborate with management against the state to block restructuring. The wretched workers in low/low sectors cannot, which in part explains firms' vaunted "flexibility."

Labor's capacity for collective action varies according to who the workers are, where they work, where they live, and what worries management about them. Workers in high/high sectors can organize easily. Such sectors demand skilled workers who represent a big, irreplaceable investment, giving them great bargaining leverage. The specialized skills such sectors require also mean that promotions take place from within, giving workers advancement opportunities, and production inflexibility means their jobs are safe even in a crisis. The facilities' size makes using selective incentives easy, since such facilities concentrate hordes of workers who pass through a few gates, share changing and dining rooms, and cannot be closely supervised. Beyond the gates, the facilities' size and concentration promote stable, homogeneous, often isolated communities that foster worker solidarity and a rich variety of social organizations that reinforce it. And given labor's small share of production costs, management can negotiate. Indeed, because of production inflexibility, management can ill afford labor unrest and may even encourage strong unions to ensure tranquillity and assist in labor coordination.

In contrast, workers in low/low sectors face insurmountable obstacles to organization. Lacking skills, they are easily replaced, so strike threats are bootless. Furthermore, they lack incentives to invest in unions to achieve long-term benefits. Unskilled work offers no advancement opportunities, and market volatility, to which firms adapt by hiring and firing, produces employment instability and limits workers' time horizons. Firms' geographical dispersion makes large-scale organizing tough, and small firm size means close supervision, barring organization at the firm level. It is thus hard to mobilize workers, monitor their actions, reward union members, or punish scabs. Workplace dispersion also means that workers live in heterogeneous communities that do not reinforce solidarity, and employment instability may force them to maintain roots in other areas, further limiting community ties and community support. Finally, management adamantly opposes unionization. Labor cost control and the ability to lay off workers are critical to firms' survival; small firm size and the unskilled nature of the work eliminate the need for unions to prevent sabotage and ease coordination.

These differences have critical implications. In high/high sectors, labor's potency is paired with low management resistance to union demands and even management support for union activity. Labor-management relations are potentially positive-sum, for both sides know they can gain from a stable, negotiated accord. As a result, neither labor nor management needs state help to achieve its ends, making it easier for both to collaborate against the state if need be. Further, high-wage, unionized labor in such sectors forces other sectors to offer similar benefits, further stunting their development. In low/low sectors, labor's impotence is paired with extreme management resistance. Labor-management relations are zero-sum, marked by often violent labor repression by management and anarchic, often violent outbursts by labor. Management needs the state to control

41

labor, and labor, lacking economic possibilities, must also turn to political action. Finally, low wages and the absence of unionization depress wages and inhibit organization in other sectors, thus facilitating their development.

Having now established the absolute capacities of state and societal actors, we can examine the autonomy and relative capacity of the state. The next section probes sectors' impact on leaders' autonomy to *formulate* restructuring policies free of sectoral and societal pressures. The last section explores how sectors shape the relative capacity of states to *implement* their policies.

AUTONOMY

Autonomy is the extent to which leaders can organizationally insulate themselves from societal pressures by controlling the channels of interest representation and thus autonomously define national tasks. For purposes of analysis, this definition is best broken into three parts: the problem of controlling channels of interest representation; the potency of sectoral and societal pressures to sway the policy process; and whether leaders can define a state interest different from sectoral interests and approximating a "national" interest.

Controlling the Channels of Interest Representation

Firms' size, the complexity of their operations, the sophistication of management and labor, specialized infrastructure requirements, and the potency of alternative sectors determine leaders' prospects for controlling the channels of interest representation. They define the extent and intimacy of state-sector contacts, the depth of sectoral representatives' penetration of the state, and whether state agencies will become advocates for sectoral actors.

In high/high cases, leaders cannot insulate decision making from sectoral pressures. Capital and labor know their interests and can mobilize for collective, even collaborative, action to defend them. The complexity of monitoring and regulating big firms demands close, ongoing relations between state agencies, management, and labor, relations facilitated by the fact that business and labor leaders are educated professionals and are agency officials' social equals. There is thus a constant interchange of personnel among state agencies and

42

management and labor organizations, there being no other source of the needed expertise. Such sectors are also attended by specialized supporting agencies with equally strong ties to management or labor or both. The resulting ties between state and sector representatives and the complexity of the issues involved give management and labor ample opportunities to influence policy formulation. Indeed, many bureaucrats come to identify with the sector and become its advocates within the state. These ties are strengthened by the absence of state agencies with ties to other sectors, which hence lack access, advocates within the state, or even knowledgeable interlocutors, and therefore cannot contest leading-sector efforts to shape policy.

In low/low cases, leaders face less daunting challenges. Capital and labor are incapable of collective action. Although the number and dispersion of firms complicate monitoring and regulation of the leading sector, the simplicity of the technologies and businesses involved minimize state dependence on it for expertise. Managers and labor leaders are unsophisticated and lack the skills to manipulate state agencies; moreover, agency officials disdain them. Firms' diversity, small size, and dispersion also mean that state support agencies are unspecialized and do not identify a given sector as their client. It is thus easy to control the channels of interest representation and insulate the policy process from sectoral pressures. In the absence of strong interest groups and intimate state-sector contacts, sector representatives lack clout, and bureaucrats have no reason to become their advocates within the state. Leading-sector clout is further weakened by the existence of other, well-developed sectors and interest groups vying for attention.

Sectoral and Societal Pressures

Leaders' ability to insulate the policy process is also a function of the pressures state institutions must bear. These reflect sectoral differences in the (in)tractability of restructuring, the implications of restructuring for different societal actors, sectors' differing capacities for collective action, the potency of alternative sectors, and the implications of their existence.

States in high/high sectors face crushing pressures from leading-sector interest groups. Production inflexibility and asset/factor inflexibility make firms obsessed with state policy. Even in good times, they cannot control many variables affecting profitability, and thus devote their energy to controlling those within their reach—such as taxes, tariffs, and transportation and ports fees. In a crisis, production inflexibility makes such efforts imperative for short-term survival, and asset/factor inflexibility makes them imperative for long-term survival, that is, for successful resistance to restructuring. In all this, such sectors are triply blessed: they are capable of effective collective action; they have access to the policy process and to allies within the state; and in the absence of alternatives, not only do their claims on the state go unchallenged by other actors but the state lacks allies to turn to in the contest.

But such states face more than special pleading by leading-sector actors. They are the target of *all* actors since, absent alternatives to the leading sector, the state is the only other source of wealth and prestige. Further, the ease of revenue extraction from high/high sectors and the periodic windfalls they produce lead to an extreme concentration of resources in the state, making it the funnel through which the national wealth is distributed. Everyone is thus preoccupied with penetrating the autonomy of the state to ensure that it directs the "funnel" their way. Leaders must develop defensive strategies for relieving such pressures—such as corporatist arrangements, pacts with ethnic power brokers, and formulas for the regional allocation of spending. Inevitably, however, these strategies compromise long-term autonomy for short-term survival. In a crisis, they give *everyone* the same interest in opposing restructuring as that of leading-sector interest groups, and similar access to the state for doing so.

States in low/low sectors face less ferocious pressures from leading-sector interest groups. In part, firms are cross-pressured: because of intense competition, they desire protection; but because each is tiny and lacks political access, they fear that such protection would favor larger firms in an unequal political contest. Firms' flexibility also means that they have less need to influence the state than firms in high/high sectors. This is just as well, since leading-sector actors are triply disadvantaged: they are incapable of collective action; they have neither access to the policy process nor allies within the state; and the vitality of alternative sectors ensures that their demands will encounter opposition and that the state will have allies to turn to in a contest.

States in such sectors also face limited challenges to their autonomy from nonsectoral actors. Alternative sectors offer opportunities for the ambitious; the dispersion of wealth, the absence of windfalls, and limited tax revenues make the state a less tempting target. "Mining"

44

the state and attacking its autonomy offer low returns and thus obsess only a few. Given limited pressures and control of the channels of interest representation, leaders can pursue exclusionary strategies that further enhance their ability to formulate policy autonomously.

Defining State and "National" Interests

Success in insulating policy from societal pressures means little alone unless we assume that leaders automatically translate the need to restructure into action, or naturally identify the state interest with the national interest; if they do not, the question Autonomy for what? remains unanswered. At issue is not the negative Can leaders insulate themselves from societal actors? but also the positive Can they define a state interest separate from sectoral interests? Indeed, the real question is: Under what circumstances will the *state* interest, defined as what leaders want, overlap with the *national* interest, defined as restructuring?

For reasons of state, the leaders of states with high/high sectors cannot define a state interest distinct from sectoral interests. Such sectors monopolize state revenues and export earnings, and stunt other sectors' growth; production inflexibility and asset/factor inflexibility mean that in the short term, the state suffers because of them and in the long term, faces intractable problems restructuring them. State institutions are built around the leading sector and are as inflexible as it is. Such states are also burdened by extensive state services and patronage systems intended to dull attacks on their autonomy and funded by these sectors' easily tapped resources. Defending state revenues and export earnings—and consequently the state's ability to fund itself, pay its debts, and service constituents—thus demands that leaders defend the leading sector. Institutionally, they can do nothing else and have no place else to turn. Even if they want to restructure, this requires reviving the leading sector; it is the only source of the vast sums needed. And however good their intentions, such efforts fail as production inflexibility and asset/factor inflexibility force leaders back to defending the state by defending the status quo. In short, leaders have independent state interests, *but they cannot be autonomous of sectoral interests*. The state interest and the national interest do not overlap, and leaders cannot autonomously define national tasks.

In contrast, low/low sectors give state leaders the *possibility* to define a state interest that approximates the national interest. Although

45

these sectors, too, dominate state revenues and export earnings, the leaders' relationship to them is very different. Production flexibility and asset/factor flexibility reduce the short-term costs that market shocks inflict and the long-term costs of restructuring; and other sectors give leaders alternative sources of revenue and foreign exchange. State institutions are flexible and can be used for monitoring, regulating, taxing, and promoting other sectors. Moreover, autonomy leaves leaders unencumbered by expensive state services or patronage systems. Defending state revenues and export earnings—and power—therefore does not demand defending the sectoral status quo; leaders can define a state interest that is autonomous of sectoral interests. This state interest need not overlap with the national interest, *but it can*. Indeed, since restructuring often increases state capacity and autonomy, leaders have statist motives to pursue the national interest.

RELATIVE CAPACITY

Autonomy is critical, but the proof of stateness lies in implementation, the key to which is relative capacity. Relative capacity is the state's ability to restructure—to alter relations between itself and society, and to reallocate resources within society. It reflects the balance between a state's interests, resources, and institutional capacity, augmented by those of its allies, and the interests, resources, and capacity of the societal groups confronted by the state in the context of a sector-specific restructuring project. An understanding of relative capacity takes us back to two subjects we have already explored: the project different sectors impose on states and societal groups; and the abilities of states and societal actors to defend their resulting interests.

Let us begin with the restructuring project that different sectors' adjustment problems impose on the state. In high/high cases, production inflexibility means that market downturns cut state revenues and export earnings, forcing state leaders to support the status quo. In the long term, too, leaders have reason to resist restructuring. Asset/factor inflexibility and the state's institutional inflexibility pose high barriers to exit, and in the absence of other sectors, restructuring must be financed by borrowing or by rejuvenating the leading sector. In low/low cases, production flexibility and the vitality of other sectors moderate the impact of market shocks and lessen leaders' need to defend the status quo. In the long term, asset/factor flexibility and institutional flexibility minimize barriers to exit, and other sectors can provide funds. In short, states in high/high sectors face severe crises and intractable restructuring projects with less flexible institutional tools, whereas their counterparts face less severe crises and more tractable restructuring projects with more flexible institutional tools.

Societal actors' circumstances are equally complex. In high/high sectors, firms and their workers must block restructuring and have the means to do so. In the short term, firms cannot adjust to market downturns because of production inflexibility; they squander their reserves to maintain full production (and employment) despite their losses. In the long term, asset/factor inflexibility poses high barriers to exit for capital and labor; restructuring puts both with their backs to the wall and gives them reason to fight. They are formidable opponents: each is capable of collective action, has potent weapons, and has access to the policy process; and both have the incentive and the ability to cooperate against the state. In low/low sectors, firms and workers are less threatened by restructuring and incapable of opposition. In the short term, production flexibility lets firms adjust to market shocks (at labor's expense), whereas in the long term asset/factor flexibility lowers the barriers to exit for both firms and labor. Furthermore, neither is capable of initiating collective action to defend the old, and each is utterly opposed to the other, making collaboration impossible.

But this picture is too simple; it is not sticky enough. Relative capacity is not the product of a discreet confrontation over the issues raised by market shocks and restructuring. It reflects an ongoing interaction of state and societal actors, and thus the effects of *past* state efforts to manage sectoral challenges. In high/high cases, state leaders pursue corporatist strategies that recognize the power of leading-sector capital and labor, but seek to manage them by creating an institutionalized balance of power structured by the state. Over time, however, such strategies stunt state autonomy and give leading-sector actors additional means to pressure the state. In low/low cases, state leaders pursue exclusionary strategies that celebrate the lack of opposition and attempt to keep it from developing. Between the extremes lie many variations. Leaders may give sectoral actors access to the state in some areas in return for state autonomy in others, or they may create patronage systems through which to distribute "national" resources to the powerful in return for support. Details aside, what matters is that although these arrangements may reflect the balance of relations between state and society at a given moment, when institutionalized, they become factors affecting states' future relative (in)capacity to restructure.

Here, then, is sectoral analysis in its entirety. It is a purely speculative but provocative construct—a powerful explanatory and predictive tool for understanding the comparative political economy of development. What remains is to apply it to the real world.

CHAPTER THREE

Zambia: The Mining Sector

"We are in part to blame," observed Kenneth Kaunda in the late 1970s, "but this is the curse of being born with a copper spoon in our mouths."[1] And Zambia is cursed. Its debts are huge; its copper industry is moribund; its ore reserves are dwindling; and no new sectors show promise. Twenty-five years ago, however, Zambia boasted a world-class mining industry and the highest per capita income in Africa. Much is unique about Zambia's sad story, but much, too, turns on copper; for Zambia is a perfect high/high mining sector case. In this chapter I examine Zambian leaders' struggle to escape from copper and their two unsuccessful attempts to restructure—one after independence in 1964, the other in the 1980s. I analyze how mining shaped policy makers' and interest groups' actions in both periods, and how the failed effort of the 1960s further constrained that of the 1980s.

Zambia is a copper economy. Copper tied Zambia to the world economy, gave it a modern infrastructure, and endowed it with huge revenues. At independence the mines accounted for 60 percent of gross domestic product (GDP), 53 percent of government revenues, and 92 percent of export earnings, and employed 20 percent of those in formal jobs. In the next decade, they generated 35 percent of GDP, 45 percent of government revenues, and 95 percent of export earnings, and continued to employ 20 percent of Zambian workers.[2] Fur-

---

[1] Kaunda quoted in *Africa Record* 23 (January–February 1978): 34.

[2] James Fry, "The Zambian Economy," in *Administration in Zambia*, ed. William Tordoff (Madison: University of Wisconsin Press, 1980), 44; Republic of Zambia (GRZ), *Zambia: Present Economic Conditions and Prospects* (Lusaka, 1985), 8; D. H. Kalyalya, "The

ther, as noted in the *First National Development Plan,* "the capital investment available to Government . . . is determined almost entirely by
revenue obtained from copper."[3] Nor did nationalization (completed
in 1975) reduce this centrality. Low prices after 1975 killed government revenues from copper and inflated foreign debt, but dependence on mining for foreign exchange rose to 97 percent. In constant
1970 dollars, mining still generates 28 to 36 percent of GDP. Agricultural, manufacturing, and mining output "rose slightly more rapidly than the GDP as a whole after 1980, [but] the increase largely
reflected the greater importance of mining."[4]

Leaders still echo the goals of the 1964 *Outline of the Government's
Industrial Policy,* which declared that "the basic principle of government policy is to support . . . the development and diversification of
the economy."[5] Since 1964 plans have stressed agricultural and rural
development, job creation through labor-intensive industrialization,
import substitution, and export diversification. They have also included warnings against diverting resources from productive purposes to welfare spending, capital-intensive projects, or subsidies.

But restructuring has failed, and the problems Zambia faces are
worse than ever. Although production is down 40 percent since 1969
and world copper prices hit a forty-year low in the mid-1980s, copper
remains central and other sectors still lag. Annual economic growth
averaged only 0.4 percent from 1975 to 1985 and has been flat since
1978.[6] Debt exceeds Zambia's ability to pay and capital spending is
down; since 1973, "half of productive investment merely financed
depreciation on the mines [and] investments in manufacturing appeared less and less supportive of self-reliant growth."[7] The manufac-

---

Mining Industry and Zambia's Economic Development," University of Zambia–
International Development Research Centre (UNZA/IDRC) Workshop on the Zambian Economy: Problems and Prospects (Lusaka, 1984), 3(a); United Nations Development Programme, International Labour Organization (UNDP/ILO), *Second Report to
the Government of Zambia on Incomes, Wages, and Prices in Zambia: Policy and Machinery,*
p. 3: *Statistical Appendices* (Geneva, 1978), secs. A, I; Irving Kaplan, ed., *Zambia: A
Country Study* (Washington, D.C.: American University Foreign Area Studies, 1979),
189.

[3] GRZ, *First National Development Plan, 1966–1970* (Lusaka, 1966), 31.

[4] N. S. Makgeta, "Investment in the Third World: The Zambian Experience,"
UNZA/IDRC Workshop, 11.

[5] GRZ, *Outline of the Government's Industrial Policy* (Lusaka, issued 1964, reissued 1966),
1.

[6] Zambia Consolidated Copper Mines (ZCCM), *Export, Rehabilitation, and Diversification Project: Five-Year Production and Investment Plan, 1985–1990* (Lusaka, 1985), 9.

[7] Makgeta, "Investment in the Third World," 12.

turing sector remains small, import- and capital-intensive, and copper-dependent; reduced revenues from mining caused it to shrink 8 percent between 1974 and 1984. Nonmineral exports are minimal. The agricultural sector cannot feed the nation, necessitating costly food imports. Population is growing more than 3 percent per year and Zambia's cities are growing still faster, but job growth is stagnant. Real wages fell 40 percent from 1974 to 1983, per capita gross national product (GNP) fell 25 percent in the same period, and social inequalities have increased sharply.[8]

When Zambian leaders tried to restructure in the early 1980s, they again called for diversification to cut Zambia's "vulnerability to external forces," and for efforts to correct "structural imbalances among sectors, between rural and urban development, as well as between excessive consumption and productive expenditures."[9] They tried to increase nonmineral exports and domestic production, stabilize exchange rates, control the deficit, cut regulation, promote parastatal efficiency, and boost agriculture. But by the time President Kaunda scrapped a final IMF austerity plan in May 1987, the effort had clearly failed. The question is, why?

THE INTERNATIONAL DIMENSION

Mining poses unavoidable challenges to all comers—corporations and countries alike.[10] The sector is marked by extreme capital intensity and economies of scale, and both production inflexibility and asset/factor inflexibility. International markets are oligopolistic, rewarding those able to surmount the high barriers to entry—and punishing those unable to manage their acute uncertainties and risks. As an unintegrated national producer, Zambia cannot pursue the necessary risk management strategies and has suffered accordingly.

Copper mining is a high-stakes, high-risk proposition. The capital intensity and extent of economies of scale are staggering, but rela-

[8] Doris Jansen, *Trade, Exchange Rate, and Agricultural Pricing Policies in Zambia* (Washington, D.C.: World Bank, 1988), 10; GRZ, *Restructuring in the Midst of Crisis*, vol. 1, *Development Policies and Objectives,* Report for the Consultative Group for Zambia (Lusaka, May 22–24, 1984), 29–31; E. C. Kaunga and P. D. Ncube, "An Overview of the Zambian Economy," UNZA/IDRC Workshop, p. 26.

[9] GRZ, "Budget Address by the Minister of Finance" (Lusaka, January 1982), 1.

[10] For a comparison of bauxite, copper, iron ore, and oil, see D. Michael Shafer, "Undermined: The Implications of Mineral Export Dependence for State Formation in Africa," *Third World Quarterly* 8 (July 1986).

tively low barriers to entry make upstream oligopoly difficult to sustain. The industry, therefore, has a "relatively large competitive fringe" over which the majors exercise only "limited domination."[11] In the short run, supply elasticity is low, but demand elasticity is high, so that demand shifts produce sharp changes in prices and market power. In the long term, however, supply elasticity is high. Thus, though price escalations occur, copper offers no hope of sustained high prices, but instead periodic busts.

The capital costs—and risks—of mining are huge. In the 1970s, locating a new nonferrous mineral deposit cost $200,000 to $500,000. Of these deposits only 2 percent merited mining, which means that firms could spend $10 million for a 50 percent chance of finding a viable ore body. Facility costs, too, are huge and rising. In 1951, new projects cost $1,300 per ton of annual capacity; by 1970 they cost $3,000 per ton; and by 1979, $6,000 to $8,000 per ton. This upward trend and the related rise in the capital intensity per unit of production continue.[12]

Extreme economies of scale also prevail. A few mines produce 20,000 to 50,000 tons of metal per year, but there are big economies of scale for operations producing 100,000 to 200,000 tons. Such mines handle more than 80,000 tons of ore per day, requiring huge mine complexes and processing facilities, rivers of water, fleets of trucks, miles of roads, entire railroads, vast power grids, special ports, armies of workers, and small cities to house them. Excluding infrastructure, they cost $500 million by the mid-1980s; with infrastructure, costs exceeded $1 billion, 95 percent of which is spent before mining begins.[13]

High capital intensity and extreme economies of scale affect all players. The size of the investments is overwhelming; in 1973, for example, Zambian mining investment, *excluding* infrastructure, was

---

[11] Walter Labys, *Market Structure, Bargaining Power, and Resource Price Formation* (Lexington, Mass.: D. C. Heath, 1980), 42, 93.

[12] Rex Bosson and Benison Varon, *The Mining Industry and the Developing Countries* (New York: Oxford University Press, 1977), 19–32; James Cobbe, *Governments and Mining Companies in Developing Countries* (Boulder, Colo.: Westview Press, 1979), 12; John Tilton, *The Future of Nonfuel Minerals* (Washington, D.C.: Brookings Institution, 1977), 61; Labys, *Market Structure*, 21, 79–80; United Nations Center on Transnational Corporations, *Transnational Corporations in the Copper Industry* (New York, 1981), 18; Ronald Prain, *Copper: The Anatomy of an Industry* (London: Mining Journal Books, 1975), 187.

[13] Labys, *Market Structure*, 27–28, 79–80; Raymond Mikesell, *Foreign Investment in Copper Mining* (Baltimore: Johns Hopkins University Press, 1975), 24.

40 percent of gross domestic investment.[14] Rising capital costs also mean that firms cannot finance development with retained earnings and private equity investment but must borrow. Thus, until the early 1970s, Zambian firms met 50 percent of their capital requirements with retained earnings and Zambia had no mining-related debt; by the early 1980s Zambia Consolidated Copper Mines (ZCCM) borrowed 80 percent of its capital and had huge debts.[15]

Long lead times and lumpiness complicate the picture. Mines take eight to ten years to start up and another ten to fifteen before showing a profit, so huge sums must be sunk under conditions of high uncertainty. Moreover, because of their size, new mines may themselves upset supply and prices. Long lead times for new capacity and high utilization rates for existing capacity mean that production cannot be increased quickly when demand surges; conversely, high fixed costs mean that it cannot be cut when supply surges or demand slumps.[16] The result is an exaggerated boom-bust cycle in prices that copper producers are helpless to control—despite depressed prices, Zambia produced "*at a loss* throughout most of the 1980s" to service huge fixed costs.[17]

Copper producers have been obsessive, and unsuccessful, in the pursuit of two strategic goals: maintaining upstream oligopoly and containing catastrophic risk. The key to both is oligopoly management. This entails limiting competition and managing supply through coordinated investment, production, and pricing policies in order to earn monopoly rents, control the market, and contain the risks that haunt high/high sectors. Failure means destructive competition or investment races among existing producers and the rise of new producers who grab market share, overexpand supply, cut prices, and destabilize the market. The keys to success are high barriers to entry, the absence of substitutes, and firms' ability to cooperate to

[14] Labys, *Market Structure*, 94.

[15] Bosson and Varon, *The Mining Industry*, 48; Marian Radetski and Stephen Zorn, *Financing Mining Projects in Developing Countries* (London: Mining Journal Books, 1979), 54.

[16] Prain, *Copper*, 52–53.

[17] Helen O'Neill et al., *Transforming a Single Product Economy: An Examination of the First Stage of Zambia's Economic Reform Program, 1982–86* (Washington, D.C.: World Bank, 1987), 18. Emphasis added. In 1982, for example, average copper prices were $0.62 per pound—and Zambia's production costs alone were $0.82 per pound. World Bank, *Zambia Country Economic Memorandum: Economic Reforms and Development Prospects*, Report no. 6355-ZA (Washington, D.C., 1986), 11, 16.

fend off new entrants and control prices and production.[18] None has existed for long in the copper industry, however.

Copper producers pursue individual and collective policies to secure the oligopoly. Firms seek to keep investment, production, and pricing in line with long-term demand and the threat of substitution. They try to secure control of new ore bodies (denying new entrants access to them) and keep them "on ice" until needed.[19] Firms have pursued horizontal integration through cartel agreements and have tried to institute a producers' price system to replace the volatile London Metals Exchange (LME) as a price-setting mechanism.[20] They also pursue informal horizontal integration by buying each others' stock, lending each other money, and sharing directors. Such measures permit firms to monitor rivals' activities and coordinate investment, production, and pricing, while giving all parties an interest in each other's well-being.[21] Joint ventures abound, permitting coordination and risk sharing, reducing competition, and moderating the market impact of bringing huge new mines on line.

But producers have never grasped either strategic goal for long; the wave of nationalizations in the 1960s and 1970s pushed both beyond reach. Despite recognition "that fluctuating markets are conducive neither to the advancement of copper consumption, nor to the orderly development of production, stability has been achieved only over comparatively short periods and at comparatively low prices."[22] The story of cartelization thus is "more a history of failure than success. No scheme yet propounded has introduced a long-term measure of price stability, at reasonable prices. . . . Indeed, most collusive agreements have retreated into acrimony and disbandment, only to be followed by damaging slides in the copper price."[23]

Two developments account for the failure of oligopoly manage-

---

[18] Theodore Moran, *Multinational Corporations and the Politics of Dependence* (Princeton: Princeton University Press, 1974), 17.

[19] David Becker, *The New Bourgeoisie and the Limits of Dependency* (Princeton: Princeton University Press, 1983), 86.

[20] Copper is priced according to the London Metals Exchange price, though most copper moves within vertically integrated firms or is sold under long-term contract. The LME is thus a very thin market in which buyers and sellers can meet their marginal needs. The LME price is therefore volatile and may not reflect "the real equilibrium position for the industry as a whole," especially in times of shortage or glut. Moran, *Multinational Corporations*, 53.

[21] Becker, *The New Bourgeoisie*, 76–77.

[22] Prain, *Copper*, 51.

[23] *Copper Studies* 1 (February 1974): 8.

ment. First, technological innovations such as fiber-optic cable, substitution of aluminum for copper, and recycling have slowed demand growth, increased competition, and eliminated monopoly rents. "With so few possibilities for dynamic growth or for upward price manipulation," firms have few incentives to invest in oligopoly management.[24] Second, the oligopoly itself has grown from seven to twenty major producers, as the continuing discoveries of new reserves, the development of new technologies permitting the exploitation of poorer ones, and the spread of mining and management know-how undermined the barriers to entry.[25] Equally important, Peru, Chile, Zaire, and Zambia (which account for 50 percent of internationally traded copper) nationalized their mines in the late 1960s and early 1970s, adding four new, independent producers to the industry. The added numbers complicated oligopoly management, and the increased production capacity exaggerated the problems posed by stagnant demand and competition for market share, thus weakening collusive price and production control, encouraging more substitution, and intensifying the boom-bust price cycle.

Firms have had to fall back on internal risk management strategies to cope with the deadly mix of high fixed costs and price volatility. The problem is that "inelasticities of supply and demand in the short run tend to shift market power abruptly from producer to consumer and back again."[26] Strikes or mining disasters can produce shortages and price surges overnight; the need to service high fixed costs then blocks production cuts when demand falls, producing gluts and price slumps. Firms must thus integrate vertically to assure themselves market outlets and internalize the market's violent price swings.[27] They may also seek "informal" vertical integration through long-term contracts, agreeing to forego high prices in times of shortage and to guarantee buyers supplies in return for buyers' agreement to forego rock-bottom prices in times of glut and to continue to take a set

[24] Quote from Becker, *The New Bourgeoisie*, 75–76. See also Robert Bowen and Ananda Gunatilaka, *Copper: Its Geology and Economics* (New York: John Wiley, 1977), 306–8; Wolfgang Gluschke, Joseph Shaw, and Benison Varon, *Copper: The Next Fifteen Years* (Boston: Reidel, 1979), 34–42; Michel Amsalem, "Bauxite, Copper, and Oil," *Columbia Journal of World Business* 19 (Spring 1984): 291.

[25] Marian Radetski, "Long-Term Copper Production Options of the Developing Countries," *Natural Resources Forum* 1 (1977): 145–46; Gluschke et al., *Copper*, 53; Moran, *Multinational Corporations*, 32–33; Labys, *Market Structure*, 88–90.

[26] Moran, *Multinational Corporations*, 50.

[27] Ibid., 38–40.

volume of copper. Similarly, producers may arrange deals with custom refiners, gaining guaranteed market outlets by guaranteeing refiners access to feedstock.[28]

This, then, is the tough world in which Zambia and other Third World copper producers operate. At issue is how successfully they can pursue the collective and individual risk management strategies required to meet its challenges—*compared with the competition.*

Nationalization

Soon after independence, Zambia took up these challenges by nationalizing its mines. Nationalization seemed to promise liberation from MNC domination, a larger share of the rents, and, as a result of cooperation with other national producers, higher, more stable prices. At home, Zambians hoped nationalization would replace the corporate profit motive with a national welfare motive, permit rational economic planning, provide the monies for restructuring, and speed Zambians' advancement into the area of mining management.

Nationalization was easy, for once mining companies' investment is sunk, they are vulnerable. In 1964 two MNCs, the Anglo-American Corporation (Zamanglo) and Roan Selection Trust (RST), controlled the Zambian copper industry and the major mining concessions. In 1968, Zambia limited company remittances to 50 percent of after-tax profits, and in 1969 reclaimed all mineral rights. In 1970, it took control of 51 percent of both firms and raised taxes to 87 percent of profits.[29] Zamanglo became Nchanga Consolidated Copper Mines (NCCM) and RST became Roan Consolidated Mines (RCM), both under the state holding company, the Zambia Industrial and Mining Corporation (ZIMCO). Zambia issued bonds for the book value of the nationalized shares and signed a management and sales agreement with the MNCs. In 1973 it redeemed the bonds and formed the Metal Marketing Corporation (MEMACO) to sell its copper. Zambia paid

[28] Becker, *The New Bourgeoisie*, 77–79; Walter Labys, "The Role of State Trading in Mineral Commodity Markets," *Les Cahiers du CETAI*, no. 79-06 (April 1979); Dani Rodrik, "Managing Resource Dependency," Harvard University Program on U.S.-Japanese Relations, Working Paper no. 81-3 (Cambridge, 1981); Raymond Vernon and Brian Levy, "State-Owned Enterprises in the World Economy," in *Public Enterprises in Less Developed Countries,* ed. LeRoy Jones (New York: Cambridge University Press, 1982).

[29] C. Fred Bergsten, Thomas Horst, and Theodore Moran, *American Multinationals and American Interests* (Washington, D.C.: Brookings Institution, 1978), 136.

off the management contracts in 1975, leaving the industry heavily indebted and self-managing just as the copper market crashed. In 1978, Zambia upped its equity share to 60 percent, and in 1981 RCM and NCCM were combined to create Zambia Consolidated Copper Mines.

But nationalization brought none of the anticipated benefits; Zambians' high hopes merely reflected "an inadequate understanding of the complexity of the world copper market."[30] National producers' capacity to capitalize on nationalization turns on their ability to pursue the collective strategies required for oligopoly management and the individual strategies required for risk management. They have been even less successful than the MNCs on both fronts, however, and have paid an even higher price for failing.

CIPEC Constrained

Zambia sought the benefits of oligopoly management through the International Council of Copper Exporting Countries (CIPEC)—and failed. Founded in 1967, CIPEC aimed to increase members' earnings; increase real prices; coordinate production, pricing, and capacity additions; and provide production and market information. But as the commercial manager of MEMACO observed twenty years later, "CIPEC today [has] no impact in terms of market stability, production or prices."[31] In part, its problems reflect depressed demand; in large measure, however, they "lie on the production side of the equation [where] producers . . . have behaved in a short-sighted and highly disruptive manner—refusing to adjust production to consumer demand and creating a huge stock of surplus copper which has undermined the market."[32] Indeed, copper prices have fluctuated more since CIPEC's founding "than in any comparable period" and in the 1980s hit a forty-year low.[33]

Some CIPEC problems are copper industry problems. To raise prices by restricting output, the absolute value of the price elasticity of demand must be less than one. The short-term elasticity of demand for CIPEC copper is only negligibly less than one, however; and

---

[30] Chisepo Mphaisha, "A Study of Zambia's Copper Policy" (Ph.D. diss., University of Pittsburgh, 1979), 3.
[31] Kataya interview.
[32] *Engineering and Mining Journal*, March 19, 1978, 69–70.
[33] Prain, *Copper*, 251–52.

long-term elasticity has been as high as -2.8, implying that efforts to raise prices by withholding supply will result only in lost market share.[34] The reasons for this are the same as those dogging MNC producers: a dynamic market in secondary copper, substitution, and big stockpiles. No less important, CIPEC controls just 35–40 percent of world copper, so it must cut production savagely to reduce supply, whereas non-CIPEC producers can expand exports to fill the void— witness the steady fall in CIPEC's market share since 1967.[35]

The creation of CIPEC also weakened the oligopoly and with it CIPEC members' prospects. The actions of CIPEC and its members led mining companies and consumers to develop new mines in politically "safe" areas. Thus, though copper investment in general declined in the 1970s because of depressed demand, "developing countries . . . experienced a disproportionate reduction in new capital formation"; all the countries for which average annual growth in copper production exceeded the average from the late 1960s to the mid-1970s were non-CIPEC members considered "safe areas for investment."[36] Zambia saw no new investment in copper.

The scramble for new sources has been bad for all concerned, but the worst effects have been felt by CIPEC members. New mines exaggerated the trend toward excess capacity, weakening the industry's ability to adjust prices and production as recession lowered demand and made such control more critical. As a result, "the industry as a whole may adjust less rapidly to price signals triggered by demand shifts, with over-production reflected in prolonged periods of relatively low prices."[37] Some of the pain borne by CIPEC members was self-inflicted, however, for many had broken long-term contracts to ride the surging prices of the late 1960s and early 1970s.[38] But they also suffered as the MNCs opened new mines and consumers developed their own suppliers. The result is a dual market in which CIPEC members are "suppliers of last resort, outside the main network of semi-integrated ties between corporate producers and consumers . . . regulated to the position of a spill-over market onto which has

[34] Kenji Takeuchi, "CIPEC and the Copper Export Earnings of Member Countries," *The Developing Economies* 10 (March 1972): 9–12; Zuhayr Mikdashi, *The International Politics of Natural Resources* (Ithaca: Cornell University Press, 1976), 95–96.

[35] Christopher Brown, *The Political and Social Economy of Commodity Control* (New York: Praeger, 1980), 168–69; Amsalem, "Bauxite, Copper, and Oil," 23; Moran, *Multinational Corporations,* 231–32.

[36] Gluschke et al., *Copper,* xxix; Tilton, *The Future of Nonfuel Minerals,* 44.

[37] Gluschke et al., *Copper,* xxvi.

[38] Kataya interview.

been shifted the burden of market uncertainty and instability for the entire industry."[39]

The problems of CIPEC result largely from barriers to collective action. Compared with most commodities, copper's "outstanding characteristic is the enormous range . . . between the lowest and highest cost producers."[40] The resulting "wide range of break-even points . . . may well defeat all CIPEC's efforts towards price stabilization," since for almost any target price, there are lower-cost producers still able to turn a profit and therefore unwilling to sacrifice, especially without a guarantee that others will as well.[41] Moreover, members are not corporations but states that depend on copper for jobs, revenues, and debt service. None can afford to cut production; all prefer to cheat and expect others to cheat, making collusion unlikely. Each produces as much as possible in the hope of selling enough to offset depressed prices.

Zambia is no exception. A senior MEMACO official asserts that CIPEC has "not much future" and that current Zambian policies reflect this assessment.[42] In the Five-Year Production and Investment Plan prepared in the mid-1980s, for example, ZCCM noted that although copper demand was likely to rise only 1.5–2.0 percent per year, ZCCM intended to increase production by 30 percent, an action justified by explicit reference to other countries' recent capacity additions.[43] In short, Zambia, like other national producers, cannot pursue oligopoly management but must pursue short-term gains at the cost of gutting CIPEC and exaggerating the long-term troubles afflicting all copper producers.

Individual Action: The Limits of Downstream Integration

Given CIPEC's failure, Zambia's prospects turn on its ability to manage risk. But as a national producer, it is structurally disadvantaged in a market dominated by vertically integrated MNC competitors. In the

[39] Moran, *Multinational Corporations*, 233–34, 241.

[40] Quote from Prain, *Copper*, 185. See also Martin Brown and John Butler, *The Production, Marketing, and Consumption of Copper and Aluminum* (New York: Praeger, 1968), 6.

[41] Quote from *Mining Annual Review*, 1974, 9. See also Stephen Zorn, "Producers' Associations and Commodity Markets: The Case of CIPEC," in *Stabilizing World Commodity Markets*, ed. F. Gerald Adams and Sonia Klein (Lexington, Mass.: D.C. Heath, 1979), 229–30.

[42] Kataya interview.

[43] ZCCM, "Summary of the Five-Year Production and Investment Plan: Export, Rehabilitation, and Diversification Project" (Lusaka, n.d.), 3.

absence of vertical integration, Zambia is open to the full force of market volatility. Vertical integration does not protect the MNCs entirely either, but their competitive advantage is not "access to capital or technology, but . . . access to markets for output." In fact, vertical integration within MNCs "tends to make the unintegrated portion [of the market] more unstable."[44] Zambia's domestic market is too small to support a fabrication industry, however, and industrial country tariffs discriminate against wrought copper products, denying Zambia an export market. Limited to its own resource base, Zambia can neither insulate itself from substitution by buying into the aluminum industry nor homogenize production costs by investing in other countries' copper mines.[45]

Zambia has had to settle for second-best risk management solutions such as long-term contracts. These agreements lower transaction costs and offer some security with regard to sales volumes, but they are constantly renegotiated as the LME price changes. Worse, "buyers commonly back away from their commitments when ore is in very easy supply." Contracts thus do little to reduce "uncertainties associated with changes in supply, demand, and price" and "provide nothing like the stability and predictability" of vertical integration.[46] Zambia has therefore tried to integrate downstream by buying stakes in European fabricators. It cannot afford investments big enough to ensure markets for its core production, however, and the effort raises questions about the wisdom of investing Zambia's limited capital in other economies.[47]

Zambia is also disadvantaged relative to its MNC competition in the area of mining finance. Until the late 1960s the copper industry attracted equity investment for new operations, and retained earnings provided "at least 75 percent of the funds required for expansion." Since then, however, rising capital costs mean that "any major new project, or . . . production expansion program," must rely on debt financing.[48] But MNC reaction to nationalization and risk-averse in-

---

[44] Quote from Cobbe, *Governments and Mining Companies,* 11–12, 31. See also Dennis Carlton, "Vertical Integration in Competitive Markets under Uncertainty," *Journal of Industrial Economics* 27 (March 1979): 207.

[45] Dorthea Mezger, *Copper in the World Economy* (New York: Monthly Review Press, 1980), 117.

[46] Vernon and Levy, "State-Owned Enterprises," 178.

[47] Radetski and Zorn, *Financing Mining Projects,* 92, 115; Kataya interview.

[48] Quotes from Gluschke et al., *Copper,* 114; and Radetski and Zorn, *Financing Mining Projects,* 138.

vestors have caused investment to be switched away from CIPEC members and have changed the investment mechanism itself to "project financing." Project financing has made capital available but is biased against national producers. Agreements may demand assured markets, for example, emphasizing their weakness in vertically integrated markets, or they may set cash flow targets, such that "until the financial results of a mining project are satisfactory, . . . host country governments are held directly liable for the debt service."[49] Further, because lenders recognize the benefits of vertical integration and joint ventures, national producers face "capital market penalties and quantity rationing," since they can pursue neither.[50]

Here lies a double problem. Rising debt payments limit producers' ability to respond to gluts and depressed prices; as a result, Zambia and other countries continued to produce at a loss for much of the decade 1975–85. Nationalization only exaggerated this problem. "As part of the 1970 takeover agreement," the Zambian state "accepted the responsibility of guaranteeing all loans raised abroad by the industry, thus tying the financing of copper development to the overall health of the Zambian economy."[51] The mines' debt service crowds out other pressing needs, but as Zambia has sunk further into debt, the cost of funds to revive the mines has soared. As a result, the mines were so starved for capital by the mid-1980s that shortages of spare parts had cut production by 40 percent, causing Zambia to drop from second place to fifth among world copper producers.[52] Thus, the question for all national producers in need of mining finance is, On what terms? For Zambia the question is, On any terms?[53]

In short, Zambia's prospects in the international copper market are not good. True, its circumstances are extreme, but they are not atypical. In good times, there are big profits to be made, but in bad times the losses are crushing. Zambia cannot realize the one or avoid the

---

[49] Quote from Radetski and Zorn, *Financing Mining Projects,* 85; See also United Nations Economic and Social Council, *Permanent Sovereignty over Natural Resources,* E/C.7/119, May 7, 1981, 17.

[50] John Stuckey, *Vertical Integration and Joint Ventures in the Aluminum Industry* (Cambridge: Harvard University Press, 1983), 170.

[51] Chukwuma Obidegwu and Mudziviri Nziramasango, *Copper and Zambia* (Lexington, Mass.: Lexington Books, 1981), 18; See also D. Michael Shafer, "Capturing the Mineral Multinationals," *International Organization* 37 (Winter 1983).

[52] Radetski and Zorn, *Financing Mining Projects,* 36–37; Mezger, *Copper in the World Economy,* 220; Kataya interview.

[53] World Bank, *Accelerated Development in Sub-Saharan Africa* (Washington, D.C., 1981), 99.

other. Pursuit of the required collective and individual strategies is impossible; the state's interests and expectations of other producers' likely behavior dictate policies antithetical to both. The only logical course of action, therefore, is to shift the sectoral base.

THE DOMESTIC DIMENSION: AN INTRACTABLE PROJECT

Zambian leaders seemed to have real advantages when they first faced the task of restructuring. Independence offered opportunities for innovation, for citizens expected them to alter the colonial political economy. And they seemed to have the money to do whatever they wanted. All was not well, however, as their advantages proved wholly insufficient when they confronted the intractability of restructuring the copper industry.

High production inflexibility is inevitable in copper mining; it reflects mining's extreme capital intensity, which burdens all firms with high fixed costs—costs exaggerated in Zambia's case by vast sums borrowed to nationalize the mines. Mining also demands investment in a big, skilled work force, an investment that Zambian mining companies have long protected by ensuring job security. Finally, Zambia's mines are prone to flooding, and "the costs of shutting down and restarting capital structures such as . . . smelting pots may be very much greater than the interest charges on idle capital."[54] Firms thus cannot cut production in times of glut but must produce, even at a loss, to cover fixed costs, retain skilled labor, and avoid mothballing facilities.

Asset/factor inflexibility is high too, reflecting the sector-specificity of infrastructure, physical plant, technology, work force, mining communities, and management. Historically, copper has driven infrastructure development, for example. Without copper, the Northern Rhodesian Railroad might have failed; without the railroad, landlocked Zambia is isolated. Thus, the colonial state devoted itself to providing rail service, roads, and power along the "line-of-rail," a pattern that continues to this day, despite efforts to develop other areas. The reason is simple: ZCCM is still Zambian Railways' dominant customer; in 1981 it used 75 percent of the electricity, 60 percent

[54] Ben Smith, "Long-Term Contracts for the Supply of Raw Materials," in *Raw Materials and Pacific Integration*, ed. John Crawford and Kiyoshi Kojima (Vancouver: University of British Columbia Press, 1978), 243.

of the coal, and 37 percent of the oil consumed in Zambia.[55] No other bulk users exist, and these specialized power grids, ore-loading facilities, and hopper cars have no other uses.

The pattern is similar for the other elements defining asset/factor inflexibility. Mines, refineries, and smelters have no other uses. Mining concentrates 20 percent of wage earners in the Copperbelt, giving them the best-paid jobs in Zambia and specialized, nontransferable skills. They and their families live in stable, homogeneous company towns whose very existence depends on mining. Mining managers possess specialized mine management skills, whereas the MNCs and ZCCM have developed specialized corporate structures to meet the needs of the industry, and they are supported by a distinct corporate culture. In sum, little of Zambia's human, social, organizational, or material investment in copper can be reallocated.

Inflexibility's effects are nasty. Production inflexibility prevents Zambia from behaving like a rational oligopolist, thus helping to destabilize the copper market and undermine CIPEC. It also ensures that when copper prices fall, Zambia will suffer immediate, catastrophic drops in foreign export earnings and tax revenues; with nationalization, there will also be a heavy financial drain from continued production at a loss. Furthermore, it means that the mining firms cannot take evasive action; consequently, they demand cuts in taxes, tariffs, and transportation and utilities rates to survive, exaggerating the pain that price drops inflict on the state.

Asset/factor inflexibility makes restructuring a nightmare. It requires writing off many of Zambia's assets, threatens a powerful industry and a powerful union, and will dislocate entire communities. And with their backs to the wall, all those concerned will fight. The political costs to the state in terms of disrupted lives and dislocated communities are too high to contemplate; in the absence of other sectors, it must build the new from scratch, without allies and under attack. No wonder the 1984 government report on the subject is entitled *Restructuring in the Midst of Crisis.*

Zambia's inflexibility is exaggerated by a bad case of the "Dutch disease," a distorted pattern of development caused by a booming staples sector. Plentiful foreign exchange and an overvalued ex-

[55] World Bank, *Zambia Country Economic Memorandum: Issues and Options for Economic Diversification,* Report no. 5000-ZA (Washington, D.C., 1984), 38.

change rate during copper's heyday encouraged imports and discouraged local manufacturing. High copper export earnings dulled incentives to develop alternative exports, and high wages in the mining industry spread throughout the economy, stifling export competitiveness. Copper revenues also "suggested that there was little need to develop agriculture to ensure adequate supplies of food or to provide foreign exchange earnings," resulting in a rise in food imports funded by copper export revenues.[56] Copper monies stimulated production of nontradables, and "services, utilities, construction, commerce, and transport . . . dominated the economy." The lack of locally produced consumer goods and agricultural inputs, combined with high tariffs on imports, savaged urban-rural terms of trade, agricultural production, and rural living standards.[57]

State policies worsened the ravages of the Dutch disease. The colonial government combined a laissez-faire ideology (which favored the copper companies, the strongest actors) with tariff, tax, agricultural pricing, and investment policies that benefited mining and contributed to its inflexibility as well as to that of the economy as a whole. The government, through the Maize Control Board, reduced food prices and thus labor costs for the mines, while taxing African producers heavily to increase production and extract the revenues needed for line-of-rail infrastructure investments. It also refused to provide loans or give tariff protection to alternative sectors facing import competition fueled by high copper export earnings. Duty-free imports of mining equipment further encouraged the rapid, capital-intensive expansion of mining.[58]

At independence, Zambia embraced large-scale, capital-intensive import substitution industrialization (ISI) based on state ownership—and made a bad situation worse. Zambia industrialized using an overvalued exchange rate, duty-free imports of capital equipment, nega-

[56] Jansen, *Trade, Exchange Rate, and Agricultural Pricing Policies,* 201.

[57] Quote from O'Neill et al., *Transforming a Single Product Economy,* p. 21. See also UNDP/ILO, *Second Report to the Government of Zambia on Incomes, Wages, and Prices in Zambia: Policy and Machinery,* pt. 1: *General Review and Recommendations,* ZAM/77/005 (Geneva, 1978), 46.

[58] Carolyn Baylies, "Class Formation and the State in Zambia" (Ph.D. diss., University of Wisconsin, 1978), 224, 251, 326–30; Alistair Young, *Industrial Diversification in Zambia* (New York: Praeger, 1973), 12–18; James Fry and Charles Harvey, "Copper in Zambia," in *Commodity Exports and African Economic Development,* ed. Scott Pearson and John Cownie (Lexington, Mass.: D. C. Heath, 1974), 195; Jansen, *Trade, Exchange Rate, and Agricultural Pricing Policies,* 56; Dennis Dresang, *The Zambian Civil Service* (Nairobi: East African Publishing House, 1975), 74–76.

tive real interest rates, and effective rates of protection as high as 2000 percent.[59] The results were disastrous, as the policy gutted agriculture, was "unambiguously biased against potential exporting industries," and increased imports' share of GDP from 8 percent to 19 percent between 1970 and 1980. The new industries offered few horizontal or backward linkages, were horrendously inefficient, and, despite huge investments, by the early 1980s still "accounted for less than 1 percent of total exports," the same as in the early 1970s.[60] The "alternative sectors" that were built to diversify the economy depended on copper earnings, and inefficiency and high prices imposed severe costs.[61]

State policy also made the industrial sector as inflexible as mining and thus posed new barriers to restructuring. It increased the incremental capital-to-output ratio of the economy from 7:1 in 1967–73 to 24:1 in 1973–79, by focusing on "capital-intensive investments . . . such as in fertilizer and textile plants and the oil refinery."[62] Their siting also increased work force concentration along the line-of-rail and in the Copperbelt. Indeed, by the late 1980s 93.3 percent of manufacturing firms and 99 percent of manufacturing jobs were concentrated along the line-of-rail; and 55 percent and 46 percent, respectively, were concentrated in the Copperbelt alone. As with mining, little of this huge investment in human capital, organization, or material can be reallocated. "Short of total economic and political collapse," argues Helen O'Neill, "it is virtually impossible to envisage [the parastatals] which dominate over three-quarters of the national

[59] O'Neill et al., *Transforming a Single Product Economy*, 45; World Bank, *Zambia Country Economic Memorandum: Economic Reforms and Development Prospects*, 13.

[60] Quotes from both O'Neill et al., *Transforming a Single Product Economy*, 39, 45, 109; and World Bank, "Improving Parastatal Performance in Zambia" (Washington, D.C., 1986), vii.

[61] Zambian industry's copper dependence is most evident in the decrease in capacity utilization since 1975 to less than 33 percent of 1973 levels. World Bank, *Zambia Country Economic Memorandum: Economic Reforms and Development Prospects*, 13. The Zambia Industrial and Mining Corporation (ZIMCO) showed no after-tax profits between 1981 and 1986; the Industrial Development Corporation's (INDECO) performance was so bad in the late 1970s and 1980s that "internal cash generation does not cover adequate plant and equipment renewal and maintenance." World Bank, "Improving Parastatal Performance," i of Annex 1; and World Bank, *Zambia: Public Expenditure Review*, vol. 1, *Executive Summary*, Report no. 6438-ZA (Washington, D.C., 1986), 19.

[62] World Bank, *Boxed in Zambia: Economic Recovery or Downward Spiral?* (Washington, D.C., 1988), 19; and World Bank, *Zambia Country Economic Memorandum: Issues and Options for Economic Diversification*, 35.

economy ceasing to wield immense power in the medium term. There are no substitutes . . . in Zambia's present economic structure."[63]

Although striking, this picture is meaningless when viewed in isolation. True, inflexibility ensures that Zambia confronts an intractable restructuring project. The issue, however, is whether the state can take on the task. Or rather, it is how the sectoral characteristics of copper shape the core elements of stateness, and therefore Zambia's prospects for success.

THE DOMESTIC POLITICAL ECONOMY OF COPPER: ABSOLUTE CAPACITY

Zambia reached independence crippled by its past. It had no national identity. The literacy rate was 29 percent; less than 50 percent of the children attended primary school, 4 percent attended secondary school, and just a hundred Zambians had college degrees. Technical education was nonexistent, and the University of Zambia would not graduate its first class until 1969. The weak civil service reflected the colonial state's law-and-order and copper industry biases. In 1964, Africans held only 39 of 1,298 senior appointments, and whites monopolized even low-level posts. Their abrupt departure gutted the bureaucracy. Even five years later, one-quarter of the civil servants had no in-service training, two-thirds of the mid-level civil servants had no high school education, and only one-quarter of the senior civil servants had finished school. Ten years later, in 1979, more than half of the permanent secretaries running ministries lacked a university education.[64]

But colonial inheritance alone is not the whole story. To explain the *pattern* of institutional development displayed by the Zambian state, as well as its peculiar strengths and weaknesses, we must turn to copper.

Resource Extraction

At the time of independence, copper seemed to promise unlimited revenues. Between 1966 and 1982, Zambia achieved the highest average tax yield of thirty-six African countries—23.7 percent of GDP,

[63] O'Neill et al., *Transforming a Single Product Economy*, 108, 137, 156.

[64] Dresang, *The Zambian Civil Service*, 24, 39; William Tordoff and Robert Molteno, "Government and Administration," in *Politics in Zambia*, ed. William Tordoff (Manchester: University of Manchester Press, 1974), 266–67.

compared with an average of 14.9 percent.[65] But the specialized tax system that had served so well in good times could not cope when copper prices crashed in 1975, nor could it support restructuring.

In 1964 Zambia had formidable resource extraction capabilities, which it soon expanded. Limited links with the outside meant that the Department of Customs and Excise required little to do its job. Zambia also had the legal and institutional means to tax mine production, foreign sales, and company earnings. But Zambian leaders wanted more. In 1966 they put a 40 percent tax on copper sales proceeds in excess of £300 per ton and raised company income taxes to 65 percent of gross profits, thus increasing mining's contribution to revenues to 54 percent and the total tax effort to 32 percent of GDP.[66] In 1969 they began to nationalize mining, and by 1975 the government had acquired 51 percent of the companies and managerial control of the industry. Ownership gave access to company records, permitting Zambia to institute a single, profits-only tax after 1970. The aim of the new tax regime was to lower the tax rate, but to raise tax revenues by encouraging investment and output.[67] It worked fine—as long as copper prices continued to rise.

Besides producing huge revenues at minimal cost, mining taxes and customs and excise taxes were "invisible." None required an intrusive, deeply penetrating institutional presence in citizen's lives. Moreover, the indirect costs of tariffs and excise taxes went unnoticed by most Zambians, and in a buoyant economy even the import-consuming rich barely felt their bite. Still better, taxing the mining companies proved immensely popular.

But when copper prices crashed, Zambia's tax system crashed as well. For beyond the inevitable, sharp revenue losses resulting from mining-sector production inflexibility, the profits-only tax regime actually made "net revenue from copper more variable with price."[68] As the finance minister lamented in 1983, "since 1975 the Government

[65] Robert Curry, Jr., "Zambia's Economic Crisis," *Journal of African Studies* 6 (Winter 1979–80): 214; World Bank, *Zambia Country Economic Memorandum: Economic Reforms and Development Prospects*, 64–65.

[66] Richard Sklar, *Corporate Power in an African State* (Berkeley: University of California Press, 1975), 53–54; Curry, "Zambia's Economic Crisis," 214.

[67] Mikesell, *Foreign Investment in Copper Mining*, 26; Cobbe, *Governments and Mining Companies*, 242–43; Marcia Burdette, "The Dynamics of Nationalization between Multinational Companies and Peripheral States" (Ph.D. diss., Columbia University, 1979), 301–6.

[68] Cobbe, *Governments and Mining Companies*, 237.

[has] received no revenue from what used to be the main traditional source, mining."[69] Real recurrent revenue fell 30 percent in 1974–75, pushing the budget, which had had a surplus equal to nearly 50 percent of recurrent expenditure, deep into deficit—where it remains. Revenues have grown 4 percent per year since 1974, but spending has grown 11.6 percent per year, and the total tax effort has plunged.[70] "Despite frequent and substantial changes in tax rates since 1975, domestic revenue fell from 29 percent of GDP in 1975 to 24 percent in 1982, which indicates the inelastic nature of the revenue structure."[71]

Nationalization made things worse. The agreement sharply reduced the effective tax rate and allowed foreign shareholders to repatriate all profits on their equity. This capped mineral revenues and *increased* the cash outflow, resulting in a "serious and growing loss for investment."[72] In the initial takeover, Zambia also issued 6 percent bonds, which it could service from dividends while meeting revenue needs only if copper prices stayed above a historically high £420 per ton.[73] In 1973 it redeemed these bonds by borrowing at 12.5–13 percent in the Eurodollar market. When prices, profits, and dividends fell after 1975, Zambia had to use general-tax receipts and borrow still more to pay the resulting debt service. Repatriated profits plus interest equaled 20 percent of gross fixed capital formation in 1970–77, "approximated 27 percent of gross national investment in 1978–82, and [were] over 50 percent in 1982 alone."[74] Copper could not fund restructuring; merely keeping the industry afloat bled the state white.

Zambian leaders need new sources of income, but the institutions that evolved during copper's heyday can neither meet the new demands nor be reformed. Given its narrow base, the Department of Customs and Excise "cannot be effective enforcing sales and excise taxes on producers dispersed all over the country"; the result has been "considerable . . . revenue loss through tax avoidance and evasion." Furthermore, authorities lack a national data base of taxpayers, the organization needed to reach them, and the auditors to check

[69] GRZ, "Budget Address by the Minister of Finance" (Lusaka, January 1983), 7.

[70] Kaunga and Ncube, "The Zambian Economy," 15.

[71] World Bank, *Zambia Country Economic Memorandum: Issues and Options for Economic Diversification*, 15.

[72] Burdette, "The Dynamics of Nationalization," 301–6; Sakala interview.

[73] ZIMCO study, cited in *Africa Confidential* 11 (September 4, 1970): 4.

[74] Burdette, "The Dynamics of Nationalization," 337–39; Makgeta, "Investment in the Third World," 20–21.

their returns. Thus, "despite very high tax rates," income taxes "have not shown any buoyancy with regard to GDP since 1980" because of "extensive tax evasion and poor tax administration."[75] Agriculture might provide new revenues, but collecting them is beyond tax authorities' capabilities. Lower copper earnings spell disaster for customs collections and for the import-intensive industrial sector—hence for its "profitability and ability to pay taxes."[76]

These problems have nasty political repercussions, too. The shift to direct, personal taxes required a more intrusive system of tax collection, but the tax authorities' weaknesses, in effect, exempt much of the population. "The bulk of the personal income tax is collected from employees in the public sector and large corporations. . . . While this might have been defensible when mineral revenues were high and other tax rates were correspondingly low, it imposes an excessive burden on a relatively narrow segment of the population now that tax rates have been raised to very high levels."[77] Being politically potent and organized, these folks have forced the state to offer exemptions (lowering revenues) and to maintain services (increasing recurrent expenditures); both cause the state to forego the funds needed to restructure.[78]

The failure to develop new revenue sources also affects restructuring directly. It has led government leaders to hope that "there is still room for increasing revenue from traditional sources."[79] The tax regime for mining is thus aimed at "extracting maximum revenue, leaving ZCCM with scarcely any post-tax net profits to finance rehabilitation investment"; higher levies on imports increased income from these sources fourfold in 1981–86, but they further biased incentives against nontraditional exports.[80] The failure to find new sources of revenue has also cut new capital investment, the key to

[75] World Bank, *Zambia Country Economic Memorandum: Economic Reforms and Development Prospects*, 72, 69, 20. Accordingly, "the current system relies on the fact that large companies have less incentive to avoid taxes, thereby facilitating the collection of personal and corporate taxes, and the sales and excise taxes" (73).

[76] GRZ, "Budget Address by the Minister of Finance" (Lusaka, January 1985), 5; "Budget Address by the Minister of Finance" (Lusaka, January 1982), 9.

[77] World Bank, *Zambia Country Economic Memorandum: Economic Reforms and Development Prospects*, 73.

[78] In 1989, for example, Zambian State Insurance Company employees struck in protest of the higher income taxes imposed to manage the budget deficit. *New York Times*, May 29, 1989.

[79] GRZ, "Budget Address by the Minister of Finance" (Lusaka, January 1984), 15.

[80] World Bank, *Boxed in Zambia*, 76; GRZ, annual budget addresses by the Minister of Finance, 1980–86.

restructuring in an economy marked by high asset/factor inflexibility. Poor collection capabilities have caused taxes on the taxable few to soar; moreover, poor parastatal performance has shifted the burden of corporate taxes to the private sector, killing capital accumulation and investment.[81] Because recurrent spending exceeded revenues every year after 1975, state capital investment plunged from 29.9 percent to 12.2 percent of the budget between 1975 and 1984. And most of the remaining state "capital investment" was used to capitalize bad loans made to existing parastatals, not to finance restructuring. Indeed, by 1985 combined public and private capital formation "had declined to only 10 percent of GDP, probably well below the level at which the capital stock could be maintained."[82]

Rising public debt, however, is only the most visible result of Zambia's inability to reform revenue extraction. Although Zambia had had a budget surplus since independence, "during 1975–85 the budget deficit averaged nearly one-third of expenditure and 13 percent of GDP. . . . The major source of finance has been domestic bank borrowing. Government borrowing has absorbed a large share of the resources available to the economy (46 percent of external loan disbursements and 77 percent of net domestic credit creation) and left few resources for public enterprises and private activities."[83] Inflation jumped from a pre-1975 average of 6.0 percent to 17.3 percent between 1975 and 1985; it hit 20.0 percent in 1984 and reached 37.4 percent in 1985. By 1986 foreign debt was $5.7 billion—$55 per capita higher than that of Brazil. Annual debt service equaled 70 percent of export earnings, but Zambia made less than 10 percent of its payments, resulting in massive compounding. By the late 1980s, Zambia's public debt relative to GDP was the highest in the world.[84]

---

[81] A 1980–81 Zambian Industrial and Commercial Association (ZINCOM) study found that in the late 1970s parastatals held 80 percent of business assets but paid 10 percent of corporate profits taxes, whereas the private sector, with just 20 percent of assets, paid 90 percent. Chabi interview.

[82] Quote from Robert Bates and Paul Collier, "The Politics and Economics of Policy Reform in Zambia," in *Political and Economic Interactions in Economic Policy Reform*, ed. Robert Bates and Anne Krueger (Cambridge: Blackwell, 1993), 390. See also World Bank, *Zambia: Public Expenditure Review*, 1: 2; Jansen, *Trade, Exchange Rate, and Agricultural Pricing Policies*, 15; GRZ, annual budget addresses by the Minister of Finance, 1980–86.

[83] Jansen, *Trade, Exchange Rate, and Agricultural Pricing Policies*, 14–16.

[84] GRZ, annual budget addresses by the Minister of Finance, 1980–86; Bank of Zambia, *Annual Report*, 1977–84; World Bank, *Boxed in Zambia*, 66; Thomas Callaghy, "Lost between State and Market," in *The Politics of Economic Adjustment in Developing*

Debt service and parastatals' import needs thus deny foreign exchange to other sectors; moreover, the heavy borrowing necessary to finance the budget deficit and the parastatals crowd out alternative-sector investment.[85] In sum, the tax system's weakness, which is traceable to the system's origins in copper as a revenue source, forces leaders to pursue policies that strengthen dependence on copper by obstructing restructuring.

Monitoring, Regulating, and Redirecting the Economy

Zambia's capacity to monitor, regulate, and promote copper production and big industry poses similar problems. Even in 1964, the state could provide large-scale power, water, and transportation infrastructures. Today ZCCM, the Copper Industry Services Bureau (CISB), and MEMACO provide all the information needed to monitor and regulate mining and copper sales. Similarly, through the Industrial Development Corporation (INDECO), ZIMCO, and the Development Bank of Zambia, leaders can promote, monitor, and regulate big industry. The University of Zambia fills the demand of the mines and parastatals for engineers and managers; corporatist labor organizations permit leaders to monitor and regulate workers in these industries.

Although few contest the importance of diversification (which ZIMCO's director of corporate planning calls "the very essence of the restructuring program"[86]), existing institutions are too specialized and inflexible to monitor, regulate, or promote other sectors. Created to service large-scale industry along the line-of-rail, they cannot reach or help tiny, widely dispersed start-ups. For example, Zambia has "no financial institution with institutionalized capacity to provide working capital to small entrepreneurs" because "the organizational structure of the Development Bank of Zambia was based on serving a [few] large-scale enterprises."[87] Similarly, though parastatals have strong

---

Nations, ed. Joan Nelson (Princeton: Princeton University Press), 46; Bates and Collier, "Policy Reform in Zambia," 389.

[85] Chabi interview.

[86] Kaunga interview.

[87] Chiselebwe Ng'andwe, "Development of Small Industries in Zambia," paper delivered at a conference on the Funding and Coordination of Small Industries' Development Programmes, Lusaka, July 28–August 1, 1986, 9–10; and Ng'andwe, "The Role of Small-Scale Industries in the Zambian Economy," paper presented to a meeting of the Institute of Bankers, Lusaka, April 4, 1985, 16–17.

foreign purchasing organizations, they lack subcontracting ties to local manufacturers. A well-developed infrastructure and the Ministry of Public Works serve the parastatals, whereas would-be entrepreneurs lack water, electricity, telephones, and transportation and are scorned by their providers. Finally, no programs provide the training, research and development, or technology needed by alternative sectors.[88]

To resolve these problems, Zambia formed the Small Industries Development Organization (SIDO) and the Export Board, but neither has flourished. In contrast to MEMACO's well-appointed offices, the Export Board operates out of a warehouse; in contrast to ZCCM's wealth of company cars, SIDO has few and its budget is so small that the staff is office-bound, despite its wide-ranging rural mission. The explanation is simple: those who staff existing agencies resist institutional challengers that undercut their missions or divert funds from their projects. The director of SIDO notes that his organization's main activity is not small-industry development but attacking—unsuccessfully—the capital-intensive bias of Zambian industrial policy, the "big project" orientation of institutions preoccupied with multimillion-kwacha investments, and the managerial elite's preference for high-prestige positions in big industry to risky jobs in untried start-ups.[89]

Copper and the Other Institutions of State

The sectoral characteristics of copper are also reflected in a range of other state institutions that today inhibit restructuring. The problem began with politicians' natural response to the deprivations of colonial rule. Despite warnings, notes a Bank of Zambia official, they ignored rising costs and the need to diversify: "As long as the copper money was coming, nobody seemed to think of other sources. There was no need. So the politicians thought up social welfare projects to make the people feel attached to them."[90] These bought political benefits but diverted resources away from diversification and saddled the state with huge recurrent expenditures it cannot now cut.

A perverse relationship between copper and party politics has long

[88] Ng'andwe, "Development of Small Industries in Zambia," 1, 5–6; Ng'andwe interview.
[89] Ng'andwe interview.
[90] Sakala interview.

existed in Zambia, born of copper's consequences for politicians' incentives.[91] By the 1940s, which saw the beginning of party organization, the Copperbelt and, more generally, the line-of-rail towns had given Zambia an urbanized industrial population. This rapidly growing concentration of readily mobilized, economically central—and economically sensitive—individuals constituted party organizers' primary target. But copper also gave rise to the powerful Mineworkers' Union of Zambia (MUZ), which challenged parties' appeal in the critical urban areas. Thus from the start, party organizers from the dominant United National Independence Party (UNIP) struggled to control the MUZ (of which more later in this chapter) and to woo urban voters. The latter task required building an extensive party organization in the cities—in 1985 UNIP's Lusaka organization alone filled 40,000 section, branch, and war offices (393)—and delivering a variety of services to urban dwellers ranging from schools, clinics, and housing to jobs and food subsidies. Further, the resulting centrality of urban constituents to the party's fortunes gave each UNIP politician political incentives to favor such services; and the desire for personal political advancement "placed a premium on endorsing the interventionist policies favored by [UNIP's] old guard" (402, 406).

Initially, copper revenues made it possible for UNIP to respond to the copper-caused problem of corraling Zambia's huge urban population. Indeed, as already noted, copper windfalls actually encouraged politicians to make more and more extravagant promises, ratcheting up popular expectations of the party and state, increasing the already strong forces drawing people into the cities, and thus exaggerating the circumstances giving rise to the incentives that characterized political competition in Zambia. But when copper revenues collapsed, UNIP's constituency base, organization, and organizational interests, to say nothing of the political and personal interests of individual UNIP politicians, all militated against restructuring. Instead, the party "heavily mortgaged future living standards" in a vain attempt to sustain the status quo (390).

Other problems resulted from lavish spending on the civil service. The weak civil service inherited in 1964 severely limited Zambia's ability to plan and implement change. Between 1964 and 1968, the state therefore expanded the civil service from 5,873 employees to

[91] Bates and Collier, "Policy Reform in Zambia," 388. The following discussion draws largely on this excellent study, but only four specific page citations are given in parentheses.

11,649 and the administration from 35 ministries and departments to 117. By 1975, the civil service had overtaken the mines as the largest employer in Zambia.[92] But this growth did little to improve state capacity, resulting instead in an incoherent and ineffective bureaucracy. In large measure, the problem is politicization. With cost no concern, politicians turned the civil service into a patronage mill, as indicated by its growth not at the bottom where services are rendered but at the politically important "super-scale" levels. Super-scale posts increased sixfold in 1962–78, twice the rate of lower-ranking posts. In fact, though growth of the civil service as a whole stalled in the 1970s, the growth in super-scale posts accelerated, driven by the need to "create high-level employment opportunities for . . . the new upper stratum."[93]

Similar problems bedeviled the parastatal sector created by the 1969 Mulungushi reforms—named after the town in which Kaunda announced them—which nationalized many foreign firms and established dozens of state corporations. But because they began operations in an era of plenty, the parastatals are capital-intensive, import-intensive, and foreign exchange–intensive, and thus depend on copper, the sole supplier of all three critical inputs. They were also expected to provide goods and services at politically acceptable but uneconomic prices and became a critical component of UNIP's organizational infrastructure for delivering benefits. (As late as 1989, twelve of ZIMCO's twenty-two directors were UNIP Central Committee members, as were the director general and head of ZIMCO.) The state therefore had to subsidize production on an ongoing basis, a viable policy only so long as copper revenues were available.[94] Rapid growth exaggerated the problems posed by Zambia's lack of trained managers, overwhelmed the state's limited managerial capacity, and opened the door to politicization.[95] Indeed, parastatal jobs became a

[92] Philip Daniel, *Africanization, Nationalization, and Inequality* (New York: Cambridge University Press, 1979), 20; UNDP/ILO, *Second Report, Statistical Appendices,* sec. K table 1.

[93] Quote from UNDP/ILO, *Second Report,* Part I, *General Review and Recommendations,* 50–51. See also GRZ, *Report of the Commission of Inquiry into the Salaries, Salary Structures, and Conditions of Service* (Mwanakatwe Commission), vol. 1, *The Public Services and the Parastatal Sector* (Lusaka, 1975), 12; Dennis Dresang and Ralph Young, "The Public Service," in *Administration in Zambia,* ed. Tordoff, 85.

[94] Makgeta, "Investment in the Third World," 8; Bates and Collier, "Policy Reform in Zambia," 401.

[95] GRZ, *Report of the Commission of Inquiry,* 1: 134–35; interviews with Mwanakatwe, Kaunga, and Mwanza.

valuable political resource; the public sector generated 55 percent of new jobs between 1966 and 1973 and by 1976 accounted for 71.5 percent of all formal-sector jobs. Nor did this growth reflect only "Zambianization" or stop when copper revenues fell. In the early 1970s more than a third of public-sector jobs created in manufacturing were in excess of Zambianization, a pattern that continued after 1975 though total public and private employment declined sharply.[96]

Zambia's civil service and parastatal sector now inhibit restructuring and drain state resources. The bureaucracy is "fragmented," "compartmentalized," and "far too big both in terms of the real needs of the country and capacity to pay"; politics infuse everything, widening "the access permitted outside groups to policymaking and implementation."[97] The National Commission for Development Planning reports that the parastatals suffer from "excessive . . . and top-heavy staffing patterns, lack of adequate maintenance of plant and equipment, inefficient operations, [and] lack of cost consciousness"; patronage has degraded their performance and politicized the parastatals.[98] The parastatals' "contribution to the economy over the years has been negligible," complained the finance minister in 1981, and they "have increasingly depended upon the Government to bail them out of financial problems." Ironically, because many of the parastatals are legal monopolies, it is politically impossible for them to turn a profit, since "they would then provoke criticism of the government for profiteering at the expense of consumers!"[99]

Zambia is in a bind: the public sector cannot promote restructuring; but the state must sustain it at terrible cost. When copper prices fell in 1975, public employees demanded and got pay increases, bigger housing allowances, lower rents, and easier access to subsidized loans. Three years later, their earnings were still rising more than 20 percent per year, and by 1978 they were 60 percent higher than those in the private sector. Although average national consumption de-

---

[96] Daniel, *Africanization,* 17; World Bank, *Accelerated Development,* 41; UNDP/ILO, *Second Report, Statistical Appendices,* sec. H, 1–10. Interviews with Ng'andu and Baynes suggest that these findings still hold.

[97] Quotes from Dresang, *The Zambian Civil Service,* 114; Mwanakatwe interview; and Dresang and Young, "The Public Service," 81.

[98] National Commission for Development Planning 1980 *Economic Report,* cited in Makgeta, "Investment in the Third World," 19. See also Michael Chaput, "Zambian State Enterprise" (Ph.D. diss., Syracuse University, 1971), 140.

[99] GRZ, "Budget Address by the Minister of Finance" (Lusaka, January 1981), 14; and Bates and Collier, "Policy Reform in Zambia," 401.

clined sharply between 1975 and 1983, the public-sector elites' consumption was not affected.[100] Indeed, there was a direct link between the two after 1975. On the revenue side, the weak tax system depended increasingly on regressive indirect taxes; on the expenditure side, the state offset the 10–80 percent pay raises for civil servants in 1980 by cutting subsidies for the poor by 70 percent. Recurrent personnel spending rose in the period 1975–84, but capital spending declined by 60 percent, overall investment fell 50 percent, and real gross capital formation declined, depressing new capital formation and "running down . . . structures and equipment in which the country has invested millions of kwachas."[101] Worse, public-sector elites have no interest in efforts to "engineer rapid and widespread economic development." This pattern of profligate spending has become "a necessary condition for the existing alignment of political forces," though it bars restructuring.[102]

CAPACITY OF CAPITAL AND LABOR FOR COLLECTIVE ACTION

The interests of Zambian copper companies and miners are defined by the same sectoral characteristics that define state interests, but whereas these conspire to limit the state's absolute capacity, they endow the companies and miners with a large capacity for collective action. And because their interests are opposed to the state's interest in restructuring, this mismatch bodes ill for Zambia. "What is remarkable about the case of Zambia," note Bates and Collier, is the divide between the UNIP and these critical societal actors, a divide that deprives the state of "a valuable resource: the ability to orchestrate economic adjustment by brokering relations among representatives of labor and industry."[103]

[100] John Markakis and Robert Curry, Jr., "The Global Economy's Impact on Recent Budgetary Politics in Zambia," *Journal of African Studies* 3 (Winter 1976–77): 419–20; UNDP/ILO, *Second Report*, Part I, *General Review and Recommendations*, 34; Morris Szeftel, "Political Graft and the Spoils System in Zambia," *Review of African Political Economy* 24 (May–August 1982): 6; Makgeta, "Investment in the Third World," 13.

[101] Quote from Kaunga and Ncube, "The Zambian Economy," 12–13, 17. See also William Byrnes, "The Elasticity of the Tax System in Zambia," *World Development* 11, no. 2 (1983): 153; Makgeta, "Investment in the Third World," i, 14–15; Jansen, *Trade, Exchange Rate, and Agricultural Pricing Policies*, 15; GRZ, annual budget addresses by the Minister of Finance, 1980–86.

[102] Quotes from both Dresang, *The Zambian Civil Service*, 164; and Markakis and Curry, "The Global Economy's Impact," 403.

[103] Bates and Collier, "Policy Reform in Zambia," 393, 399.

In 1964, two huge firms dominated Zambian copper production, and both dwarfed the new state. In Zambia, RST and Zamanglo had similar concerns about the complex infrastructure needed for production and export, and about the tax and regulatory regimes under which they operated. Internationally, they shared an interest in oligopoly management. Collaboration on both domestic and international fronts was easy: each firm was so large that even solitary action yielded high returns; furthermore, mining's concentration in the Copperbelt and the limited rail links to the outside areas made it easy for each firm to monitor the other's compliance with any collusive agreements they struck. In fact, in 1964 they were colluding successfully. Facing weak demand in 1957, they and other MNC producers had agreed to cut production 10 percent. When this proved insufficient, they cut it another 5 percent in 1960, and the three largest producers began buying copper on the LME. By 1963 these efforts had stabilized prices. When the market improved in 1964 they reversed course, capping prices to protect future demand.[104]

This capacity for collusion in the market generalized easily to the political sphere. The size and centrality of RST and Zamanglo gave them huge resources, and their worldly, well-connected managers had important advantages over Zambian policy makers. Nationalization only increased the copper companies' capacity to defend mining and thwart restructuring.[105] Locating RCM and NCCM in ZIMCO (which they dominated) in 1970 eliminated any remaining barriers to collective action and offered them direct access to government. Combining them into ZCCM in 1981 culminated this process; ZCCM's managing director was placed on ZIMCO's board of directors where, as the director of corporate finance put it, ZCCM is "in a very strong position vis-à-vis any other claimants."[106] Mining's complexity has limited politicization, leaving ZCCM, unlike other parastatals, managed by competent professionals who have risen through the ranks, identify with the company, and share a strong corporate culture.[107]

[104] Gluschke et al., *Copper*, 12; Bowen and Gunatilaka, *Copper*, 299; Sklar, *Corporate Power*, 52–53.

[105] Noted a former finance minister in 1986, "The nationalized companies operate exactly as do the MNCs. They go directly to the president and make their case which is then forced on the others in much the same way as the [MNCs] used to do" (Mwanakatwe interview).

[106] Baynes interview.

[107] Interviews with Yamba-Yamba, Chanda, Sichula, and Ng'andu. For comparative figures on levels of "unproductive" employment, see UNDP/ILO, *Second Report, Statistical Appendices*, sec. H, Table 5, 9.

There is also no mistaking Zambia miners' capacity for collective action. Starting with strikes in 1935 and 1940, the miners led the labor organization movement in Zambia, winning recognition for their union, the Mineworkers Union of Zambia, in 1949. Its success is evident in miners' living standards. In the 1950 and 1960s, miners' average income was twice the national average (until 1966 the lowest wage paid in mining topped the highest wage paid elsewhere), and mine employment guaranteed miners and their families good housing and free hospital care. Even today, mining wages are 40 percent higher than the national average and 45 percent higher than manufacturing wages.[108] No less important, MUZ's continued autonomous existence attests to its tenacity in the face of intense efforts by the state to control it.

Miners' capacity for collective action derives from the sectoral characteristics of mining employment. Beginning in the 1930s, the copper companies sought to create a permanent work force in order to preserve their growing investment in worker training. The monthly turnover rate fell to 50 percent by 1940 and 0.6 percent by 1967, where it remained through the 1980s; miners' average length of service was 6.5 years in 1960 and more than 11 years in 1986.[109] Specialized skills acquired on the job have afforded miners advancement opportunities and leverage with the companies; job security has given them the incentive to invest in a union. The concentration of large numbers of miners without close supervision has facilitated the organizing of individual mines, dues collection, and scab bashing; moreover, the concentration of mining in the Copperbelt and the existence of transportation and communications infrastructures servicing the mines have simplified industrywide organizing.

Company efforts to create a stable work force have created stable, closed mining townships that reinforce miners' shared identity. Housing is distributed by seniority and need, not pay level, thus emphasizing residents' common identity as miners. Prior to independence, the racial divide between African and white townships reinforced this identity and miners' shared sense of apartness; since independence attacks on the relative luxury of the townships by envious nonminers

[108] Michael Burawoy, "Another Look at the Mineworkers," *African Social Research* 14 (December 1972): 267, 278; World Bank, *Boxed in Zambia*, 15.

[109] Copper Industry Services Bureau, *Zambia Mining Yearbook 1978* (Kitwe, Zambia, 1979), 32–34; CISB, *MINDECO Mining Yearbook 1970* (Kitwe, Zambia, 1971), 44–46; interview with Kampamba.

have had the same effect. Long-term residence in the townships, the distribution of housing according to mining-related criteria, not ethnicity, and a shared identity as miners minimize the salience of ethnic divisions in the union and miners' rural ties. Finally, other township organizations ranging from churches to coffee klatches bind miners, their families, and the union.[110]

Nor is management averse to unionization. Indeed, because high fixed costs require uninterrupted production, management must maintain its skilled work force and labor discipline, and thus needs a strong union with which to negotiate.[111] As ZCCM's director of human resources puts it, "without a solid union, labor management in the copper industry would be impossible" because of wildcat strikes, lack of labor discipline, and sabotage.[112] And because labor costs are a tiny proportion of total costs, management can negotiate. The MNCs and ZCCM have therefore encouraged MUZ's development, and through good-faith bargaining have established MUZ's effectiveness in miners' eyes and fostered a strong labor-management relationship separate from the state.

Miners' capacity for collective action has serious political and economic implications for the state and other actors. The superior ability of MUZ to win lucrative contracts for its members, for example, diverts mining-sector monies away from restructuring, a process that would favor workers in other sectors. And though a few enterprise unions operate in manufacturing, construction, and commerce, their geographical dispersion, the high cost of organizing, and cross-cutting identities have stymied the organization of these industries at the national level.[113] Politicians have long vied for MUZ's support, but they have ignored other unions, which therefore are not credible allies for the state as it tries to restructure. Paradoxically, MUZ's success has aided other unions, though again to the detriment of restructuring. MUZ is a model for other unions; it has helped them organize and, by forcing the state to adopt a policy of "one industry, one union," has helped them achieve a unity they could not have achieved

[110] Robert Bates, *Unions, Parties, and Political Development* (New Haven: Yale University Press, 1971), 111–19; interview with Mazyopa. Mazyopa and others confirm the irrelevance of ethnicity for an otherwise homogeneous, permanently urbanized industrial workforce.

[111] Interviews with Sichula, Chanda, and Yamba-Yamba.

[112] Sichula interview.

[113] Gilbert Mudenda, "The Process of Class Formation in Contemporary Zambia," in *Beyond Political Independence*, ed. Klaas Woldring (Hawthorne, N.Y.: Mouton, 1983).

on their own.[114] The success of MUZ in increasing miners' wages has spilled over into other sectors, pushing wages up faster than the cost of living and productivity to levels three times those in neighboring countries, and badly hurting more labor-intensive industries.[115] Even when Zambia was facing economic collapse in April 1985, MUZ led a successful drive for an 18 percent wage hike for all unionized workers.

But the real battle has pitted MUZ against the state, stymieing restructuring and dividing the state and a critical ally. It was not always so. Before 1964 what mattered was winning independence and, in mining, ending racial job reservation, which barred Africans from many positions, and racial wage structures, which paid Africans a fraction of what whites earned. In this, UNIP and the union had a common cause; UNIP needed the miners to win, and miners saw their "bad conditions of service as synonymous with colonialism."[116] Independence solved these problems, but it set MUZ and the state at loggerheads. The state wanted wage restraint to boost productivity, and it wanted to use the company profits to raise the funds needed to diversify. "It is the patriotic duty of the unions," declared Kaunda, "to pursue constructive and responsible policies because it is these policies which will serve the people in their struggle for economic progress."[117] But having built a union to defend their interests, miners had no desire to see it enlisted in an effort to make them bear the cost of restructuring. Thus, beginning in 1964 MUZ mounted a series of strikes that in 1966 forced a 22 percent pay increase. Nor did the union reverse itself with nationalization, despite Kaunda's claim that "now there is a clear identity of interests between workers and Gov-

[114] Shengamo interview.

[115] Sichula interview; Fry and Harvey, "Copper in Zambia," 201–5; Young, *Industrial Diversification in Zambia*, 259; Robert Molteno and William Tordoff, "Independent Zambia," in *Politics in Zambia*, ed. Tordoff, 363; GRZ, *Second National Development Plan, January 1972–December 1976* (Lusaka, 1971), 10–11.

[116] Mazyopa interview; W. Richard Jacobs, *The Relationship between African Trade Unions and Political Organizations in Northern Rhodesia/Zambia, 1949–1961* (Geneva: International Institute for Labor Studies, 1971), 12–13; Bates and Collier, "Policy Reform in Zambia," 396.

[117] Kaunda to the Zambia Congress of Trade Unions (ZCTU) General Council, November 29, 1965. Thus, he continued, "we had to regard the revenues that flow from the copper industry as the means by which we could get developed. . . . This revenue will be the basic investment in our development plans which will produce the extra employment, extra schools, extra factories, which are so desperately needed." Cited in ZCTU, *Report of the Working Party Appointed by the General Council to Enquire into the Structure of Trade Unions in Zambia* (Kitwe, Zambia, 1972), 15.

80

ernment."[118] MUZ still has "the ultimate sanction"—a strike against Zambia's copper heart—and it has a seat on the ZCCM board.[119] Rhetoric aside, therefore, "government policy towards employment in the mining sector . . . leans heavily towards political expediency rather than the dictates of [restructuring]."[120]

MUZ also challenges state authority in other key areas. As the saying goes on the Copperbelt, "UNIP to UNIP and Union to Union."[121] The formation of MUZ predated the nationalist movement; indeed, the Copperbelt bred it. But whereas miners supported UNIP, MUZ's strength came from the shop floor and an ability to resolve bread-and-butter issues. Union leaders therefore rejected involvement in politics "except labor legislation," fearing it would compromise their ability to defend miners' interests or would open MUZ to political control.[122] Since 1964 they have battled the state over resources as well as over who commands the miners' allegiance and who should set national development policy. The issue came to a head beginning in 1968 when the Copperbelt was the locus of first intra-UNIP and then interparty conflict, and "the loyalty of the labor movement, including the miners, became crucial not only for the government's position, but for the maintenance of authority itself."[123] Kaunda met the challenge by making Zambia a one-party state in 1972, and thus heightened the state-MUZ conflict by making labor the only viable opposition.

Since then, the state has sought to control access to union office and decision making by cajolery and force, and it has tried repeatedly to reduce MUZ to a "mass organization" on a par with the Women's Brigade.[124] Neither coercion nor co-optation worked, however. The state co-opted much of MUZ's national leadership and stopped official union strikes. But the victory proved Pyrrhic. Miners came to distrust and often ignore top union officials, control of the union became increasingly decentralized, and wildcat strikes plagued the industry. At the same time, miners came to view the state as the enemy

[118] August 1969 speech in which he announced governmental takeover of 51 percent of the mining companies. Cited in Robert Molteno, "Cleavage and Conflict in Zambian Politics," in *Politics in Zambia*, ed. Tordoff, 83.

[119] Mwanakatwe interview.

[120] Kalyalya, "The Mining Industry," 5–6.

[121] Cherry Gertzel, "Labour and the State: The Case of Zambia's Mineworkers' Union," *Journal of Commonwealth and Comparative Politics* 13 (November 1975): 293.

[122] Mazyopa interview.

[123] Gertzel, "Labour and the State," 295; Bates and Collier, "Policy Reform in Zambia," 397–99.

[124] Interviews with Tempo, Mazyopa, Lungu, and Shengamo.

and the government as ineffective and illegitimate, views that only strengthened their already adamant opposition to restructuring.[125] The struggle, however, brings us to the question of autonomy: How does copper affect Zambian leaders' ability to insulate themselves organizationally and to define national policy autonomously?

AUTONOMY: CONTROLLING THE CHANNELS OF INTEREST REPRESENTATION

Zambian leaders cannot control the channels of interest representation. Copper industry groups know their interests and can mobilize to lobby for them. More important, ZCCM has penetrated to the heart of ZIMCO and the state. Until 1991 President Kaunda was chairman of ZIMCO, and his son was the chief executive officer (CEO) of ZCCM and a member of the ZIMCO board, making "ZCCM management virtually autonomous," for its managers can "bypass ZIMCO's board and management" and "go directly to the President to make their case, which is then forced on the others."[126] Likewise, MUZ has a seat on the ZCCM board, and the Zambia Congress of Trade Unions (ZCTU), of which MUZ is the key member, has a seat on the ZIMCO board, allowing MUZ to "exercise considerable power behind the scenes in government councils."[127] But more is at issue than the organization of the parastatal sector.

The centrality and complexity of mining ensure constant, unequal interactions between sectoral actors and the state. Mining's technical complexity and the difficulty of managing a company of ZCCM's size force the state to depend on the industry for the expertise needed to monitor and regulate it. Thus, though investment proposals must be submitted to ZIMCO's board for approval, ZIMCO cannot autonomously assess ZCCM's submissions and "has no technically qualified personnel competent to monitor ZCCM's operations."[128] Although

[125] Interviews with Mazyopa, Chanda, and Shengamo.

[126] Quotes from World Bank, "Improving Parastatal Performance," iii; O'Neill et al., *Transforming a Single Product Economy,* 132; and Mwanakatwe interview. The chief financial officer of ZCCM explains that when ZCCM completed its rehabilitation plans, they were taken to Kaunda for his approval; "with this, no real alliances could organize against the five-year plan, although many individuals did oppose it." Baynes interview.

[127] Sakala interview.

[128] Quote from O'Neill et al., *Transforming a Single Product Economy,* 132. See also Kaunga interview.

ZCCM is Zambia's biggest debtor, it has equally one-sided relations with the Bank of Zambia and the Ministry of Finance, as well as with the Zambia Electricity Supply Corporation (ZESCO), the energy parastatal, from which it buys 60 percent of total Zambian energy production. Indeed, ZCCM provides consulting services to the state, ZESCO, Zambian Railways, and other parastatals.[129]

Other sectors' ineffectiveness increases ZCCM's access to the policy process. Other industries fell under the control of political hacks, for example, but "the useful myth of technical complexity scared many would-be meddlers off, leaving the [mining] industry to those who had risen through the ranks."[130] Although politicians controlled project choice, siting, financing, and manning decisions in other industries, management initiated 86 percent of NCCM projects in the 1970s; it implemented only three government-initiated projects and blocked implementation of others.[131] With the exception of the parastatals, the problems of other sectors are still greater. Peasant farmers, for instance, who constitute half the population and offer the best hope for restructuring, have pressing needs; they are widely scattered and divided by ethnicity and language. They also lack a sense of common interests and a capacity for collective action, making it easy for the state to establish agricultural policy autonomously. Their silence amplifies the voice of mining, however, and deprives the state of a key ally in restructuring.

Sectoral and Societal Pressures

Zambian leaders' limited autonomy is also a function of the overwhelming pressures exerted by societal actors. Even during the fat decade, mining interests resisted efforts to restrain wages and foster diversification. But when copper prices collapsed, the pressure intensified. Given production inflexibility, ZCCM and MUZ could not help themselves, nor could the state protect them in the international market. They therefore used their capacity for collective action and their access to the policy process to pressure the state to do what it could:

[129] World Bank, *Zambia: Public Expenditure Review,* vol. 2, *Main Report,* Report no. 6438-ZA (Washington, D.C., 1986), 100; and World Bank, "Improving Parastatal Performance," 25–26; Kampamba interview; ZCCM, *Annual Report,* various years.

[130] Chanda interview.

[131] George Simwinga, "Corporate Autonomy and Government Control" (Ph.D. diss., University of Pittsburgh, 1977), 169, 240–45, 259.

offer tax and debt relief, cut transportation and energy costs, and ease payment terms. Thus, when the state tried to raise the rates charged by parastatals in order to reduce the need for subsidies, ZCCM forced Zambian Railways to reduce its rates, refused to pay higher ZESCO electricity rates, and delayed payments to AGIP-Zambia, the national oil distributor, by sixty to seventy days.[132] The problem goes far beyond the mining sector, however.

In Zambia, the state is *the* target of all individuals and interest groups; it is a funnel through which huge revenues flow, the allocator of the national wealth. From colonial times, when Africans were barred from conducting business, to the present, when copper stifles all other sectors, the state has been the mother lode to be mined by the ambitious. Beyond mining, access to the state alone offers power and wealth. It is, therefore, the object of fierce competition over access to power, money, and jobs, and attacks on its autonomy are everyone's chief concern.

These attacks have prompted leaders to pursue not diversification but survival strategies intended to deflect the pressures. Lulled by seemingly limitless copper revenues, they have paid off potential opponents—witness the rapid increase of super-scale posts in the civil service and the parastatal sector to accommodate the would-be middle class. UNIP has established a vast patronage system in which access to state resources is traded for political support on the basic principle of "No UNIP, No Job." (See the section "Copper and the Other Institutions of State.")[133] To manage regional and ethnic demands, Kaunda dropped the role of "grand policy maker and assumed the role of "arbiter among the contending factions." He resorted to ethnic and regional balancing in the cabinet and Central Committee and then, to escape the limits this imposed, began rotating officials at short, irregular intervals.[134]

But these efforts have proved doubly damaging. On the one hand, they have undermined state capacity. They politicized the administration; devalued hard work, merit, and probity; and left Zambia to face restructuring with institutions, a civil service, and a parastatal sector that are themselves a large part of the problem. On the other hand,

---

[132] World Bank, "Improving Parastatal Performance," 22.

[133] *Times of Zambia*, January 28, 1969. See also Bates and Collier, "Policy Reform in Zambia," passim.

[134] Quote from *Zambia: A Country Study*, 40. See also Dresang and Young, "The Public Service," 86–87.

they have spurred societal groups to *increase* their efforts to penetrate the state and made it easier for them to do so. "Politics became more a means to wealth and position than an end in itself [and] the Party . . . [became] a pressure group vis-à-vis government institutions, extracting from them material rewards."[135] Public-sector growth has meant "an enormous increase in the influence of senior civil servants, trade union leaders [and] parastatal managing directors," whose inflated salaries give them a vested interest in preserving the status quo.[136] Regional and ethnic balancing have made the distribution of projects among sectional interest groups, not diversification, the focus of "development planning."[137]

In sum, inflexible state institutions, mining-sector groups' access to the policy process, intense societal pressures, and the effects of efforts to manage those pressures have barred Zambian leaders from autonomously pursuing the national interest—restructuring—because the state's interests cannot be separated from the interests of the mining sector or other groups that depend on access to the state. The state's very ability to fund itself depends on the continued viability of copper; and politically and economically the state is "aligned with the leading, best organized social forces in the country." For reasons of state, government leaders cannot "break out of this mutually supportive but inherently debilitating inter-relationship" but must continue it, even at the cost of crippling the restructuring effort.[138]

RELATIVE CAPACITY: TAKING ON THE CRISIS

The test of a state is successful implementation, the key to which is relative capacity. For Zambia, the test began in 1975 when copper prices crashed. In one year, copper's terms of trade fell 50 percent, export receipts declined 40 percent, and revenues from mining decreased 80 percent (further decreasing to zero in the period 1977–79). The balance-of-payments deficit jumped to 30 percent of GDP,

[135] Bornwell Chikulo, "Elections in a One-Party Participatory Democracy," in *Development in Zambia*, ed. Ben Turok (London: Zed Press, 1979), 202.

[136] Quote from Ian Scott, "Party Administration under the One-Party State," in *Administration in Zambia*, ed. Tordoff, 148. See also Dresang, *The Zambian Civil Service*, 164.

[137] Interviews with Mtonga, Siame, and Mwanza; Bates and Collier, "Policy Reform in Zambia," 401.

[138] Kenneth Good, "The Reproduction of Weakness in the State and Agriculture," *African Affairs* 85 (April 1986): 255.

and a budgetary surplus became a deficit equal to 24 percent of GDP. The government cut the budget deficit in half between 1976 and 1979 by slashing recurrent and capital spending 25 percent and 75 percent, respectively, and trimmed the balance-of-payments deficit by borrowing heavily and cutting imports by 45 percent.[139] But external debt and commercial payments arrears soared, and capacity utilization and production plummeted. Copper production dropped 33 percent in the period 1976–85; in 1976–79, the industrial-sector growth rate fell from 17.6 percent to −20.5 percent. Unemployment rose, living standards fell, and real per capita income dropped 44 percent between 1974 and 1984.[140]

Still, policy makers did not panic, believing that copper prices would rebound quickly and that Zambia could borrow against future copper receipts "to get through the temporary balance of payments problem." They thus did not consider devaluation, reordering industrial policy, reorganizing the parastatals, or restructuring.[141] Then came the second oil shock in 1979, a surge in international interest rates, and a further decrease in the demand for copper. Something had to be done. As noted in the 1985 *Guidelines for the Formulation of the Fourth National Development Plan*, "the more Zambia persists in operating the existing structure of the economy, the deeper she will go into foreign debt without making any significant impact on the growth of real output, employment and incomes in the domestic economy. The need to restructure the economy and make it self-reliant has never been greater than it is at the present juncture."[142] Another 1985 report included the warning that "the copper industry is entering a new phase of declining production leading to the . . . exhaustion of known ore reserves" in fifteen years.[143] Having failed to restructure when it was flush, Zambia now faced the task stone broke. If ever there was a crisis to give new policies, sectors, and institutions a chance, this was it. But stickiness prevailed.

[139] GRZ, *Restructuring in the Midst of Crisis*, vol. 1, 1–2; and "Budget Address by the Minister of Finance" (Lusaka, January 1981), 8–9.

[140] GRZ, *Zambia: Present Economic Conditions*, 14–15, 25–27; World Bank, *Zambia Country Economic Memorandum: Economic Reforms and Development Prospects*, 8; "Budget Address by the Minister of Finance" (Lusaka, January 1986), 3; "Budget Address by the Minister of Finance" (Lusaka, January 1981), 5; Bank of Zambia, *Report and Statement of Accounts* (Lusaka, 1977), 12–13; GRZ, *Guidelines for Formulation of the Fourth National Development Plan* (Lusaka, 1985), 2.

[141] Kaunga interview.

[142] GRZ, *Guidelines*, 3.

[143] GRZ, *Zambia: Present Economic Conditions*, 1.

Restructuring in the Midst of Crisis

Zambia sought "to restructure the economy, reduce its heavy dependence on the mining sector, and accelerate . . . social and economic development." The policy was aimed at promoting: "the diversion of an increasing share of resources from non-productive to productive uses; the increased utilization of local materials; the increased efficiency and competitiveness of the mining sector; the development of a wider range of exports and import-competing industries; [and] the improved performance of the agricultural sector."[144] The restructuring program called for tariff and exchange rate liberalization, lower budget subsidies, redirection of public investment to favor agriculture and export-oriented industry, parastatal reform, improved institutions of economic management, an end to import licensing, decontrol of bank interest rates, civil service cuts, a new investment code, and tax reform.

But the reform sputtered and died. Some parts of it were implemented: tariffs were revised, the kwacha was devalued briefly, farm gate prices were raised and agricultural marketing was streamlined; some parastatal prices were decontrolled; and limited encouragement was offered to the private sector.[145] Nothing was fundamentally changed, however. Failure to increase revenues and cut spending led to unchecked internal borrowing and inflation; by the mid-1980s the weight of Zambia's foreign debt "virtually assure[d] negative transfers of capital" well into the future.[146] Recurrent spending's share of the budget has continued to rise, capital investment's share has continued to fall, and what little investment has been made has gone into capital-intensive parastatals and the mines.

Kaunda abandoned the restructuring effort in May 1987, having given in to pressure to protect UNIP's core constituencies of urban township inhabitants, civil servants, and parastatal managers, and reintroduced traditional interventionist policies that "defended immediate consumption at the expense of longer-run growth."[147] He reimposed import licensing, control of foreign exchange allocations, and

[144] GRZ, *Restructuring in the Midst of Crisis*, vol. 1, iv.
[145] Interviews with Sakala, Ng'andwe, Kaunga, and Mtonga; GRZ, *Restructuring in the Midst of Crisis*, vol. 1, 52–53, 75; GRZ, *Zambia: Present Economic Conditions*, 9–10; GRZ, *Guidelines*, 10–11.
[146] World Bank, *Zambia Country Economic Memorandum: Issues and Options for Economic Diversification*, 55.
[147] Bates and Collier, "Policy Reform in Zambia," 429.

overvalued exchange rates; reintroduced price controls; reasserted a commitment to subsidies; and scrapped plans to cut the bureaucracy and freeze government salaries. For a moment, the gamble seemed to have paid off: copper prices soared in 1988 and a bumper harvest filled the granaries. A falling dollar lowered debt service fees and increased returns from sterling-denominated copper sales. The GNP rose 2.2 percent; export earnings increased; and imports poured in, increasing capacity utilization. But rapid population growth left Zambia with a negative per capita annual GNP growth rate, and the windfall did not relieve the huge debt burden, nor did it solve the economy's structural problems.[148] Indeed, the boom reinvigorated the mining industry, dulling the impetus for change. And by 1990 the boom was clearly a bust. So how do we explain Zambia's second failure to restructure?

Haunted by the Past

Facing the future, Zambia bears the double burden of the past: the consequences of copper dependence and of state actions taken to counter them. State institutions that were conceived in the fat decade have been unable to adjust. Zambia's tax authorities, deprived of copper revenues, have failed to broaden the revenue base, for example. As a result, revenues still depend on traditional sources, forcing leaders to maintain, not dismantle, the old. Despite ZCCM's need for funds to rehabilitate its facilities and reverse declining production, state officials have even tried to raise ZCCM's taxes. Similarly, ZIMCO exists to service the parastatals and cannot restructure existing firms or promote smaller, more competitive ones in the private sector. Moreover, its efforts to do either meet intense internal opposition from bureaucrats who are committed to ZIMCO's original mission and are advocates of its parastatal clients.[149]

The predominance of copper and the influence of past policy have also deprived the state of the productive options necessary for restructuring. Strong copper export earnings and an overvalued kwacha meant an abundance of cheap imports and stifled local production; "mining the state" offered risk-free opportunities to would-be entrepreneurs. The state responded by creating parastatals, thus

---

[148] *New York Times,* May 29, 1989.
[149] Ng'andwe and Kaunga interviews.

preempting private initiative. Ideological attacks on private enterprise led many either to forego all business ventures or to pursue short-term, self-liquidating commercial ventures, not long-term productive ones.[150] Zambia thus lacks a latent private productive capacity that is easily galvanized by policy changes; and overmanning, inefficiency, and past protection have rendered the parastatals incapable of turning a profit, let alone exporting.[151] Not surprisingly, even after years of trying, in 1986 nontraditional goods accounted for less than 5 percent of total exports and still show little promise.[152]

Those Zambians who might form the basis of a new economy cannot voice their needs, and their weakness robs the state of an ally with which to counter vested interests.[153] Peasant farmers are voiceless. Commercial farmers and Zambia's few business leaders see the need for a collective voice, but there is a "very strong business fear of public representation and pressure" as a result of past government attacks; there is also "no surety that all the liberalizations will last," not least because business leaders recognize the very real incentives encouraging politicians to resist or sabotage restructuring. Thus, policy makers struggle in vain "to convince economic agents that the government could commit itself to policies that would harm the interests of the townships, favor private business or commercial farmers, and curry favor from foreign capital." Business organizations, too, are cross-pressured, split between importers and exporters, and dominated by parastatals (most of which oppose restructuring) and MNCs (which address the government directly).[154]

By contrast, all the major interest groups created or served by past policy oppose restructuring, and they have both the capacity for collective action and the access to the state necessary to succeed. From the start, the effort to restructure was marked by "the coherence, pervasiveness, and institutionalized nature of the opposition to it," as interest groups battled to get "their people into key positions of formal power over the economic reforms."[155] Thus, even before 1987, when Kaunda reversed course, policy often contravened restructur-

[150] Interviews with Chabi, Ng'andwe, Namushi, and Mphepo.

[151] Interviews with Sakala, Ng'andwe, Mtonga, and Kaunga.

[152] Interview with Banda; GRZ, *Restructuring in the Midst of Crisis*, vol. 1, 91.

[153] For this argument in full, see Bates and Collier, "Policy Reform in Zambia," 393–400, 406–30.

[154] Quotes from Chabi and from Bates and Collier, "Policy Reform in Zambia," 406. Supporting material from Namushi and Mphepo interviews.

[155] Callaghy, "Lost between State and Market," 56.

ing; "expenditures seem to have been cut where public and political opposition would be felt least, typically at the primary level, in the more remote rural areas, and on the capital budget and nonwage part of the recurrent budget." Indeed, "as financial resources became more constrained, expenditures [became] more skewed in favor of higher level services which benefit middle and upper income groups."[156]

In the absence of alternatives and new allies, the state has had to depend on ZCCM and MUZ, both of which are committed to renewing the mining industry, not restructuring the economy. As pointed out in *Restructuring in the Midst of Crisis,*

> For any long-term growth strategy to succeed, the mining industry, which is the major provider of foreign exchange, must . . . be restored to previous levels of efficiency to make it once again profitable and competitive in world markets. Without a rehabilitated mining industry providing foreign exchange and budget resources, GRZ's restructuring and diversification efforts are likely to fail for lack of resources.[157]

This, however, is precisely the task Zambia had failed to achieve under far more auspicious circumstances twenty years earlier.

The key to ZCCM's resurgence was the company's Export, Rehabilitation, and Diversification Project, begun in 1985. The five-year plan addressed a backlog of managerial, manpower, financial, and technological problems caused by insufficient foreign exchange, poor cash flow, and a limited ability to borrow.[158] As noted in the final report, ZCCM got carte blanche to remedy its problems: "The Government is fully aware of these factors and recognizes that the industry's return to financial health is critical to the success of its own plans for economic development. The Government has therefore made a commitment to cooperate with the Company and ease the external constraints under which ZCCM operates as far as possible."[159] The government thus agreed to let ZCCM reduce its labor force, rational-

---

[156] World Bank, *Zambia Country Economic Memorandum: Economic Reforms and Development Prospects,* 58.

[157] GRZ, *Restructuring in the Midst of Crisis,* vol. 1, 4.

[158] ZCCM, *Export, Rehabilitation, and Diversification Project;* GRZ, *Restructuring in the Midst of Crisis* vol. 1: World Bank *Zambia Country Economic Memorandum: Issues and Options for Economic Diversification.*

[159] ZCCM, *Export, Rehabilitation, and Diversification Project,* 2.

ize operations, and close uneconomic facilities; committed itself to reduce ZCCM's taxes; and guaranteed ZCCM the foreign exchange and investment capital it needs.

But here was the catch. Even though ZCCM suffered a foreign exchange and investment drought after 1975, it still fared better than other sectors. Mining absorbed 70 percent of total foreign exchange. "Merely keeping the mines from falling further behind the international competition absorbed the lion's share of productive investment after 1975," and though this "failed to revitalize the industry, it prevented significant diversification."[160] The five-year plan promised ZCCM $350 million per year—far more than it had received in the recent past. This sum was more than 50 percent of the total available for parastatal investment and, according to ZIMCO officials, made efforts to diversify "unsustainable."[161] The plan also promised ZCCM the foreign exchange needed to proceed. It did not get all it asked for, but in 1985, for example, ZCCM received 84 percent of its request, whereas ZIMCO and the manufacturing sector received just 52 percent and 41 percent of theirs, respectively.[162] In fact, ZCCM's foreign exchange allocations were so big that they were said to "threaten the government's ability to meet its own debt service requirements." When asked how it could extract so much, ZCCM's director of corporate finance declared: "We could force them to agree because they had no choice. . . . Without ZCCM the country wouldn't stand a chance for anything."[163]

Nor was this all; ZCCM used its power to evade taxes and prey on other parastatals. Although ZCCM's nominal tax rate increased, it was allowed "unlimited carry-over of losses and investment allowances from previous years," which were expected to "almost entirely eliminate ZCCM's tax liabilities" well into the 1990s. It also enjoyed "generous investment allowances, limited exemptions from import taxation, and especially favorable electricity prices," all of which "undermine the objective of diversification of resources from mining to other uses

[160] Quote from Kalyalya, "The Mining Industry," 18. See also Makgeta, "Investment in the Third World," 10–11.
[161] World Bank, *Zambia: Public Expenditure Review* 1: 26, 20; ZCCM, *Export, Rehabilitation, and Diversification Project*, 16; Kaunga interview.
[162] World Bank, "Improving Parastatal Performance," 5.
[163] Baynes interview. When the draft plan was finished, ZCCM officials went to the government and said, in effect, "look chaps, we've got a mine to run, and if you want it to run, we need the following" (Ng'andu interview).

with greater contributions to the national economy."[164] And, of course, ZCCM simply refused to pay higher freight rates to Zambian Railways or higher electricity rates to ZESCO, though it is the largest and costliest customer of both parastatals.[165]

ZCCM even invested in the company's future at the expense of Zambia's. Enjoying "virtual autonomy" from ZIMCO supervision, it extracted funds not only for mining but to buy an executive recruitment agency, an office temporaries agency, and a travel agency in London, and to invest in commercial agriculture and a chain of safari lodges in Zambia.[166] The director of corporate planning at ZIMCO argues, however, that because of its sector-specific management expertise, ZCCM cannot run such businesses profitably and is wasting scarce resources. The entire effort, he asserts, proves that ZCCM has a "disproportionate, distorting impact within ZIMCO" and that its managers occupy a "privileged spot" and can "do what they want because of their very special relationship to government, in spite of what ZIMCO management may think or want."[167]

The MUZ has done less well than ZCCM, but it remains a potent force. Restructuring plans required labor discipline to maintain production, and wage restraint to free mining-sector monies for diversification. Zambian leaders also worried that 19 percent of the national work force belongs to a union "capable of bringing the Government to its knees."[168] They therefore renewed attacks on the MUZ—even accusing it of ties to the Central Intelligence Agency and to South African and CIA-backed insurgent groups operating in Angola and Mozambique—and sought tough new labor laws.[169]

But MUZ survived. Indeed, state efforts to control it resulted instead in widespread discontent and wildcat strikes. More important, the inclusion of MUZ's general secretary, Timothy Walamba, on ZCCM's board in an effort to mollify miners allowed ZCCM and MUZ

---

[164] World Bank, *Zambia Country Economic Memorandum: Economic Reforms and Development Prospects,* 66–67; and "Improving Parastatal Performance," Annex 1.

[165] World Bank, "Improving Parastatal Performance," 22; *Zambia: Public Expenditure Review* 2: 100; and *Zambia Country Economic Memorandum: Issues and Options for Economic Diversification,* 38.

[166] ZCCM, *Export, Rehabilitation, and Diversification Project,* 15; World Bank, "Improving Parastatal Performance," iii, 25–26; and *Zambia Country Economic Memorandum: Economic Reforms and Development Prospects,* 41.

[167] Kaunga interview.

[168] Quote from Sichula; interviews with Chanda, Mazyopa, and Lungu.

[169] Shengamo interview; and Kaunda in the *Times of Zambia,* April 4, 1987.

to mount a combined attack on the state. From serving on the board, Walamba learned that ZCCM finances could not bear a wage hike and thus throw MUZ support behind ZCCM's push to cut its taxes—and its contribution to diversification. For its part, ZCCM management worried about wildcat strikes, lack of labor discipline, and the MUZ leadership's weakening position. It therefore lobbied for higher wages and opposed new labor legislation intended to "deal a death blow to labor," since this would have made labor management impossible and destroyed company productivity.[170] In approaching the sensitive issue of closing uneconomic facilities, ZCCM excluded politicians, preferring to deal solely with MUZ. Thus, whatever the broader consequences of mine closings, ZCCM and MUZ have, as in the past, kept mining matters to themselves, effectively excluding the state.[171]

What explains Zambia's inability to restructure? The shortest answer is copper; the slightly longer one is relative *in*capacity. In the 1960s, the Zambian state had neither the autonomy nor the institutions to implement restructuring when confronted by organized and capable leading-sector interests. In the 1980s, it had far greater capabilities, born of policies intended to increase state capacity—but it failed again because it was still too weak relative to societal actors that were also stronger, largely because of the very policies that had been undertaken to increase state autonomy and capacity. More generally, Zambia's predicament, then as now, offers a clear picture of the overwhelming challenge confronting states bound to world markets by a high/high mining sector: how to manage an intractable restructuring project with weak, poorly insulated state institutions, and in the face of intense societal opposition.

[170] Quote from Sichula; interviews with Chanda, Yamba-Yamba, and Shengamo.
[171] Interviews with Baynes, Sichula, Kampamba, Yamba-Yamba, and Shengamo.

CHAPTER FOUR

Korea: The Light
Manufacturing Sector

In contrast to Zambia, Korea is a model held up for other Third World countries to emulate. Thirty years ago, it was a resource-poor agricultural country and the despair of its American advisers. Today it is vying for a place in the fraternity of industrialized countries, having grown from an exporter of duck feathers and seaweed to a world-class producer of steel and supertankers. No less important, Korea is today taking the first steps toward democracy. But as it does, it is also threatened by labor revolt, by political protest, and by staggering economic performance.

As with Zambia, much is unique about the Korean story, but sectoral analysis can explain a lot, and Korea offers a natural experiment for testing it. In the 1960s Korea's economy fit the light manufacturing ideal type; in the 1970s Korean leaders used their autonomy and capacity to shift the sectoral base of the economy to high/high heavy manufacturing. The results were startling. Having thrived economically in the 1960s and 1970s despite intense international competition, Korea now faces tougher problems, the solutions to which may be beyond its reach. Moreover, the restructuring project confronting Korean leaders today is less tractable than the one managed so convincingly in the 1960s and 1970s. And despite continued institutional growth, the state's relative capacity to take the project on has declined because of the increased capacity of business and labor for collective action, resulting from altered sectoral circumstances.

This chapter begins with some explanations for the "Korean miracle," followed by a sectoral analysis of Korea in the heyday of light manufacturing. I then examine the changes wrought by the Heavy

94

and Chemical Industries Development Plan (HCID) in the 1970s and the consequences of the resulting sectoral shift in the Korean political economy. In short, sectoral analysis is employed to examine change in Korea, and Korea is used to test sectoral analysis.

THE KOREAN MIRACLE

Given Korea's dazzling economic growth since the early 1960s, it is easy to forget the pessimism about its prospects that prevailed at the time. In 1945 Korea emerged from Japanese rule politically and economically divided. Its mineral wealth and Japan's industrial investment were located in the north. The south, in contrast, was agricultural with only a tiny light manufacturing sector. Without power or inputs from the north, production in the south plummeted, and partition deprived southern producers of their traditional markets. The Korean War inflicted appalling human costs, demolished the infrastructure, destroyed 20 percent of net capital stock and 42–44 percent of manufacturing capacity, and left Korea burdened with a huge military that annually consumed 56 percent of the government budget. From 1953 to 1962, the United States lavished aid on Korea, but 38 percent of this aid was military; 75 percent of the economic aid financed commodity imports and 10–15 percent was used to rebuild infrastructure—thus leaving little for productive investment.[1] As reconstruction was completed, aid dried up, leaving Korea to face the 1960s only slightly better off economically than it had been in the 1950s and wracked by political turmoil culminating in the 1961 coup that unseated Syngman Rhee.

Then the Korean economy took off. In a sharp reversal, investment surged—and stayed at an *average* level of 26.5 percent of GDP from 1965 to 1980. During the first five-year plan (1962–66), real GNP rose an average of 7.8 percent per year; the average rate during the second plan (1967–71) was 10.5 percent. Exports increased from $55 million annually to $3.2 billion in the period 1962–73, fueling 40

[1] Edward Mason et al., *The Economic and Social Modernization of the Republic of Korea* (Cambridge: Harvard University Press, 1980), 182, 432–33; Kwang Suh Kim and Michael Roemer, *Growth and Structural Transformation* (Cambridge: Harvard University Press, 1980), 33; Paul Kuznets, *Economic Growth and Structure in the Republic of Korea* (New Haven: Yale University Press, 1977), 105; Stephan Haggard, "Pathways from the Periphery" (Ph.D. diss., University of California, Berkeley, 1983), 116.

percent of GNP growth and the accompanying economic transformation.[2]

Korea's base for this export-led growth drive was labor-intensive light manufacturing. In the 1960s, light manufacturing accounted for more than 70 percent of production in a manufacturing sector that in 1960–70 grew from just 7.2 percent of GDP to 29.1 percent. Exports of light manufactures also dominated. In the same period, they increased from 24.2 percent of total exports to 60.3 percent, whereas exports of primary products decreased from 63.5 percent of total exports to 11.3 percent. Much of this increase came from firms with ten workers or less, whose contribution to total exports grew from 18.6 percent to 31.4 percent between 1963 and 1968. As exports increased, output became increasingly concentrated in labor-intensive industries and, within industries, in labor-intensive products.[3]

Neither Korea's export growth nor its industrial development stopped here, however. A maker of wigs and stuffed toys in the 1960s, Korea has become the eighth largest steel producer in the world, the second largest shipbuilder, the third largest producer of large-capacity memory chips, and a major supplier of cars and computers. Manufacturing now accounts for 30 percent of GDP, the same percentage as in Japan, and a far higher percentage than in the United States (20 percent) or the average for industrialized market countries (23 percent). Machinery, transport equipment, and other manufactures jumped from 17 percent of total exports in 1960–62 to 85 percent of a far larger volume of exports in 1974–76; by the mid-1980s they constituted almost 95 percent of a flood of exports worth nearly $30 billion. As Korean exports have increased, so too has heavy

[2] Robert Wade, *Governing the Market* (Princeton: Princeton University Press, 1990), 307; Young-Ho Lee, "The Politics of Democratic Experiment," in *Korean Politics in Transition*, ed. Edward Wright (Seattle: University of Washington Press, 1975), 30; Anne O. Krueger, *Perspectives on Trade and Development* (Chicago: University of Chicago Press, 1990), 264; Hyug Baeg Im, "The Rise of Bureaucratic Authoritarianism in South Korea," *World Politics* 39 (January 1987): 244–45; Mason, *The Economic and Social Modernization*, 103.

[3] Sang Chul Suh, "Policies for Industrialization and Regional Development," *Journal of Asiatic Studies* 21 (July 1978): 6; Gary Fields, "Labor Market and Export-Led Growth in Korea, Taiwan, Hong Kong, and Singapore," Seminar Paper Series, no. 82-01 (Seoul: Korean Development Institute, 1982), 6; Yung Bong Kim, "The Growth and Structural Change of the Korean Textile Industry," Working Paper no. 7710 (Seoul: KDI, 1977), 65; Suk Tai Suh, "Import Substitution and Economic Development in Korea," Working Paper no. 7519 (Seoul: KDI, 1975), 54; Gustav Ranis, "Industrial Sector Labor Absorption," *Economic Development and Cultural Change* 21 (April 1973): 404; Kuznets, *Economic Growth and Structure*, 161–62.

industry's contribution to total exports, rising from just 13.7 percent in 1971 to 59.7 percent in the mid-1980s. Today, tiny Korea is the thirteenth largest industrial exporter in the world, selling more than three times as many manufactures abroad as Brazil.[4]

No less important, private consumption has risen rapidly, absolute poverty has declined sharply, income distribution remains excellent by Third World standards, and the poor "have participated more or less proportionately in the fruits of development."[5] Exports of labor-intensive manufactures resulted in a doubling of industrial employment between 1963 and 1971, cutting unemployment from 8.3 percent in 1962 to 4 percent in 1973, where it remained through the 1980s. Real wages climbed 45 percent in the 1960s, doubled in the 1970s, and rose another 20 percent in the first half of the 1980s. Between 1963 and 1980, the number of self-employed and unpaid family workers fell from 78.5 percent of the work force to 52.7 percent, and more people held more highly skilled, better-paying jobs. The number of workers with no schooling fell from 44.7 percent to 16 percent of the work force in 1960–80, and the proportion with high school and university educations rose from 8.6 percent to 28.5 percent.[6]

All this stands in contrast to the economy's poor showing in the 1950s and the state's inability to improve it, despite having been "born strong." Built around a colonial bureaucracy and police, backed by the United States, and free of rural threats as a result of land reform undertaken in the late 1940s, Syngman Rhee's government had great administrative and coercive capacity. It was not, however, used for economic development. Rhee worried constantly about the weakness of his ruling coalition and therefore compromised state autonomy and capacity by building a vast system of patronage requiring constant manipulation of the economy for political ends. He blocked development of strong institutions for economic planning and management that might limit his control. He also pursued a policy of overvalued

[4] *New York Times*, October 6, 1985, and May 28, 1990; *Los Angeles Times*, December 23, 1983; Krueger, *Perspectives on Trade and Development*, 264; Wade, *Governing the Market*, 36, 44–45, 317; Alice Amsden, *Asia's Next Giant* (New York: Oxford University Press, 1989), 58.

[5] Quote from Fields, "Labor Market and Export Led Growth," 33. See also Sang Muk Suh, "The Patterns of Poverty in Korea," Working Paper Series, no. 79-03 (Seoul: KDI, 1979), 30, 38–39.

[6] Amsden, *Asia's Next Giant*, 72; Fields, "Labor Market and Export Led Growth," 9–13, 21–22, 26, 33; Krueger, *Perspectives on Trade and Development*, 266.

exchange rates to reduce import costs, offered low or no tariffs on favored imports combined with political controls on their allocation, imposed high tariffs on imports that competed with domestic production, and fought for foreign aid. These stymied development, but control of foreign exchange, imports, tariff protection, and aid monies provided an underpinning for his Liberal Party and its patronage net.[7]

From Rhee's perspective, the system worked well until the late 1950s; but it had bad economic consequences. Reconstruction was finished, some import-substituting industrialization occurred, and manufacturing grew rapidly, albeit from a tiny base. In the main, however, "more energy was spent plundering the existing surplus than producing more."[8] Rhee's policies bred not productive investment but zero-sum arbitrage, and an industrial sector that was too small to influence the overall growth rate; suffered from severe capacity underutilization and a high degree of import dependence; generated few jobs, no exports, and less foreign exchange; and offered no hope of future export expansion.[9] When foreign aid peaked in 1957, this aid-based economy began to stagger, but because of the regime's dependence on powerful clients and because of past efforts to limit institutional capacity, it could not respond. The GNP growth rate dropped, Rhee's coalition unraveled, opposition increased, and finally student riots forced Rhee from office in February 1960. His government was followed by the still weaker "Second Republic," which was subsequently ousted in the Park Chung Hee coup of 1961. Given such a starting point, how was the Korean miracle achieved?

Alternative Explanations of the Miracle

Explanations abound, most of them useful but none satisfactory. First are those that identify critical, enabling conditions such as the

[7] David Cole and Princeton Lyman, *Korean Development* (Cambridge: Harvard University Press, 1971), 187; Anne O. Krueger, *The Developmental Role of the Foreign Sector and Aid* (Cambridge: Harvard University Press, 1979), 4. For an excellent analysis of the political economy of the Rhee period (1948–60), see Jung-en Woo, *Race to the Swift* (New York: Columbia University Press, 1991), chap. 3.

[8] Amsden, *Asia's Next Giant*, 38–39.

[9] Kim Kyong-Dong, "Political Factors in the Formation of the Entrepreneurial Elite in South Korea," *Asian Survey* 16, no. 5 (1976): 467–69, 474–75; Duk-Choong Kim, "The Role of Entrepreneurs in Korea's Economic Development," in Korean Development Institute, *Industrialization and Rural Change* (Seoul: KDI, 1985), 13; Kuznets, *Economic Growth and Structure*, 98; Krueger, *The Developmental Role*, 167, 57.

land reform forced on Rhee by the United States, American aid, or extensive foreign investment. Thus, land reform gave Korea an egalitarian distribution of assets, expanded the domestic market, eliminated agrarian elites as political players, removed the last issue around which the left could have built rural support, neutralized the peasantry, and ironically began its destruction, producing an exodus to the cities where displaced farmers provided the cheap labor needed in labor-intensive manufacturing.[10] But though land reform may have been a necessary condition, it does not explain the explosive growth that began more than a decade later.

American aid, too, helped lay the foundations for growth. Between 1953 and 1961, the United States provided $1.56 billion in military aid and $2.58 billion in economic aid. These monies, which equaled nearly 80 percent of fixed capital formation and 8 percent of GNP during this period, rebuilt Korea's infrastructure and financed nearly 70 percent of its imports. Since domestic savings could have maintained the war-depleted capital stock but not per capita income levels, this aid was "necessary to permit such economic growth and recovery as took place," and the fact that it was in the form of grants meant that Korea embarked on the 1960s debt free.[11]

But U.S. aid did not *cause* Korean growth. Some 75 percent was allocated to commodity imports to slow inflation and meet welfare needs; of the 25 percent devoted to project assistance, more than half was spent on infrastructure and social services projects and less than 15 percent (4 percent of total aid) went to productive investments in agriculture and industry.[12] Aid peaked in 1957 and fell rapidly thereafter; "70 percent of investment growth from 1960–62 onwards was financed by Korea's efforts . . . fueled largely by the growth of both exports and national savings, which were substantial enough to support large increases in output while simultaneously replacing foreign savings as the dominant factor in development."[13]

[10] Larry Westphal, "The Private Sector as 'Principal Engine' of Development," *Finance and Development* 19, no. 2 (1982): 37; Silvio de Franco, *Korea's Experience with the Development of Trade and Industry,* Economic Development Policy Seminar Report no. 14 (Washington, D.C.: World Bank, 1988), 2; Cole and Lyman, *Korean Development,* 2; Jang Jip Choi, "Interest Conflict and Political Control in South Korea: The Labor Unions in Manufacturing Industries, 1961–1980" (Ph.D. diss., University of Chicago, 1983), 74–75.

[11] Quote from Krueger, *The Developmental Role,* 208–10. See also Mason et al., *The Economic and Social Modernization,* 182–86.

[12] Haggard, "Pathways from the Periphery," 116.

[13] Kim and Roemer, *Growth and Structural Transformation,* 51, 58.

Finally, there is the role of foreign direct investment (FDI). Some dismiss Korea as an export platform for foreign MNCs.[14] But since the early 1960s, control of investment has been in Korean hands, for Korea has used commercial borrowing, not FDI, to build industry. Even assuming that all FDI went into manufacturing, in 1970 it financed "no more than 5 percent of the capital stock."[15] Indeed, despite a burst of HCID-related FDI in the mid-1970s, FDI financed just 1.2 percent of gross domestic capital formation between 1962 and 1979, peaking at 2.2 percent in 1972–76 and falling to 0.6 percent by 1979.[16]

The minor role of FDI is reflected in equally limited foreign control over management, jobs, and exports. In 1980, 13.9 percent of all foreign-invested firms (7.8 percent excluding the Free Trade Zone [FTZ]) were wholly owned subsidiaries, and accounted for 22.9 percent of FDI (18.5 percent excluding the FTZ). These percentages are lower than those for Japan. Between 1968 and 1980, the proportions of foreign-invested firms that were wholly owned and majority-owned decreased from 18.6 percent and 24.8 percent to 13.9 percent and 12.2 percent, respectively, as the increase in the number of large Korean firms exceeded the number of foreign affiliates established in *every* manufacturing sector between 1962 and 1978. As a result, foreign-invested firms' share in value added (weighted to reflect joint ventures) was 0.4 percent in food and beverages; 3 percent in textiles, apparel, and basic metals; 4 percent in metals and transport equipment; 5 percent in machinery; 8 percent in chemicals; and 16 percent in electrical machinery.[17] In 1978 foreign-invested firms provided just 2.3 percent of total jobs and 9.5 percent of manufacturing jobs, and these positions were concentrated in a few industries where Korean firms dominated.[18] In 1970–71, firms with *any* foreign participation generated just 11–14 percent of exports, a situation little altered by

[14] Martin Landsberg, "Export-Led Industrialization in the Third World," *Review of Radical Political Economics* 11 (1979): 50–63.

[15] Larry Westphal, "The Republic of Korea's Experience with Export-Led Industrial Development," *World Development* 6, no. 3 (1978): 361.

[16] Clive Hamilton, *Capitalist Industrialization in Korea* (Boulder, Colo: Westview Press, 1986), 45; Amsden, *Asia's Next Giant*, 100–101.

[17] Bohn-Young Koo, "New Forms of Foreign Investments in Korea," Working Paper Series, no. 82-02 (Seoul: KDI, 1982), 38–40, 45–47, 71–75; Chung Lee, "U.S. and Japanese Investment in Korea," *Hitosubashi Journal of Economics* 20 (1980): 26–41.

[18] Koo, "New Forms," 30–32.

the introduction of FTZs in 1970, for "FTZ exports . . . have never exceeded 10 percent of . . . total exports."[19] The HCID briefly increased foreign-invested firms' share of total exports to 18.7 percent in 1978, but even in industries such as consumer electronics, where domestic firms' share of production fell from 68 percent to 36 percent in 1970–75, Korean firms rebounded and accounted for 58 percent of production and 53 percent of exports by 1981.[20]

But if limited MNC penetration explains Korea's success, how did Korea limit and direct FDI? The immediate answer is state policy. Korean planners defended the home market for domestic firms by channeling FDI into export sectors or into import-substituting industries whose technical requirements were beyond the capabilities of local firms. Following a revision of the Foreign Capital Inducement Law in 1973, the FDI screening committee also limited foreign ownership in labor-intensive industries and made local participation a government priority even in high-technology industries. Export requirements kept foreign firms outward-looking, and even the FTZs helped by separating foreign investors from the local market.[21] But this answer simply prompts a deeper question: how could Korea undertake such policies, when most other Third World states have failed?

The most common explanations of the Korean miracle focus on Park's strong state and the policies it pursued. David Cole and Princeton Lyman, for example, argued in the early 1970s that "the ability of the government to pursue its economic policies with such success, and of the country to make the transition in economic outlook and performance that it did by 1966, point . . . to the importance . . . of the government's political-military strength, on the one hand, and its particular convictions, on the other."[22] More recently, Robert Wade has emphasized the importance of Korea's "hard state," which was "able not only to resist private demands but actively to shape the economy

[19] Quote from Yung Whee Rhee, "Instruments for Export Policy and Administration," World Bank Staff Working Paper no. 725 (Washington, D.C., 1985), 17–18. See also Westphal, "Korea's Experience," 361; Deepak Nayyar, "Transnational Corporations and Manufactured Exports from Poor Countries," *Economic Journal* 88 (March 1978).

[20] Korea Exchange Bank, *Monthly Review,* November 1980; Koo, "New Forms," 80–82.

[21] Stephan Haggard, *Pathways from the Periphery* (Ithaca: Cornell University Press, 1990), 198–99.

[22] Cole and Lyman, *Korean Development,* 93. See also Mason et al., *The Economic and Social Modernization,* 244; Westphal, "'Principal Engine,'" 38; Amsden, *Asia's Next Giant.*

and society"; Alice Amsden emphasizes the importance of "an interventionist state" in making Korea "Asia's next giant."[23] And both the state and the policies it pursued *are* critical.

Park realized that Korea had no future if it did not alter its insular, yet dependent, stance and develop a capacity to earn foreign exchange—and that *he* had no future if he could not legitimize his rule. Therefore, he made economic growth the measure of political performance and the symbol of Korea's progress.[24] In 1962 he launched a policy of "guided capitalism" in which the state would "directly participate in or indirectly render guidance to the basic industries and other important fields."[25] To implement guided capitalism, Park revitalized the bureaucracy by stressing "achievement, technical proficiency, and Western methods of organization and administration"[26] and built strong, insulated institutions for economic management. Most important among them were the Economic Planning Board (EPB), chaired by a deputy prime minister and charged with planning, screening FDI, coordinating aid, and overseeing the budget; and the Economic Secretariat, located in the Blue House, the Korean presidential mansion, and directed by a vice-minister. These institutions increased the amount and quality of information available to policy makers and gave Park the means to manage the economy.

Park also pursued effective policies. He did not, as is often suggested, pursue neoclassical policies of minimal state intervention and untrammeled free trade.[27] Instead, he initiated a system of "government-directed development" in which "the hand of government reaches down rather far into the activities of individual firms with its manipulation of incentives and disincentives."[28] His policies included a major devaluation in 1964 and adoption of a floating unitary exchange rate in March 1965, an increase in interest rates, liberalization of import controls, implementation of export promotion policies that "set relative prices deliberately 'wrong' in order to create profitable investment opportunities" in targeted industries, the "setting [of] stringent performance standards in exchange for the

[23] Wade, *Governing the Market,* 337; Amsden, *Asia's Next Giant,* 8.

[24] Woo, *Race to the Swift,* 98.

[25] Republic of Korea, *Summary of the First Five Year Economic Plan* (Seoul, 1962), 28.

[26] Cole and Lyman, *Korean Development,* 46.

[27] See, for example, E. K. Y. Chen, *Hyper Growth in Asian Economies* (London: Macmillan, 1979); Milton Friedman and Rose Friedman, *Free to Choose* (New York: Harcourt Brace Jovanovich, 1980).

[28] Mason et al., *The Economic and Social Modernization,* 254.

subsidies," and even exercising "a strong element of coercion" to force compliance with the state's export promotion program.[29]

Park's policies protected infant industries and promoted exports of labor-intensive light manufactures. In this process, the state "not as much *picked* winners as *made* them . . . by creating a larger environment conducive to the viability of new industries—especially by shaping the social structure of investment so as to encourage productive investment and discourage unproductive investment, and by controlling key parameters on investment decisions so as to make for greater predictability."[30] Park's policies did not depoliticize the economy, nor did they stop corruption. Rather, they redefined the political context of economic activity and made business success the key to government support. As Alice Amsden reports, "To qualify as a regular customer of the government for long-term subsidized credit [and for all other forms of government largesse], objectively necessary, if not sufficient, conditions had to be met . . . : Big firms and small firms, young firms and old firms, *chaebôl* [conglomerates] and non*chaebôl* had to export."[31]

Guided capitalism, however, gave all Koreans a personal stake in state actions, and therefore required "a state strong enough to battle whoever stood to suffer from a loss of government support."[32] After all, the policy shift hurt those already in business: interest rate reforms increased the cost of money for disfavored sectors; import-substituting firms found their profits squeezed by rising costs and import competition; and everyone had to compete according to certain economic criteria. Not surprisingly, businesspeople became obsessively interested in policy. Likewise, the push to labor-intensive light manufacturing turned on an ability to control labor and labor costs, which gave the burgeoning working class an equally strong interest in policy.

What is striking, then, is how little influence business and labor wielded, for "the silent counterpart with this concern for the state . . . is the absence of countervailing social power."[33] Despite the importance of business success for the regime, government had "the whip hand." Indeed, "private enterprise has been merely a delegate of state

[29] Westphal, "Korea's Experience," 350–51; Amsden, *Asia's Next Giant*, v–vi, 13–14, 69.

[30] Wade, *Governing the Market*, 334.

[31] Mason et al., *The Economic and Social Modernization*, 266–67; Amsden, *Asia's Next Giant*, 74.

[32] Amsden, *Asia's Next Giant*, 18.

[33] Woo, *Race to the Swift*, 14.

power and the principal agent of the state directed development."[34] Representatives of big business were contacted for information, but according to the first EPB director, their influence was "negligible."[35] Workers also had no say in economic policy because despite their numbers, labor organization, protest, and power were negligible until the late 1970s.

But such explanations are incomplete. It is not enough to cite coercive capacity, since as Rhee's failure shows, the existence of an authoritarian state does not guarantee development. Nor is it enough to add a stated leadership interest in development, for the experience of would-be Latin American Newly Industrializing Countries (NICs) suggests that even export-oriented authoritarians may fail. And it is not enough to cite the policies pursued; they have been tried in many other places, only to be abandoned. At issue are questions of timing and of state-society relations over time.

These have been raised under the rubric of "development sequencing." In this debate, two arguments have been offered. The first emphasizes the supposedly auspicious timing of Korea's entry into the world economy. According to this argument Korea, in contrast to would-be Koreas today, was blessed by the simple accident of adopting an export-led growth strategy at a moment marked by a rapid expansion in world trade, "relatively favorable access to industrial country markets, dramatically increased access to international finance, . . . increasing relocation of production by multinational corporations to low wage sites," and remarkable stability in the world economy.[36] No less important, Korea did so at a time when most Third World countries were still pursuing inward-looking strategies, and thus faced little competition.

But such an argument is not entirely satisfactory. As we will see later in the section on "Beating Protection: Testing Korea's Flexibility," Korea's adoption of an export-led growth strategy coincided almost perfectly with the imposition of the first multilateral protectionist regime in textiles, Korea's export of preference. Furthermore, international lending continued to surge until the late 1970s, and the increase in international trade competition has, if anything, encour-

---

[34] Quotes from both Mason et al., *The Economic and Social Modernization*, 262–63; and Choi, "Interest Conflict," 328–39.

[35] Chung interview. Business leaders confirm this assertion. See LeRoy Jones and Il Sakong, *Government, Business, and Entrepreneurship in Economic Development* (Cambridge: Harvard University Press, 1980), 74, 137.

[36] Wade, *Governing the Market*, 346–47.

aged even more relocation of production to low-wage areas. The common contention that other Third World countries cannot follow Korea's path because their doing so would glut the market for light manufactures is also hollow for the simple reason that very few other developing countries have succeeded in getting to the market at all.[37]

The second, more compelling development-sequencing argument focuses on domestic conditions. The import substitution industrialization period in Korea was so short that the state did not face an entrenched ISI coalition when it switched to export promotion. Moreover, the dependence of the few big ISI firms on the Rhee regime left them vulnerable to state pressure after the coup. Because of these firms' role in the economy, Park could not punish their chief executives as he had originally planned. "Who, if not businessmen, would finance the governing party, regime consolidation, and growth?"[38] Park was, however, able to forge a development-oriented business-government relationship dominated by the state. The "deep pockets" thus stayed at center stage, but "in a kneeling position," for the state could and did demand that even the biggest firms meet exacting performance standards of its making.[39] The small size of the Korean business community in 1961 and the fact that its growth followed the implementation of export promotion policies further limited business power since most firms were new, small, and weak. Finally, Park's reforms preceded the development of strong organizations able to express business interests.[40]

Labor was limited by a repressive labor regime that predated the export drive and that permitted policy makers to "channel and restrain demands placed on the state as these demands grew" with industrialization.[41] The labor movement was crushed in the late 1940s and its remnants incorporated into the Liberal Party as "a political instrument to buttress Rhee's rule" without "any meaningful rank and file organizational base."[42] On taking power, Park imposed his own organization to guarantee political control. He formed a national labor organization, the Federation of Korean Trade Unions (FKTU), but kept enterprise-level unions, thereby disarticulating the labor movement internally. Furthermore, the very speed of industrialization—

[37] See, for example, Robin Broad and John Cavanaugh, "No More NICs," *Foreign Policy* 72 (Fall 1988): 81–103.
[38] Woo, *Race to the Swift*, 83–84.
[39] Amsden, *Asia's Next Giant*, 72, 74.
[40] Interviews with Chung, Whang, Cha, and Lim.
[41] Wade, *Governing the Market*, 339.
[42] Choi, "Interest Conflict," 46.

which between 1962 and 1977 prompted an urban influx of more than 7 million people, or 20 percent of the population—produced a first-generation working class that lacked a class identity.[43] Park thus could exclude labor because, in the absence of previous labor mobilization, he had no incentive to include it and because it became important only as a result of the growth sparked by Park's reforms.

But development-sequencing arguments about the lack of business and labor opposition are misleading. They imply that, given this leg up, the state is forever favored, and therefore they offer no way to understand changes in state-society relations or the consequences of state action for them. To compensate for these limitations, let us turn to sectoral analysis.

THE INTERNATIONAL DIMENSION

Light manufacturing is a low/low sector marked by high production flexibility and asset/factor flexibility. There are few barriers to entry: capital requirements are slight; economies of scale are unimportant and production is divisible; skill requirements are low; technology is standardized and available; access to distribution channels is easy; and infrastructure requirements are unspecialized. Easy entry means that new firms arise quickly when demand surges, thus barring windfall profits. It also discourages MNC investment, leaving an even field for all producers. But being open to all, the market is extremely competitive, a competitiveness exaggerated by high buyer concentration and low switching costs. Profit margins are tiny and firms are demand driven. Neither firms nor countries can control the market; what matters is a capacity to conform to it.

Despite interindustry variations, capital intensity is low in all segments of light manufacturing. In apparel, textiles, and footwear, which are critical industries in Korea, labor accounts for as much as 25 percent, 60 percent, and 33 percent of production costs respectively, and fixed capital costs may be less than 10 percent.[44] New equipment can be expensive, but small producers with low labor costs can compete using secondhand machines—witness the success of small Korean manufacturers that often employ double or triple shifts to

[43] Ibid., 78, 104.
[44] David Morawetz, *Why the Emperor's New Clothes Are Not Made in Colombia* (New York: Oxford University Press, 1981), 92; David Yoffie, *Power and Protectionism* (New York: Columbia University Press, 1983), 173.

spread capital costs, maximize the benefits of low-cost labor, and minimize the disadvantages of old equipment.[45]

The prevalence of small firms also indicates limited economies of scale. In the 1970s, for example, Third World firms employing forty-nine workers or less generated 37–38 percent of value added and accounted for 46–53 percent of light manufacturing jobs; the percentages for firms with nine workers or less were 16–20 percent and 32–34 percent, respectively. Moreover, small firms' productivity came close to the average productivity of firms of all sizes, and in Korea, as well as in other developing countries, it exceeded the average. In Korea specifically, EPB figures from the mid-1970s also show that though value added per employee rises with firm size in textiles and apparel, the curves are nearly flat.[46]

The reasons for low economies of scale vary by industry, but they overlap. Light manufacturing industries are not "process" industries, and production is thus divisible, permitting small-scale operations.[47] Where economies of scale exist, they are in the length of production runs, which reduce downtime (to change tooling) and increase labor productivity (with practice). These too do not exclude small firms which are equally capable of long production runs. Finally, labor productivity increases "not as a result of quantum leaps in the type of machinery used, but rather through . . . many small improvements in particular operations or in the organization of the production process." Again, since productivity gains "involve changing ways of doing and organizing things, rather than introducing new machinery," small firms are not disadvantaged.[48]

Consider the case of textiles, which in Korea drove early export growth and supplied the apparel industry. Even in 1968, most textile machinery in the Third World was fifty years old, suggesting that "technological obsolescence . . . does not necessarily imply economic obsolescence."[49] Textile equipment also lends itself to multiple shifting, which allows firms to spread investment costs and compensate for

[45] Mason et al., *The Economic and Social Modernization*, 160.
[46] Ranadev Banerji, "Small-Scale Production Units in Manufacturing," *Weltwirtschaftlishes Archiv* 114, no. 1 (1978): 71–73; Kim, "Korean Textile Industry," 112.
[47] C. F. Pratten, *Economies of Scale in Manufacturing Industry* (Cambridge: Cambridge University Press, 1971), 241–42.
[48] Morawetz, *The Emperor's New Clothes*, 85–86.
[49] United Nations, Economic Commission for Latin America, *Choice of Technologies in the Latin American Textile Industries*, E/CN.12/746 (1966), p. 21. See also International Labor Organization, Textiles Committee, *Labor Problems in the Textile Industry in Developing Countries* (Geneva, 1968).

old equipment by using cheap labor in quantity. Thus, in 1965 Korean firms worked spindles and looms an average of 135 hours and 123 hours per week, respectively—the equivalent of 20 hours and 18 hours a day, seven days a week—and on average employed 25 percent more labor per unit than firms in countries belonging to the Organization for Economic Cooperation and Development (OECD), which ran spindles and looms an average of 77 hours and 67 hours per week, respectively.[50] Especially when they used older equipment, textile firms had limited economies of scale, and small firms predominated, as they did even in western Europe.

Dramatic changes have occurred in the world textiles industry since then, and although they affect Korea today, they did not in the late 1960s. Beginning in the 1950s, rising competition, labor costs, and Third World imports drove technological progress in the OECD countries, increasing machine speeds and cutting labor needs by as much as 75 percent. Investment costs in Europe and the United States for new plant jumped from $6,600 per operator in the 1950s to $12,700 per operator in 1960, and to $20,000 in 1965; total costs were several million dollars, 90 percent of which were fixed. Technological change also increased the extent of economies of scale; by the mid-1960s, the minimum efficient scale for a new, integrated mill in the OECD had increased to 30,000–40,000 spindles and 500 looms.[51] But whereas the continued importance of variable costs forced American firms in particular to invest heavily in new technology to offset high labor costs, Korean firms felt no such pressure. An "analysis of the structure of production costs in an integrated spinning and weaving mill shows that the variable cost components represent between 60 and 80 percent of total costs. . . . The reduction of fixed costs, which are those most affected by production scales, would therefore have to be very great for economies of scale to be achieved."[52] Labor costs and lengths of production are the "decisive cost components in

[50] ILO, *Labor Problems*, 42–43; United Nations Industrial Development Organization, *Industrialization of Developing Countries: Problems and Prospects, Textile Industry*, UNIDO Monograph on Industrial Development no. 7, 1969.II.B.39 (Vienna, 1969), 68; Organization for Economic Cooperation and Development, *Modern Cotton Industry* (Paris, 1965), 66.

[51] UNIDO, *Industrialization of Developing Countries*, 47–48; ILO, *Labor Problems*, 20–21; ILO, *The Effects of Structural and Technological Changes on Labor Problems in the Textile Industry* (Geneva, 1968), 3–4, 10–11, 24–27; United Nations, *Choice of Technologies*, 9–10, 30–31; Pratten, *Economies of Scale*, 231–32.

[52] United Nations, Economic Commission for Latin America, *Economies of Scale in the Cotton Spinning and Weaving Industry*, E/CN.12748 (1966), 1.

economies of scale in the textile industry"; therefore, "it is more effective to lower production costs by improving labor efficiency and capacity utilization than to lower investment costs per unit of annual production by constructing new plants of economically optimum size."[53]

In light manufacturing, Korea and Korean firms confront conditions different from those faced by Zambia. Limited fixed costs and the divisibility of production allow firms to adjust to changes in the market. As a result, the characteristics of production do not exaggerate market moves as they do in the boom-and-bust cycle typical of minerals markets. Low barriers to entry also discourage vertical integration by MNCs in the international market; consequently, Korean firms are not structurally disadvantaged vis-à-vis competitors. Low barriers to entry encourage large numbers of firms to enter the fray, however, so the international market for light manufactures is characterized by vicious competition. In many markets critical for Korea, high buyer concentration intensifies competition. By the late 1960s, for example, a few OECD firms, such as Sears, J. C. Penney, and Marcor, were buying billions of dollars' worth of Asian light manufactures. These big buyers save small firms the trouble of finding markets, provide product designs, help organize production, and supply working capital. But because they "place enormous orders and are often able to book 60–100 percent of [firms'] capacity for one or two years," they can dictate prices, since "in such a situation the loss of an order is much more serious than accepting a very low price."[54]

Under such conditions, ologopolistic, market-control strategies are out and market-conforming strategies are in. There are no monopoly rents to be had and no incentives for collusion, which is barred anyway by the large number of firms and the intense competition. What matters is firms' capacity to seize marginal advantages when ephemeral opportunities appear and to survive inevitable market downturns. Firms must be price competitive, able "to comply with clients' detailed specifications, to implement and maintain a stringent system of quality control, and to ensure that all shipments meet their tight delivery

[53] Quotes from ibid., 57; and UNIDO, *Perspectives for Industrial Development in the Second United Nations Development Decade: The Textile Industry*, 1971.II.B.14 (Vienna, 1971), 22. See also Pratten, *Economies of Scale*, 226–30.

[54] Angus Hone, "Multinational Corporations and Multinational Buying Groups," *World Development* 2 (February 1974): 148.

dates."[55] And, given the market volatility, the seasonal nature of demand for many products, and the constant changes in style and technical specifications, firms cannot seek efficiencies in specialization but must cultivate flexibility.

Firms can pursue either external flexibility or internal flexibility. To achieve the former, firms must diversify product lines and customer base to cut dependence on specific products, market segments, and buyers.[56] But such efforts are often beyond the powers of small firms. Few can produce more than one product at a time; product variety reduces economies of scale resulting from longer production runs; and the high costs of finding new markets leave most firms dependent on the big buyers. Internal flexibility is thus the key to success. Compared with mining firms, light manufacturing firms are flexible by virtue of their lower debt, fixed costs, and specificity of assets. But since these advantages are common to all light manufacturing firms, "competitive flexibility" depends on the quality of management and labor.

Here firms can attack all three elements of competitiveness: cost, quality, and on-time delivery. Indeed, "the shopfloor tends to be the strategic focus of firms that compete on the basis of borrowed technology."[57] Firms must have the managerial flexibility to absorb new designs and move them rapidly into production, the technical flexibility to adjust production lines quickly, and a skilled work force to make fast changes without adversely affecting quality.[58] Low labor costs are also important, but not as important as labor productivity, which depends on "the skill of the workers; the intensity of the workers' work effort; the efficiency with which production is organized . . . ; and the quality of the machinery and its maintenance."[59] Contrary to claims that cheap labor explains Korea's success, "the macroeconomic indicators point strongly to an increasingly efficient manufacturing sector, with rising productivity of both labor and capital leading economic growth."[60] Finally, quality control and on-time delivery depend on workers' skill and the quality of shop floor management.

[55] Morawetz, *The Emperor's New Clothes*, 33.
[56] H. Igor Ansoff, *Corporate Strategy* (London: Sidgewick and Jackson, 1986), 56–58.
[57] Amsden, *Asia's Next Giant*, 5.
[58] Donal Keesing, "Linking Up to Distant Markets," *American Economic Review* 73 (May 1983): 340.
[59] Morawetz, *The Emperor's New Clothes*, 133.
[60] Kim and Roemer, *Growth and Structural Transformation*, 66–68.

But what could the Korean state do to enhance national firms' ability to meet these challenges, outperform the competition, and generate the benefits of export-led growth? Luckily for Korea, the answer is a lot, for the dominance of market-conforming strategies locates all the critical variables within the grasp of firms and the state. Thus, the state "created an enclave of relative stability for long-term investment decisions through its control of key parameters (foreign exchange rates, interest rates, and aggregate demand); modulated the economy's exposure to international competitive pressures in the domestic market; restricted the activities of foreign companies in Korea so as to keep control in Korean hands; aggressively pushed exports; and exercised leadership in selected industries."[61]

Korea Takes on the Challenges of Light Manufacturing

Korean policy makers sought to ensure that market signals reached firms undistorted, developed policies and institutions to support them as they took up export production, and intervened to assist targeted industries and individual firms. Although the latter step has attracted the most attention, "Korea's successful export performance . . . derives primarily from initiatives taken by firms acting within a decentralized system and in response to generalized incentives."[62] Let us therefore focus on the initiatives that established the policy environment in which all would-be exporting firms operated.

In a market where price, quality, and on-time delivery are critical, firms must receive timely, undistorted market signals. In this, openness is essential, and a key element of openness is the exchange rate. Without consistent, competitive exchange rates, firms cannot compete—as Korean firms could not under the exchange rate regime maintained by the Rhee government. The establishment of a unitary floating rate in 1965, however, gave firms accurate signals on prices and removed exchange rate disincentives to export production, thus launching the export boom.

Firms also require timely access to equipment and quality inputs at competitive prices. Because of the seasonal nature of light manufactures, late delivery of inputs can spell disaster, and poor materials or equipment can lead to the rejection of shipments by buyers. More-

---

[61] Wade, *Governing the Market*, 307.

[62] Westphal, "'Principal Engine,'" 36. For detailed studies of East Asian industrial policy, see Amsden, *Asia's Next Giant*, and Wade, *Governing the Market*.

over, despite high labor intensity, raw materials account for 35–60 percent of production costs; if they are unavailable at competitive prices, firms are lost.[63] Again, under the Rhee government, import restrictions and firms' dependence on high-cost, poor-quality local goods killed exports. After 1961, however, Korean firms received tariff exemptions on equipment and raw materials for export production, were given a choice between domestic and imported inputs, and were even allowed an automatic credit for the purchase of imported inputs upon receipt of an export contract.[64] Together with the new exchange rate regime, such measures put Korean firms on an equal footing with firms located elsewhere. But equality alone is not enough to succeed; a competitive edge is required.

In Korea, state institutional measures provided this edge. Robert Wade notes that "until brandnames become established in the market, foreign buyers judge a product less by its manufacturer than by its country of origin. Hence the shoddy quality of a single product can penalize producers of other products from that country." This being the case, the state established compulsory quality inspection schemes for certain important exports in order to protect markets for all Korean firms.[65] But because they were small, inexperienced producers far from potential export markets, Korean firms faced uncertainty about the benefits of abandoning domestic markets and a bewildering array of financial, managerial, technical, marketing, bureaucratic, and manpower problems. The state, however, could—and did—help them overcome these problems by providing incentives and by implementing institutional measures that favored all would-be exporters.

Policy makers first had to get firms to try exporting. To accomplish that, they shifted incentives to favor production for export and assured exporters high initial profits, thus considerably reducing their reluctance to make the leap. On top of the tariff exemptions already mentioned, exporters received exemptions from business and commodity taxes, 50 percent reductions in corporate and income taxes on export earnings, accelerated depreciation allowances for fixed capital used in export production, and permission to use export earnings to

[63] United Nations, *Economies of Scale*, 44: Morawetz, *The Emperor's New Clothes*, 92; UNIDO, *Industrialization of Developing Countries*, 56.

[64] Tai Suh Suk, "The Effects of Export Incentives on Korean Export Growth, 1953–79," Working Paper Series, no. 81-07 (Seoul: KDI, 1981), II-23-4; Jones and Sakong, *Government, Business, and Entrepreneurship*, 94–96; Bela Balassa, "Export Incentives and Export Performance in Developing Countries," *Weltwirtschaftliches Archiv* 114, no. 1 (1978): 27–28.

[65] *Governing the Market*, 144–45.

buy still-prohibited imports, which they could sell for high profits.[66] These measures "provided businessmen with immediate net gains from investments" in exporting without which few would have risked the shift to export production.[67]

But to succeed, would-be exporters also needed help to meet the challenges of light manufacturing. Over the course of the 1960s, therefore, the Park government intervened to enhance firms' competitiveness by reducing their production costs. It offered low-cost investment funds and ensured the timely provision of working capital by establishing the Small and Medium Industry Bank, created a fund to convert firms to export production, and financed the purchase of imports needed to meet export orders. It granted exporters discounts of 20–30 percent on electricity and railway freight rates. It sought to improve firms' management by establishing the Technological Improvement Program at the Ministry of Technology, the Korea Productivity Center, and business education programs; and by offering management consulting services. In an attempt to upgrade technology, increase the productivity of installed technology, and improve product quality, it established the National Technical Research Institute and helped firms reorganize production. Later it established the Korea Advanced Institute of Science and Technology to foster industry-supporting research and development, and the Korea Institute of Electronics Technology to promote semiconductor research and development and to coordinate the importation, assimilation, and dissemination of semiconductor design and production-related technologies.[68] Finally, although the government was restraining unions and limiting wage increases, it pursued policies "including education and training and work incentives [which] played a major role in productivity gains."[69]

Other initiatives cut transaction and information costs and helped

[66] de Franco, *Korea's Experience*, 7; Jones and Sakong, *Government, Business, and Entrepreneurship*, 94–96; Krueger, *The Developmental Role*, 104, 183–85; Kim and Roemer, *Growth and Structural Transformation*, 75.

[67] Interview with Whang.

[68] Interviews with Whang and Han; Chang Ha Lee, "Co-operative Marketing Activities of Small Industries in the Republic of Korea," and Jang Shur Park, "Basic Directions of Small Industry Development Policy in the Republic of Korea," *Small Industries Bulletin for Asia and the Far East*, UN.66.II.F.12, 4 (1966): 70–72, 135; Jones and Sakong, *Government, Business, and Entrepreneurship*, 94–95; Mason et al., *The Economic and Social Modernization*, 131; Bela Balassa, "Industrial Policies in Taiwan and Korea," *Weltwirtschaftlishes Archiv* 106, no. 1 (1971): 63; Wade, *Governing the Market*, 280, 313, 353.

[69] de Franco, *Korea's Experience*, 13–14.

firms penetrate distant markets by lowering downstream barriers to entry. Monthly export promotion meetings at the Blue House reduced delays; expedited customs-clearing procedures cut red tape; and a "one-stop service" system brought together officials from all interested agencies to minimize paperwork.[70] The state invested heavily in the transportation, communication, and power infrastructures needed for an efficient export-manufacturing sector, thus cutting firms' costs and increasing their ability to operate overseas.[71] Industrial parks provided access to support infrastructure, reduced start-up and operating costs, and gave small firms "facilities of large-scale economy that would otherwise be unavailable to them."[72] The state also encouraged associations of exporters and created the Korean Trade Promotion Corporation (KOTRA), which, along with the Ministry of Commerce and Industry, the EPB, and Korean embassies abroad helped exporters identify markets and develop products; understand foreign standards, tastes, and distribution systems; enter international trade fairs and design packaging and catalogs; and build distributor, service, and repair networks.

Beating Protection: Testing Korea's Flexibility

Rising protection in markets for light manufactures is the best test of Korean firms' flexibility and the Korean state's capacity to manipulate the variables critical to success. Especially worrisome for Korea are Voluntary Export Restraints (VERs) and Orderly Marketing Arrangements (OMAs). These impose quantitative restrictions on "labor-intensive, low-priced goods, products such as textiles and footwear, where a developing country has the greatest comparative advantage [and] involve bilateral negotiations that isolate the weak, developing country in a one-on-one confrontation against a powerful developed state or the EC [European Community]."[73] But despite the host of VERs and OMAs aimed at it, Korea has *increased* exports of the protected goods. In the six years after the United States imposed the

[70] Krueger, *The Developmental Role,* 126; Susumu Watanabe, "International Subcontracting, Employment, and Skill Promotion," *International Labor Review* 105 (May 1972): 443–44.

[71] Interviews with Whang and Han; Kae H. Chung, "Industrial Progress in South Korea," *Asian Survey* 14 (May 1974): 446.

[72] Park, "Basic Directions," 135–36.

[73] David Yoffie, "The Newly Industrializing Countries and the Political Economy of Protection," *International Studies Quarterly* 25 (December 1981): 572.

first VER on cotton textiles and apparel in 1962, for example, Korean exports of these products to the United States increased sevenfold, and despite the additional imposition of the first multifiber VER in 1971, Korean textile and apparel exports to the United States increased a staggering 4060 percent between 1962 and 1976.[74] The question is how.

The immediate explanation is found in the nature of protection itself.[75] Protection is a myopic, adjustment-avoidance strategy to defend saturated, slow-growth, low-end market segments for uncompetitive firms. Korean firms initially were concentrated in these markets because that is where their comparative advantage lay, because they were short-run profit maximizers, and because they were unaware of the greater opportunities existing in high-end markets. The irony of protection is that it forced Korean firms "to allocate resources more efficiently, diversify markets, and upgrade product lines." The imposition of quantitative restrictions in the form of VERs and OMAs gave Korean firms and the Korean state incentives to trade up—to upgrade exports to escape protected, saturated markets and thus earn more selling fewer, but higher-value, goods (23–24). Korea's success with such policies is evident in its response to VERs on textiles and footwear, both key exports.

Unfortunately for Korea, its outward reorientation coincided with imposition by OECD countries of the 1961 Short Term Agreement and the 1962 Long Term Agreement, which established a multilateral protectionist regime in cotton textiles. Korea had to maximize earnings from cotton goods in the short term, while seeking long-term growth in the dynamic and unrestricted synthetics market. To do so, firms had to upgrade their products "in order to charge the maximum possible price" for what cotton items they could export. This demanded that they "modernize production, keep up with fashion trends, and bargain well with importers" (117). The future was in synthetics, however; and beginning with the first five-year plan (1962–66), attention focused on rapid expansion of synthetics production. Exports of synthetics to the United States alone rose from 2.5 million square yard equivalents (MSE) in 1964 to 254.0 MSE in 1970, putting Korea in "the forefront of the synthetic fiber industry" (113, 120).

---

[74] UNIDO, *Perspectives for Industrial Development*, 29; Yoffie, *Power and Protectionism*, 207.

[75] The following discussion derives from Yoffie, *Power and Protectionism;* specific page citations are given in parentheses.

Korean success added to pressures by OECD producers for broader protection, which resulted in the more restrictive 1972 Multifiber Agreement (MFA)—and an equally successful response. Korean firms more than doubled prices "to capture scarcity rents and recoup losses from reductions in quantities" (159). Then with state support they improved the quality of their products to such an extent that despite a 25 percent drop in exports of synthetics to the United States in 1971–74, the value of textile and apparel exports rose 52 percent. Again with state aid, they diversified their markets, and by 1977 had redirected 20 percent of textile exports to Japan. These measures expanded the Korean textile industry, as, ironically, Korea's response to multilateral protection nearly tripled global earnings between 1971 and 1973 (160).

By the late 1970s, such success had produced pressure for still greater protection, and OECD producers obtained it in the form of the even more restrictive MFA-3. Korea again held its own, pursuing a strategy similar to that used in the past. It also began to push beyond upgrading, to abandon textiles and shift resources to higher-value-added industries.

The footwear story is similar. Having combined with other producers to block an OMA in the mid-1970s, Korean firms knew by 1977 that one was inevitable. In anticipation, they increased shipments and prices to capture expected scarcity rents; and when the OMA went into effect in July of that year, they cheated. These efforts allowed the industry to avoid serious short-term losses that would have resulted from the OMA, but the industry's growth resulted from upgrading, which the state encouraged by, for example, giving preferential tax treatment in 1978 to higher-priced footwear. In July 1977, when the OMA took effect, 87 percent of Korean shoe exports sold for less than $5.00; by December 1978 only 16 percent did. Average unit value jumped 81 percent in 1977–80, so that despite a 12 percent drop in volume, export earnings rose 53.1 percent (180, 195–99).

The question remains: how did Korea do it? In part, the effort to expand exports despite restrictions succeeded because the government, KOTRA, and the Korean Traders Association (KTA) waged a tough campaign to combat protection. The KTA's Trade Cooperation Department does nothing but follow developments affecting Korea's export markets. In the United States, its representatives lobby Congress, organize trade delegations to all fifty states, and target Korean investment to create political allies against would-be protectionists or

116

to gain a pro-Korean voice in key congressional districts. Since such efforts are not fail-safe, KTA also promotes market diversification to reduce dependence on the OECD.[76]

But the key has been Korea's ability to restructure: to trade up and reallocate resources to new industries. To grasp how the state was able to restructure, however, we must shift our focus from the international realm to the domestic political economy of light manufacturing.

THE DOMESTIC DIMENSION

The place to start is with the relative ease of restructuring, for light manufacturing's high production flexibility and asset/factor flexibility mean that restructuring posed fewer problems for Korean officials than for their Zambian counterparts. Production flexibility reflects the core characteristics of light manufacturing and the firms' own efforts to survive. Small capital requirements and low fixed costs mean that firms can cut production to adapt to market downturns without jeopardizing debt service. Workers are unskilled and easily trained, leaving firms free to hire and fire as demand dictates. Light manufacturing facilities are unaffected by shutdowns and there are few costs associated with temporary closings if demand slumps. Further, because most light manufacturing is divisible without loss of economies of scale, firms can partially shut down without suffering greatly increased unit costs.

Asset/factor flexibility is also high, and the barriers to exit when the market shifts or the state provides incentives to do so are low. Although Korea built an extensive transportation, communication, and power infrastructure, it is neither specialized nor concentrated. Similarly, light manufacturing technology, capital equipment, and facilities are unspecialized and can often be redeployed at little cost. This advantage does not, of course, apply to power looms, for example, but the wide range of textiles that they can produce (and the heterogeneity of light manufactures generally) increases flexibility. Because their skills are limited and widely applicable, workers have little attachment to specific jobs or industries. Small firm size and the wide geographical distribution of production permitted by the absence of a need for specialized infrastructure mean that working-class commu-

[76] Interview with Sung.

117

nities are heterogeneous and far-flung, and the impact of restructuring is therefore widespread. Firms' small size and recent origins also mean that most have rudimentary management organizations and that managers have only general business skills. Thus, investments in neither complex organizations nor specialized training inhibit change.

Flexibility was a boon to Korea. Production flexibility enabled firms to respond quickly to shocks with market-conforming behavior and thus to remain competitive. It also softened and delayed the financial impact on the state, because firms with the internal flexibility to survive in light manufacturing could take evasive action and help themselves without costly state aid. The heterogeneity of light manufacturing firms and products also meant that market downturns seldom touched all segments simultaneously or to the same degree, further easing the impact on export earnings and state revenues.[77] And when firms needed help, they required not protection from the effects of market shifts but more of the same competitiveness-enhancing policies that were central to the export-promotion program. Thus, even aid to firms in trouble could be an investment in future growth and competitiveness.

Asset/factor flexibility had equally important long-term benefits because it permitted Korea to restructure in the face of protection. The lack of specialized infrastructures meant that little had to be written off to accommodate change. Cheap, incremental improvements such as road widening and improvement of freight facilities bought a lot, for major new investments could be limited to a few specialized facilities such as a new port to service the Pohang iron and steel complex. Similarly, because they could utilize general-purpose equipment and facilities, and because progress largely involved improved ways of organizing and doing rather than investment in fancier machines, firms could trade up incrementally and at low cost. The management skills honed to achieve internal flexibility were also those needed to trade up and even to change businesses; unskilled workers, too, were mobile and could be trained incrementally and at low cost.

Asset/factor flexibility had political benefits. Limited sunk investments in equipment, skills, and organization meant that restructuring did not put business leaders' backs to the wall. Indeed, the low cost of modernization, low barriers to exit, and the state's export-promotion

---

[77] Princeton Lyman, "Economic Development in South Korea," in *Korean Politics in Transition,* ed. Wright, 249.

package—generous depreciation schedules, cheap investment funds, management consulting services, marketing assistance—gave business reason to view the state as a partner in development.[78] And when they *were* hurt, firms needed more of the same, not adjustment-dulling protection. The pain for workers could be severe, since they bore the burden of adjustment. But the heterogeneity and geographical distribution of light manufacturing and working-class communities meant that even big changes did not dislocate whole regions, towns, or neighborhoods, or provoke sharp opposition.

THE DOMESTIC POLITICAL ECONOMY OF LIGHT MANUFACTURING: ABSOLUTE CAPACITY

But the relative tractability of the restructuring project Korean policy makers faced is only part of the answer to our question. We also must examine how light manufacturing influences the state's capacity and autonomy to undertake it.

When the export drive began in 1961, the Korean state already had an autonomous, powerful, cohesive, competent, deeply penetrating bureaucracy. Park further broadened and extended its reach. To supplement the coercive powers of the police and military, for example, he created the Korean Central Intelligence Agency (KCIA), with powers to control political opposition, business, and labor. With the help of a small cadre of economists, who, by the late 1950s had established the basis for an export-led growth strategy, Park created the new agencies and instruments necessary to implement it.

But the state's initial institutional endowment alone does not explain its exceptional absolute capacity. It explains neither the pattern of institutions developed to support export-led growth nor their capabilities. It does not explain the flexibility they subsequently showed when called on to support restructuring. The sectoral characteristics of light manufacturing, however, help explain all three.

Resource Extraction

The Park government inherited little extractive capacity from its predecessors. The economy of the 1950s was small; and between 1953 and 1960 the annual tax yield from it averaged just 7.5 percent of

---

[78] Jones and Sakong, *Government, Business, and Entrepreneurship,* 75.

GNP, a low figure by international standards.[79] Abundant foreign aid dulled concern about revenues and permitted Korea to spend far more than it raised. Rhee depended on indirect taxes and customs duties for between 61.9 percent (1954–55) and 63.8 percent (1959–60) of revenues.[80] Customs duties and import restrictions in particular provided a steady revenue stream and paid big political dividends in the form of scarcity rents that could be doled out to supporters. But this meant that revenues were hostage to powerful political actors; furthermore, dependence on indirect taxes prevented the use of fiscal policy to manage the economy and high tariffs killed exports, leaving Korea dependent on foreign aid.

All this changed under Park. Between 1962 and the early 1970s, annual tax receipts increased fifteenfold and the annual tax yield doubled to 15.5 percent of GNP; in one study of the tax efforts of fifty-two less developed countries (LDCs), Korea advanced in rank from forty-eighth (1963–64) to eighteenth (1974–76).[81] The soaring GNP and more efficient tax collection pushed revenues through the roof. Indeed, despite a growing budget (government spending rose from 14.8 percent of GNP to 23.5 percent between 1964 and 1972) and the virtual end of foreign aid, by 1964–65 current revenues exceeded current expenditures.[82]

In part, rising revenues reflected the continued importance of indirect taxes and of customs duties on a greatly increased volume of imports. Indirect taxes still accounted for 38.5 percent of annual revenues in 1969–70, and customs duties totaled 8.2 million won in 1964 and 50.9 million won in 1970, or 18.7 percent and 14.8 percent of annual revenues, respectively.[83] The reason was unadorned expediency: indirect taxes and customs duties are easy to assess and collect; income and wealth are hard to assess and tax. Still, officials feared indirect taxes' market-distorting impact and tariffs' threat to the competitiveness of exports with a high import content and thus to

[79] Ibid., 111.

[80] Mason et al., *The Economic and Social Modernization*, 316.

[81] Jungsae Kim, "Recent Trends in the Government's Management of the Economy," in *Korean Politics in Transition*, ed. Wright, 267; Jones and Sakong, *Government, Business, and Entrepreneurship*, 111; Jorgen Lotz and Elliot Morss, "Measuring 'Tax Effort' in Developing Countries," *IMF Staff Papers* (November 1967), 478–99.

[82] Kim and Roemer, *Growth and Structural Transformation*, 54; Mason et al., *The Economic and Social Modernization*, 107; Kim, "Recent Trends," 266.

[83] Suk, "The Effects of Export Incentives," II-17; Kim, "Recent Trends," 267; Mason et al., *The Economic and Social Modernization*, 316.

export-led growth. They therefore cut the effective tariff rate from the 23.5 percent that prevailed in 1960 to 9.5 percent in 1964 and 8.3 percent in 1970, and increased direct taxes' share of annual revenues from 30 percent in 1963–64 to 38.3 percent in 1969–70, a take from direct taxes that was 50 percent higher than would be expected for a country of Korea's income level.[84]

The increase in direct taxes depended on the state's ability to collect corporate and personal income taxes—administratively and politically the most costly of all taxes. The key was the deeply penetrating, highly flexible Office of National Tax Administration (ONTA) created in 1966. Its aim was to raise revenues and improve tax administration by stopping corruption, tax evasion, and arbitrary assessments.[85] ONTA opened offices throughout the country, expanded the cadre of tax collectors and auditors, modernized assessment and collection procedures, and built a computerized data base of corporate and individual financial records. The organization's semi-autonomous status protected its operatives from interference, while it set "tax collection targets or quotas by geographic area and tax items" and rewarded or punished them "for exceeding or falling short of the targets."[86] New laws, too, gave ONTA a big stick to wield because tax evaders could now be threatened with fines, public denunciation, and criminal prosecution.

Why create such an institution? Given a light manufacturing base, the folks to be taxed were mostly poor, and the firms to be taxed were numerous, small, marginally profitable, and widely scattered. Individuals' returns were thus small, which meant that raising revenue by means of direct taxes required a countrywide presence and a very fine-grained database. Moreover, because individuals were poor and firms were pressed by competition, everyone had a strong incentive to evade taxes, which meant that the state required an extensive audit and enforcement capacity, too. (A campaign to punish tax evaders in the 1970s began with an audit of 14,864 firms' returns![87]) The hetero-

[84] Suk, "The Effects of Export Incentives," II-17; Mason et al., *The Economic and Social Modernization*, 316; Raja Chelliah, "Trends in Taxation in Developing Countries," *IMF Staff Papers* (July 1971), 278, 283.

[85] Mason et al., *The Economic and Social Modernization*, 270, 316; Kim, "Recent Trends," 266; Jones and Sakong, *Government, Business, and Entrepreneurship*, 113–14.

[86] In-Joung Whang, "The Role of Government in Economic Development in Korea during the Sixties and Seventies," in Korean Development Institute, *Industrialization and Rural Change* (Seoul: KDI, 1985), 14.

[87] Jones and Sakong, *Government, Business, and Entrepreneurship*, 114–15.

geneity of light manufacturing required that ONTA personnel be trained as generalists and that ONTA be able to assess and collect taxes from a wide range of industries and businesses.

ONTA also enhanced the state's capacity to use fiscal policy to direct—or redirect—development. Limited efforts to do so had begun in 1961 with tax cuts on export earnings and accelerated depreciation allowances for fixed capital used in export production, but without ONTA such policies were at best clumsy. The Law on the Regulation of Tax Deductions and Exemptions, passed in 1965, gave the state broad powers to favor selected industries. Creation of ONTA in 1966 made the law's implementation possible and set the stage for such measures as the 1967 provision of investment tax credits for targeted industries, the 1969 tax credit for foreign market development costs, the 1973 tax credits for losses on operations in foreign markets, the many tax incentives offered as part of the HCID, and the 1978 provision of preferential tax treatment for higher-priced footwear.[88]

Finally, ONTA's flexibility protects the state from catastrophic revenue losses and ensures revenues even during restructuring. In Zambia, revenues follow the roller coaster of copper prices. But ONTA's ability to tax a wide range of firms softens the impact of downturns in individual market segments; it also allows the state to offer relief to depressed industries and find replacement revenues elsewhere. In Zambia, the copper-dependent tax system leaves the state without revenue when it most needs it, thus forcing it to rebuild mining to survive. The existence of ONTA permits Korea to increase revenues even while restructuring. Thus, revenues from light manufacturing continued to increase in the 1970s, permitting the extension of huge tax credits to firms that invested in heavy industries—and sustaining the state when it found itself overextended in the early 1980s.

Monitoring, Regulating, and Redirecting the Economy

The Korean state can also monitor, regulate, and redirect the economy. In part, this capacity reflects past circumstances. When the Park government embarked on export promotion, for example, it already had a rough input-output matrix and a model for projecting the effects of its policies. "All the pieces were in place" in 1961, ready to

---

[88] Ibid., 94; Kim, "Recent Trends," 267.

be assembled by the EPB, with its control over planning, budgeting, foreign borrowing, and direct investment, and by the Blue House Economic Secretariat, with its direct access to Park.[89] These institutions gave officials the data necessary to monitor and regulate developments affecting the economy and enabled them to intervene to redirect those developments as they saw fit. Although the institutions were used initially to serve the light manufacturing sector, they improved the state's general capacity for economic management.

These institutions' general purpose nature reflects the characteristics of light manufacturing. Korea's brief experience with ISI left the state unencumbered by institutions devoted to servicing big firms, and the Park government showed "a sophisticated bias . . . toward the promotion of light consumer-goods industries amenable to small investments and simple technical processes."[90] The large number and small size of the firms that sprang up, and the wide range of industries they represented and of markets they serviced, made direct government control impossible. Thus, though private investment soared under the revised first five-year plan (1964–66), government investment fell far below target, confirming "a retreat from guided capitalism . . . and a greater role for the private sector."[91] Government policy aimed instead to establish "a permissive framework for the realization of comparative advantage," a goal included in the third five-year plan (1972–76), which stressed "policies which will lead to the desired allocation of resources within the framework of private decision-making in response to price incentives."[92]

To achieve this end, the Korean state required highly flexible institutions very different from those required to manage a high/high sector. The differences are exemplified by the contrast between Zambia's MEMACO, and KOTRA and the KTA.[93] The purpose of KOTRA, like that of MEMACO, is to promote exports, but KOTRA promotes *all* Korean exports, the diversity of which forced it to develop a general, export-supporting organizational mission and capabilities. Assisting KOTRA are the KTA, which is organized not along industry lines but along functional lines—export promotion and

---

[89] Chung interview.
[90] Kim, "Recent Trends," 257.
[91] Ibid., 259.
[92] Quotes from Haggard, *Pathways from the Periphery*, 67; and Jones and Sakong, *Government, Business, and Entrepreneurship*, 52.
[93] Lim interview.

trade cooperation—and below it, associations representing different export industries. These associations provide the state and their members with timely, detailed information about production, sales, exports, and foreign markets. They also extend the state's regulatory arm to all the export industries at little cost. Unlike MEMACO, which is inflexibly copper-specific, KOTRA, the KTA, and the industry associations give the Korean state the ability to monitor domestic and foreign developments relevant to all current and potential exports; they also regulate firms' export activities and redirect them if necessary by helping to identify new opportunities and by minimizing the costs of entering new markets.

Light Manufacturing and the Other Institutions of State

Korea's sectoral base in the 1960s helps to explain the limited growth of other state institutions and the low institutional barriers to restructuring that existed in the 1970s. In the early 1960s no export bonanza saddled officials with more revenues than they could spend. To the contrary, whereas foreign aid had allowed Rhee to invest in ISI and to distribute political patronage without regard to efficiency or cost, the Park government confronted restructuring at a time of plummeting foreign aid, when there was a serious threat from the north, and it had only the revenues it could wring from the fledgling light manufacturing sector. Lavish spending on grandiose state projects and extensive social service institutions was out of the question.

Government spending reveals the officials' priorities. Defense accounted for 33 percent of spending in 1960, 29 percent in 1965, and 21 percent in 1970—the decrease reflecting that nondefense spending increased more rapidly than did total spending between 1965 and 1972. During these years "an average of 27 percent of total government expenditure went to investment and loans for economic development," indicating that their priority was equal to that of defense. In contrast, "merely 2.5 percent went for social security and welfare programs," thus releasing "budgetary resources for investment in economic infrastructure."[94] Limited spending on social services, the small size of institutions for delivering them, and low public expectations gave the Korean government added flexibility when faced with

[94] Quotes from Mason et al., *The Economic and Social Modernization*, 21, 307; and Choi, "Interest Conflict," 430–31. See also Chuk Kyo Kim, "The Growth Pattern of Central Government Expenditure in Korea," Working Paper no. 7702 (Seoul: KDI, 1977), 15.

revenue downturns and restructuring because there was less pressure to divert funds from directly productive uses.

Limited revenues and the imperative for economic development if such revenues were to increase also kept the state small and the parastatal sector efficient. The Korean civil service, in contrast to that of Zambia, remains a tiny, closed fraternity that has contributed little to job creation, especially relative to the burgeoning private economy.[95] Even more striking is that though the size of the parastatal sector "parallels that of many countries advocating a socialist pattern"— twelve of the sixteen biggest industrial firms were parastatals in 1972—there was and is little political featherbedding. Rather, Korean parastatals represent a "pragmatic . . . response to the various market imperfections that are virtually synonymous with low levels of economic development." They are efficient; some are even profitable. And though "most of the government's deficit has been accounted for by public corporations," observes Alice Amsden, the parastatals have "spent on long-term investment, not on short-term consumption" as in Zambia.[96] Again, the absence of huge windfalls limited patronage and payoffs. The resulting leaner, meaner state, unencumbered by a bloated bureaucracy or by inefficient but politically potent parastatals, meant that policy makers had more flexibility when they confronted restructuring.

INCAPACITY OF BUSINESS AND LABOR FOR COLLECTIVE ACTION

To understand the Korean state's success in restructuring, we must also consider the interests of business and labor and their capacity for collective action. Here, too, sector matters. But whereas in Zambia the characteristics of the mining industry undermined the state and strengthened business and labor, in Korea we find the opposite. Although the characteristics of light manufacturing helped make the Korean state strong and flexible, they hobbled business and labor.

In the early 1960s business's weakness was partly circumstantial. The ISI effort had not become so entrenched that Korea was stuck with a large, inefficient industrial sector able to demand protection by

[95] Cole and Lyman, *Korean Development,* 20.
[96] Wade, *Governing the Market,* 178; Jones and Sakong, *Government, Business, and Entrepreneurship,* 141, 151–55, 161; Amsden, *Asia's Next Giant,* 92.

virtue of its size and weakness. The fall of the Rhee regime also temporarily discredited the so-called deep pockets. And though such organizations as the Korean Chamber of Commerce and Industry (KCCI) and the KTA existed, they were small, divided, and disinclined to lobby. Moreover, the business community was still tiny; its explosive growth followed the outward reorientation of government policy. But these initial disadvantages do not explain business's continuing weakness. The characteristics of light manufacturing do.

Korean growth was based on the production of a huge number of small firms. In 1963, 98.7 percent of Korea's 18,310 registered firms had fewer than 200 workers. These firms provided 66.4 percent of employment and 52.8 percent of the value added, whereas firms with fewer than 20 workers generated 29.0 percent of employment and 19.3 percent of the value added. By 1966, firms with 10 workers or less employed 43 percent of the work force and firms with 50 workers or less employed 50 percent.[97] These firms were largely family businesses—sweatshops equipped with primitive technologies—and 80 percent of their production went to the domestic market; the remainder constituted 40 percent of Korean exports. Indeed, firms with fewer than 10 workers produced 18.6 percent of exports in 1963; they produced 31.4 percent of a far larger total in 1968. Such firms are widely dispersed; just 17 percent are in Seoul—a percentage that increases rapidly with small increases in firm size.[98]

These characteristics barred collective action. Low barriers to entry, combined with government policy, enticed thousands of entrepreneurs into the ring. They all suffered the plight of small firms in a tough international market, but their numbers and the heterogeneity of their products and markets limited contact among them and encouraged freeriding. Worse, although their number increased 40 percent from 1962 to 1974, life at the bottom of the entrepreneurial pyramid was nasty, brutish, and short.[99] The result was cut-throat competition for survival, not collusion, and plaints by business executives that Korean firms were too competitive with one another to

[97] Leroy Jones, *Jae-Bul and the Concentration of Economic Power in Korean Development,* Consultant Paper Series, no. 12 (Seoul: KDI, 1980), 53; Harry Oshima, "Labor-Force 'Explosion' and the Labor-Intensive Sector in Asian Growth," *Economic Development and Cultural Change* 19 (January 1971): 165.

[98] Han interview; Ranis, "Industrial Sector Labor Absorption," 404; Oshima, "Labor-Force 'Explosion,'" 167–68.

[99] Jones and Sakong, *Government, Business, and Entrepreneurship,* 170–71. In the period 1966–69, for example, 2,142 firms opened—and 1,988 folded.

cooperate in lobbying. Further, the KCCI, the KTA, and the Korean Federation of Small Business could not help because firms in similar markets would not cooperate, and the heterogeneity of light manufacturing and of association members' interests left these groups internally cross-pressured.[100] Whatever their entrepreneurial talents, small business entrepreneurs also lacked the time, skills, resources, and contacts to lobby.

The Park government had early advantages over labor, too. The unions had been broken in the late 1940s and repressed and co-opted by Rhee in the 1950s. Moreover, because labor was weak, Park did not need its support and could attack it at will.[101] Despite a burgeoning industrial work force, miserable working conditions, and low wages, collective bargaining failed in the 1960s, strikes fizzled, and employers violated labor laws with impunity. Although real wages rose after 1968 as a result of a tightening labor market, productivity increases outstripped wage growth, indicating a declining share of profits for labor.[102]

But labor's real problem was that growth, especially job growth, occurred in light manufacturing, the sectoral characteristics of which undercut collective action, insulating business and the state from labor pressure. Thus, labor protest has been limited to skilled workers in heavy industry, whereas 70–75 percent of the employment growth in the 1960s occurred in the light manufacturing export sector, which employed unskilled labor and was marked by labor-intensive, small-unit production.[103]

Workers in light manufacturing face towering barriers to collective action. The smallness and dispersion of firms, exaggerated by labor laws requiring firm-based unions, discourage worker solidarity and encourage free riding. Close supervision and potent traditional authority, especially in family firms, further hamper organization.[104] In 1973, 56 percent of all firms employed fewer than 16 workers; these

[100] Interviews with Lim, Cha, Han, Wan-Kee Minn, and Choong-Kee Minn.

[101] Bruce Cumings, "The Origins and Development of the Northeast Asian Political Economy," *International Organization* 38 (Winter 1984): 1–40; Choi, "Interest Conflict," 129.

[102] George Ogle, "South Korea," in *International Handbook of Industrial Relations*, ed. Albert Blum (Westport, Conn.: Greenwood Press, 1981), 504–5; Frederic Deyo, "Export Manufacturing and Labor," *Labor in the Capitalist World-Economy*, ed. Charles Bergquist (Beverly Hills, Calif.: Sage, 1984), 270; Choi, "Interest Conflict," 480.

[103] Ogle, "South Korea," 503.

[104] Eberhard Leibau, "Labor-Management Relations in the Republic of Korea," Consultant Paper Series, no. 7-A (Seoul: KDI, 1980), 8.

firms accounted for 11 percent of all manufacturing jobs, but none of their workers were unionized; 95 percent of all firms employed fewer than 200 workers; such firms accounted for 44 percent of all manufacturing jobs, and only 9 percent of their workers were unionized. In 1979, no workers in firms with fewer than 16 workers were unionized, compared with 6 percent unionization in firms with 16–200 workers, 24 percent in firms with 200–1,000 workers, and 48 percent in firms employing more than 1,000 workers.[105]

There is nothing to encourage light manufacturing workers to organize. Firms hire and fire their unskilled employees at will, leading workers to see each other as competitors, not companions.[106] Without job security, hope of promotion, or leverage with management, workers have no incentive to invest in a union. They exhibit little job commitment and weak attachment to work groups; their average turnover rates are 95–240 percent per year—rates that rise as firm size decreases. This is especially true of the young women who, in the 1960s, came to constitute 35 percent of the industrial work force and 80 percent of the workers in the light manufacturing export industries.[107]

The nature of Korean working-class communities only aggravated workers' difficulties. The dispersion of workplaces, even in urban areas, and the rapid influx of new workers in the 1960s resulted in highly heterogeneous communities unconducive to organization. Further, employment instability, high turnover rates, the high incidence of target employment, and the ability of many workers to fall back on the resources of their families in rural areas meant that workers had only limited commitments to their communities. They thus invested little in establishing the social ties and organizations necessary to support labor organization.[108]

Intense competition, the centrality of labor costs, and the need for flexibility made owners fight unions tooth and nail. Poor prospects

[105] Choi, "Interest Conflict," 66.

[106] Young women entering the apparel industry can be trained in a few weeks; workers in the electronics industry can be trained on the job in one month. Frederic Deyo, *Beneath the Miracle: Labor Subordination in the New Asian Industrialization* (Berkeley: University of California Press, 1989), 175.

[107] Ibid., 190–91; Sookon Kim, "Employment, Wages, and Manpower Policies in Korea," Working Paper Series, no. 82-04 (Seoul: KDI, 1982), 31–32; Ogle, "South Korea," 503; Choi, "Interest Conflict," 83–100.

[108] Deyo, *Beneath the Miracle*, 185, 194–95; George Ogle, "Labor Unions in Rapid Development" (Ph.D. diss., University of Wisconsin, 1973), 385–86.

for survival in the short term led them to discount the future value of the increased labor productivity that a stable work force provides. Thus, the smaller the firm, the higher was the turnover rate; owners used temporary labor to "maintain work force flexibility and reduce seniority-increments to their wage costs."[109] They also regularly fired potential organizers or turned to the police and the KCIA for help.

The large degree of intersectoral variation in unionization, protest, and wages in Korea indicates the importance of sectoral characteristics and challenges strong state explanations that predict the universal weakness of labor. In 1974, 50 percent of the miners and 37 percent of the workers in such heavy industries as chemicals, petroleum, rubber, and cement were unionized, but just 18 percent of the workers in the textile and apparel industries were. In 1974, 3,000 striking Hyundai shipyard workers maintained their unity even in the face of intense pressures, quitting only when attacked by 1,000 riot police. By contrast, protests in light manufacturing have been small, scattered, unorganized, and marked by despairing acts of symbolic violence such as self-immolation that suggest the lack of effective means of protest. Wages are lowest in light manufacturing; textile and apparel workers make one-half as much as shipyard workers. In fact, Korea "has one of the largest manufacturing wage dispersions between light and heavy industry" in the world.[110]

But the Korean state's capacity to restructure was not merely a matter of its absolute capacity, nor was it simply a result of the incapacity of business and labor. What counts is the relationship among the state, business, and labor. To understand that, we must examine state officials' autonomy in formulating policy and their relative capacity to implement it.

AUTONOMY

Circumstances and sectoral characteristics gave the Korean state considerable autonomy. As Rhee's heir, Park commanded a bureaucracy designed by the Japanese to be immune to demands from below. He benefited from the neutralization of the peasantry and rural elite

[109] Quote from Deyo, *Beneath the Miracle,* 179. See also Kim, "Employment, Wages, and Manpower Policies," 31–32.

[110] Deyo, "Export Manufacturing and Labor," 282–83; and Deyo, *Beneath the Miracle,* 176. Quote from Amsden, *Asia's Next Giant,* 10.

as a result of land reform, from the delegitimation of the Left by the war, and from the taming of the unions. The coup itself broke existing state-society ties, for Park arrested or banned many politicians, attacked business elites, replaced union leaders with KCIA appointees, and built a centralized system with himself at the apex. Even with the return to nominally civilian, democratic rule in 1964 his autonomy remained intact. These unique circumstances alone do not explain the high degree of state autonomy, however.

Sectoral characteristics are critical. The lack of effective organizations and of lobbying skills on the part of business and labor hindered interest articulation and facilitated state control of the channels of interest representation. The state's active role in fostering industry and the simple technologies that light manufacturing industries employ minimized state dependence on business for expertise and thus the exchange of personnel, limiting the access of business to policy making. Indeed, in Korea as in Taiwan, "familiarity with engineering concepts even at the top levels of industrial policy-making has made for an easy translation from the broad choices to what exactly must be done to get specific projects off the ground."[111] The general-purpose nature of the institutions serving light manufacturing and the sector's heterogeneity further limited access to policy making by minimizing the risk that state institutions would be captured by business and by depriving industries of advocates within the state. The small size and large number of industry groups also meant that none could demand attention.

Sectoral characteristics also explain the limited pressures by business and labor to penetrate the state's autonomy. International competition led to the intense interest of both groups in state support for industry—but of the sort already being provided. More generally, the dynamism of the export economy and the abundant opportunities existing in the private sector minimized incentives to "mine the state"; the state's travails with revenue extraction and the openness of the foreign exchange and trade regimes minimized the profitability of doing so. In short, because they were inaccessible and under only limited pressure, state officials could make policy without reference to special pleading by societal actors, as evidenced by their capacity to

[111] Jones and Sakong, *Government, Business, and Entrepreneurship*, 67. Quote from Wade, *Governing the Market*, 220. Wade quotes a vice-chairman of Taiwan's Council for Economic Planning and Development: "Because of the small size of companies, they are not as well informed as government in deciding what is best for them."

use state "power to discipline not just workers, but the owners and managers of capital as well," and to invest rather than spend the state's resources.[112]

This autonomy allowed Korean leaders in the 1960s and 1970s to define the state interest in terms compatible with restructuring. In part, they were motivated by political necessity. They faced decreasing foreign aid and needed to legitimize their rule, both of which demanded fundamental economic change. They also saw the economic—and political—logic of export promotion.[113] But sectoral characteristics explain their ability to act, for asset/factor flexibility cut the costs of trading up, and the sector's heterogeneity ensured that even in transition the economy would continue to thrive. The flexibility of the ONTA ensured that revenues would increase, too, and other agencies' flexibility meant that restructuring harmed no bureaucratic interests and that the state could manage it. In short, restructuring threatened neither state revenues nor institutions, freeing officials to define a state interest that approximated the national interest.

EXERCISING RELATIVE CAPACITY

By the late 1960s, however, Koreans had reason to worry despite rapid economic growth. Of special concern were the economic and political vulnerabilities born of success and overspecialization. Real wages were rising, thus reducing competitiveness vis-à-vis such "second-tier" NICs as Malaysia and Thailand, and success in OECD markets was provoking increased demands for protection. Most worrisome were American pressures to slash Korean textile exports to the United States, since in 1970 textiles accounted for "one-third of total Korean manufacturing, [for] 38 percent of total exports . . . [and about] 32 percent of the manufacturing population."[114] Inflation was on the rise, but devaluing to control it aggravated balance-of-payments and debt service problems that resulted from heavy foreign borrowing and dependence on imported raw materials and capital equipment. As a result, dozens of big firms that had once been sustained by "impossible debt-equity ratios through export subsidies and unreasonable fiscal and financial policies" faced bankruptcy, threaten-

[112] Amsden, *Asia's Next Giant*, 64.
[113] Chung and Kim interviews.
[114] Woo, *Race to the Swift*, 126.

ing the state-owned banking system.[115] Finally, the Nixon administration's 1971 call for troop cuts led Korean officials to weigh the need to build an arms industry.

Park responded to the resulting tensions with a preemptive exercise of state power that culminated in the authoritarian Yushin Constitution of 1972. Along with related measures, it dissolved the National Assembly, banned political parties, prohibited strikes, further restricted unions, and imposed price controls in order to permit Park to bail out failing firms and pursue "industrial rationalization." But only continued growth coupled with redistribution, not coercion, could solve Park's problems. Indeed, in the short term all he could hope for was that a new growth spurt would legitimize his actions as it had following the 1961 coup.[116] The need for new growth, however, also meant confronting Korea's changing international position.

For Park and his advisers, the challenge was to deal preemptively with an increasingly difficult world economy, and with the anticipated passing of Pax Americana and the once certain protection it provided. To meet this double challenge, they believed that Korea had to restructure its economy—to change from being a producer of light manufactures and a final processor of export goods to being a world-class producer of steel, ships, machine tools, chemicals, and weapons. And they had the means to effect the changes they believed were necessary, for the developments of the 1960s had given them "a state that was iron-fisted at home and, therefore, capable of restructuring the domestic economy and supporting sustained growth."[117] Their blueprint for Korea's restructured future was contained in the Heavy and Chemical Industries Development Plan announced in 1973.

The aim of the HCID was to reposition Korea in the international division of labor by shifting the sectoral base of the economy. The HCID targeted steel, nonferrous metals, ship building, machinery, electronics, petroleum refining, fertilizers, industrial chemicals, pulp, and cement. The plan did not follow Korea's comparative advantage but used state interventions to lead the market, break dependence on exports of light manufactures, increase self-sufficiency (especially in capital goods), and enhance Korea's international competitiveness. It sought to upgrade technology in traditional export sectors and promote diversification into new industries such as steel, shipbuilding,

[115] Ibid., 109.
[116] Kim interview.
[117] Woo, *Race to the Swift*, 116.

machine tools, and computers. The HCID policies encouraged monopolistic production to achieve workable economies of scale, reduced tariffs on capital equipment, protected infant industries, offered incentives for both research and development and worker training, and created a National Investment Fund to provide low-interest loans to meet the new industries' huge investment needs.[118]

The HCID radically redistributed incentives for business. Reports Jung-en Woo: "The main goal of Korea's finance was to hemorrhage as much capital as possible into the heavy industrialization program." To do so, the state "set financial prices at an artificial low to subsidize import-substituting heavy, chemical and export industries."[119] Between 1977 and 1979, "80 percent of total investment in manufacturing went to heavy industry, which consumed 97 percent of total planned investment in the first three years of the fourth five-year plan [1977–81]," an allocation managed only by gutting investment in light manufacturing.[120] As noted in a government report, "labor intensive manufacturing . . . has been left to fend for itself."[121] Foreign investment, too, was redirected. FDI in textiles, for example, fell from 14 percent of total investment in 1967–71 to nil in 1977–80, whereas FDI in machinery rose from 3.2 percent of total investment to 10.9 percent.[122] More generally, policy favored big firms over the small ones on whose success the first phase of Korean growth had depended.[123]

There is an irony in the Korean state's success in pursuing the HCID, however. The state's absolute capacity, its autonomy from small firms, and their inability to defend their own interests made restructuring possible. After all, the "Big Push," as it was called, "was a big shove by a big government that bullied workers, coerced entrepreneurs, and distorted the market."[124] But the state's success in restructuring—in shifting the economy's base from a low/low sector to a high/high sector—also had economic costs. More important, it

[118] Sang Mok Suh, "Development Strategies" (Seoul: KDI, n.d.), 14–15.

[119] Woo, *Race to the Swift*, 159.

[120] Stephan Haggard and Chung-In Moon, "Industrial Change and State Power," paper presented at the Annual Meeting of the American Political Science Association (Washington, D.C., August 27–31, 1986), 11–12.

[121] Korea Exchange Bank, *Monthly Review*, December 1980.

[122] Haggard, *Pathways from the Periphery*, 202, Table 8.1.

[123] For evidence of the bias against light manufacturing, see Woo, *Race to the Swift*, 166–67.

[124] Ibid., 148.

changed the interests and improved the collective-action capabilities of business and labor, giving both the ability to hit back and also reducing state autonomy and relative capacity.

Reaping the Dragon's Teeth

The HCID had major economic consequences, both good and bad. Whereas the higher short-term profits of smaller-scale light manufacturing would have discouraged investment in heavy industry, thus *reinforcing* Korea's existing position in the international division of labor, the HCID offered businesses powerful incentives to invest in establishing a *future* comparative advantage in heavy industry. These incentives—combined with stringent and harshly enforced performance criteria—increased investment's share of GNP from 26 percent to 37 percent in 1976–78; it also increased heavy and chemical industries' share of manufacturing output from 39 percent to 51 percent between 1971 and 1979, and their share of total exports from 15 percent to 38 percent.[125] The steel industry absorbed 40 percent of all government loans to heavy industry from 1975 to 1982, but steel production capacity increased fourteenfold in that period, and Korea is today one of the most efficient and profitable steel producers in the world. The shipbuilding industry, a major consumer of steel, also received massive state support—and flourished as it "surmounted the global slump of the early 1980s and then proceeded to capture more than 20 percent of all new orders in the world market." Korea's machine tool, automobile, defense, chemical, and electronics industries have fared equally well.[126]

Even economically, however, the HCID created important problems. Although the World Bank now argues that "in a comprehensive, dynamic perspective, it is difficult to demonstrate that an alternative policy would have worked better," Korea suffered in the short term.[127] In part, the causes were exogenous—the second oil shock in mid-1978, the related leap in interest rates, and a poor harvest in 1980. The HCID itself, however, promoted overinvestment in capital-

[125] Tun-jen Cheng and Stephan Haggard, *Newly Industrializing Asia in Transition,* Policy Papers in International Affairs, no. 31, Institute of International Studies (University of California, Berkeley, 1987), 16–17.

[126] Quote and steel statistics from Woo, *Race to the Swift,* 133–38. See, too, Amsden, *Asia's Next Giant,* chaps. 11 and 12; and Wade, *Governing the Market,* 306–20.

[127] World Bank, *Korea: Managing the Industrial Transition,* vol. 1 (Washington, D.C., 1987), 45.

intensive industries, distorted domestic prices, widened the productivity gap between protected and unprotected industries, and aggravated threats to Korea's comparative advantage in labor-intensive industries. Real wages rose 67 percent from 1976 to 1978—twice as fast as the increase in labor productivity, thus eroding Korea's international competitiveness. Inflation shot up from an annual average of 16.1 percent in 1962–78 to an annual average of 26.4 percent in 1979–81; average annual economic growth rates fell from 9.9 percent to 2.2 percent; real growth in total exports dropped from an annual average of 27.4 percent to an annual average of 7.5 percent; foreign debt escalated from $4.3 billion in 1973 to $20.0 billion in 1979; and the current account deficit grew from $1.1 billion in 1979 to $4.4 billion in 1981.[128]

By late 1978, there were many demands for change. The OECD trading partners wanted Korea to cut aid to exporters and open its markets, and many in government called for liberalization to reignite growth and reduce the threat of protection. In April 1979, the EPB advanced a plan to cut inflation and undo the monopolistic structure of HCID-sponsored heavy industries by liberalizing trade and increasing the market's role in pricing and resource allocation. Its implementation was interrupted by the second oil shock in July and Park's assassination in October, but Park's team of planners remained in the Chun Doo Hwan government and the effort continued.

The Chun government's stabilization and restructuring policies were remarkably successful. A devaluation in 1980 increased competitiveness; growth in government spending was cut from an annual average of 28 percent between 1962 and 1980 to nil in 1984; a virtual wage freeze was imposed in the public sector; thousands of public servants were fired; real wages were cut in 1980–81 and wage increases were held below labor productivity gains from 1982 to 1984. Inflation dropped from 28.7 percent to 2.3 percent in 1980–84, and the balance-of-payments deficit improved from $4.4 billion to $1.37 billion in 1981–84, as growth rates rebounded to 5.6 percent in 1982, 9.5 percent in 1983, and 7.5 percent in 1984, and total exports increased from $20.67 billion to $26.35 billion.[129] The state also began a "second outward turn" in 1980 and made an effort to correct HCID-

[128] Suh, "Development Strategies," 11, 16–17; Kim, "Employment, Wages, and Manpower Policies," 64, 76–77; Stephan Haggard and Chung-In Moon, "Institutions and Economic Policy," *World Politics* 42 (January 1990): 216.

[129] Haggard and Moon, "Industrial Change and State Power," 20–22, 36.

induced distortions. It enacted the Monopoly Regulation and Fair Trade Law, liberalized import controls, rationalized industries with excess capacity, shifted lending priorities to again favor light manufacturing, and abolished preferential tax rates for heavy industry.[130]

How were these successes achieved? In part, the damage done and the difficulty of undoing it were limited by the HCID's short life and the fact that although the state offered lavish support, it exacted a high level of performance as well.[131] In part, too, success reflected the continued autonomy and capacity of a centralized economic management machinery with powerful policy instruments at its command. But it also reflected the continued importance of advantages deriving from the sectoral characteristics of Korea's economic base. The state could impose adjustment costs on the largest firms because, despite the HCID, it had allies in the still vital light manufacturing sector.

The HCID supplemented, rather than supplanted, the established core of the economy. Despite heavy industry's growing share of GNP and exports, light manufacturing firms remained at center stage, for the growth in their productivity and output exceeded that of the big firms in the 1970s.[132] Thus, though motor vehicle exports, one of the most visible successes of industrial deepening, increased from $300 million to $1,000 million between 1979 and 1985, the toy exports of tiny firms increased in that period from $300 million to $670 million. The textile industry "still employed 30 percent of manufacturing workers, churning out 39 percent of total exports and 22 percent of value added," and shoes and apparel accounted for another 13 percent of exports. Of 6,804 exporters in the mid-1980s, 6,047 firms sold less than $100,000 worth of goods per year—a total of 12.2 percent of exports.[133] More generally, although light manufacturing was starved of investment and otherwise disfavored, it continued to be substantially more profitable than heavy industry throughout the 1970s and 1980s.[134] The vitality of light manufacturing permitted the state to reverse course when the costs of the HCID were perceived. Such a reversal also offered political benefits because it seemed to divorce

[130] Kim interview; Haggard and Moon, "Institutions and Economic Power," 219–20.
[131] Kim interview.
[132] Chuk Kyo Kim, "Industrial Growth and Productivity Trends in Korea," in *Essays in Memory of Sang Chul Suh* (Seoul: Korea University Press, 1985), 59.
[133] Quote from Woo, *Race to the Swift,* 131. See also Broad and Cavanaugh, "No More NICs," 87; Cheng and Haggard, *Newly Industrializing Asia,* 6; Lim interview.
[134] Amsden, *Asia's Next Giant,* 89.

136

Chun from his predecessor and also cut the power of big business, while contributing to employment and helping the middle class, both of which are closely tied to light manufacturing.[135]

Despite these successes, it is also clear that restructuring *reduced* the relative capacity of the state by increasing the capacity of business and labor for collective action. The change is most evident in the increasingly central role of the *jae-bul,* or conglomerates, in the economy. Employment and value added in big firms (more than 200 workers) doubled during the 1960s, then leveled off in the 1970s. Jae-bul growth accelerated in that period, however, spurred by the HCID. The top five jae-bul grew at a real compound annual rate of 31.6 percent, and the top forty-six grew at a rate of 24.2 percent, whereas the economy grew at a rate of just 9.9 percent. Thus, by the end of the 1970s a few jae-bul dominated the Korean economy. Indeed, by 1981 "Korea [had] acquired one of the world's most concentrated economies."[136] These developments proved costly, because the growth of jae-bul resulted not from economies of scale or greater efficiency but from preferential access to artificially cheap HCID-provided capital. "In reality," observes Woo, "they are creations . . . of the state and the Korean financial structure."[137] More important, however, are the political consequences of jae-bul growth.

The increase in jae-bul strength altered state-business relations. In the early 1960s, the state faced thousands of fledgling companies and a few vulnerable big ones; now it faces huge firms organized in a unified, potent lobbying organization, the Federation of Korean Industries (FKI).[138] Jae-bul dependence on tariff protection, monopoly markets, cheap loans, preferential tax treatment, and export subsidies gives the conglomerates an intense interest in state policy. But the jae-buls' precarious financial position and importance in the economy, and the small firms' dependence on them for marketing and subcontracting relationships, limit state leverage and force the state "into the role of lender of last resort," since jae-bul bankruptcy "would threaten not only the financial but the economic stability of

[135] Han interview.

[136] Amsden, *Asia's Next Giant,* 121.

[137] Jones, *Jae-Bul,* 21, 50–61, 94–97, 104–5. Woo, *Race to the Swift,* 14–15, 150. Raymond Vernon argues that jae-bul growth reflected a superior capacity to manage uncertainty and imperfect capital markets (personal communication). Even if this view is correct, however, it does not alter the following argument regarding the impact of jae-bul growth on relative capacity.

[138] Interviews with Lim, Cha, Kim, Chung, and Cho.

the country."[139] Further, the jae-bul now have access to the state. Public-private joint ventures, high asset/factor inflexibility, and the related growth of specialized state agencies and ties between big business and bureaucrats have opened direct and indirect channels of communication and provided the jae-bul with advocates inside the state. The Ministry of Commerce and Industry, for example, which helped draft the HCID, is a staunch FKI ally, defending heavy industry against the EPB's efforts to restructure.[140]

The jae-bul have joined the policy process and can resist policies that hurt their interests. "Park Chung Hee had eradicated the distinction between public and private when he pumped the jae-bul, back in 1973, as the muscle of the Big Push. By the end of the decade the chickens were coming home to roost."[141] In contrast to the 1960s and early 1970s, the government now accepts 90 percent of FKI's policy recommendations.[142] Jae-bul power is also evident in the reversal of ONTA's progress, for direct taxes' share of revenues ceased to grow in the mid-1970s, declining in importance compared with regressive indirect taxes.[143]

What is striking, however, is that the jae-bul forced concessions to be made in the stabilization and restructuring program. A key aim of that program was to staunch the flow of preferential loans that had induced the overcapacity plaguing heavy industry. But when the jae-bul felt the pinch, the FKI howled and the state had to offer bailout loans. After all, by 1985 the average debt-equity ratio of the fifty largest jae-bul was conservatively estimated at 458.4 percent—and nonperforming loans, overwhelmingly attributable to the jae-bul, equaled 17.0 percent of domestic credit or two to five times the paid-up capital of Korea's major banks.[144] Thus, when the state cut credit to the private sector, "the relative share of preferential financing out of total bank credit . . . increased [and] the primary beneficiaries of the new policy loans were, once again, big business. . . . A further credit squeeze was enforced on all other sectors, including particularly

[139] Woo, *Race to the Swift*, 149.
[140] Kim interview.
[141] Woo, *Race to the Swift*, 169.
[142] Cho interview.
[143] Choi, "Interest Conflict," 431; Mason et al., *The Economic and Social Modernization*, 316; Hagen Koo, "The Political Economy of Income Distribution in South Korea," *World Development* 12, no. 10 (1984): 1034–35.
[144] Woo, *Race to the Swift*, 170.

small and medium-sized firms."[145] In short, the jae-bul forced an outcome that was diametrically opposed to the state interest in rebalancing the relationships between big and little firms and among sectors.

Ironically, liberalization—"the means by which the new military leaders and economic advisers hoped to discipline big business and reverse the legacy of two decades of state controls"—has also backfired because of the jae-buls' state policy–induced power.[146] Some trade liberalization did occur, but only in return for the state's acquiescence to jae-bul demands that it relax its control of the financial system. The state thus reduced regulation of nonbank financial intermediaries, many of which were and are controlled by the big jae-bul, and began to privatize banking. As a result of deregulation, the deposits of these intermediaries soared and, despite formal limits on equity ownership, the big jae-bul managed to gain control of individual banks. Armed with vast new financial resources, the jae-bul went on a buying spree, sharply *increasing* economic concentration as well as their political power. "Korea, Inc." had given way and the relative capacity of the state was reduced—"the government's forcefulness and credibility declined and private business groups augmented their power."[147]

The reduction of state strength relative to that of labor is no less striking. In the early 1980s, unions still could not defend workers. The Chun government cut real wages and purged labor leaders; it asserted the right to control collective bargaining, prohibit unions from striking without approval, and bar even FKTU organizers from factories. But the growth of high/high heavy industry had already fundamentally altered the conditions affecting labor's capacity for collective action. In the new heavy industries, the large workplaces facilitate organizing. Workers in the new industries are highly skilled and often have received extensive on-the-job training; therefore, they possess considerable leverage. Furthermore, their stable employment prospects and good advancement opportunities give them strong incentives to invest in labor organization. Finally, stable employment, the geographical concentration of heavy industry, and the firms' size have led to the creation of stable working-class communities, many of which are company towns as homogeneous as the mining compounds of the Zambian Copperbelt.

[145] Haggard and Moon, "Industrial Change and State Power," 32–33.
[146] Amsden, *Asia's Next Giant*, 133.
[147] Ibid., 134–36.

Managers' attitudes toward labor changed, too. Big investments in training, the need for labor discipline and uninterrupted production, and the vulnerability of production to sabotage gave managers a vital interest in worker retention and loyalty; labor's small share of production costs gave them room to negotiate. Thus, grudgingly but steadily, Korea's heavy industrial firms have allowed the growth of unions to "stabilize a highly mobile work force by providing new sets of organizational and interpersonal commitments and by providing institutional alternatives to quitting in response to job-related problems or grievances."[148] The number of union shops and union members soared in the 1970s. Today union density is highest in chemicals, automobiles, mining, and metals, and there is even a Korean Employers Association (representing the jae-bul) to foster industrial peace through "cooperation with the FKTU."[149]

State-labor relations changed, too. The exclusionary labor regime of the 1960s was gradually replaced by one that was more corporatist in orientation—in favor of heavy industrial workers. Since the mid-1970s, FKTU leaders have been consulted by, and even included in meetings of, the Economic Plan Coordination Committee, which prepares the five-year plans, and the Export Promotion Conference chaired by the president. These changes reflect officials' recognition of heavy industry workers' potential power and are intended to offset it. They also grant labor access to the policy process, however.

Waves of successful strikes against Korea's biggest firms during the 1980s demonstrate heavy industrial workers' clout. Whereas light manufacturing workers' protests fizzled, even during the stormy period between Park's death in August 1979 and the Chun coup in May 1980, strikes wracked heavy industry. In April 1980, for example, strikers closed the Tongwon coal mine, seized a nearby town, and occupied police headquarters. They won higher wages, doubled their bonuses, got management to pay all damage claims resulting from the strike, and extracted more state spending on housing, roads, and amenities for miners and their families. Elsewhere, strikes had similar

[148] Deyo, *Beneath the Miracle*, 146.

[149] Ibid., 77. Quote from Choi, "Interest Conflict," 55, 165–66, 387–91. The Korean Employers Association was formed in 1970, but talks with the FKTU started only in 1975 when implementation of the HCID began. The association has since become part of the Labor-Management Friendly Meeting and the Central Labor-Management Friendly Meeting, state-labor-management groups that are the key forums in which industrial relations are discussed at the national level.

results—even when, as at the Dongkuk steel mill, they involved clashes with riot police.[150] Intense repression then stopped strike activity until 1984, when it exploded again as heavy industrial workers demanded not only material gains but changes in the repressive labor regime and in the political system itself. They formed independent, regional labor associations such as the Circle Movement in the Seoul-Inchon area to help them organize.[151] They also forged ties to student, church, and other potential opposition groups, thus giving these organizations the manpower and economic clout they had long lacked.

The best proof of the state's reduced relative capacity is the tidal wave of strikes that swept Korea in 1987 and helped force a return to democracy. They did not mobilize the workers in light manufacturing on whose backs the Korean miracle was built, however. They mobilized the skilled workers of the biggest, most modern firms in the new heavy industries built under the aegis of the state's own restructuring program. Strikes closed the Changwon industrial complex, Daewoo Heavy Industries, the Hyundai shipyards, and dozens of other huge firms, crippling the economy. Workers took on the state and big business—and when business balked, the state actually supported labor. Workers won better wages and benefits, and the right to organize independent unions, even at Daewoo, Samsung, and Hyundai, where not even company unions had been allowed. They demanded, and got, humiliating public apologies from the CEOs of Korea's biggest companies. Most important, along with their student and middle-class allies, they made the demand for democracy irresistible.

The Korean story brings us full circle. Although sectoral analysis acknowledges the role of circumstantial variables, it lets us explain what other analytical methods explain—and also what they do not. In particular, it helps us to appreciate why the international market and the domestic restructuring project faced by Korean officials were more tractable than those confronted by their Zambian counterparts. Sectoral analysis also enables us to explain change, even unexpected change. For what could be more ironic than President Roh Tae Woo's current predicament? He heads a democratic government born of the

---

[150] Deyo, *Beneath the Miracle*, 78–79; Kim, "Employment, Wages, and Manpower Policies," 64.

[151] Haggard and Moon, "Institutions and Economic Policy," 233–34.

protests of heavy industrial workers and their middle-class allies who were angered but also empowered by the old authoritarian state's unrestrained exercise of power in restructuring the economy. He is also the embattled leader of a ruling coalition held hostage by a new party founded and led by the head of Hyundai, a party dedicated to reducing state control over business.

CHAPTER FIVE

Sri Lanka: The Industrial Plantation Crop Sector

Sri Lanka[1] is a land of contrasts. When it won independence in 1947, it boasted a world-class tea industry and a strong democracy. The World Bank suggests that Sri Lanka "may be unique among mixed economies in achieving a massive transfer of resources from the elite to the poor," and despite widespread poverty its "record on life expectancy, literacy and fertility . . . is one of the best in the world." But growth has been "extremely low and disappointing," for the tea industry has withered, government economic policy has stunted development, and welfare gains have come at the expense of future generations.[2] These contrasts are unique to Sri Lanka, but Sri Lanka is also a perfect high/high industrial plantation crop case. This chapter begins a discussion of the international tea market, which has long shaped Sri Lanka's prospects. I then analyze policy makers' attempts to escape from a dependence on tea in the 1960s and again after 1977, examining how tea influenced societal and political actors' interests, capabilities, and actions during the process of restructuring, and how the failed policies of the 1960s complicated the restructuring effort in the late 1970s and 1980s.

Plantations have made Sri Lanka what it is today and have tied it to the international economy. Coffee came first. Beginning in the 1820s,

---

[1] Historically called Ceylon, the island adopted the name Sri Lanka in 1972. To avoid confusion, I use "Sri Lanka" throughout.

[2] World Bank, *Sri Lanka and the World Bank* (Washington, D.C., 1987), 5; and World Bank, *World Development Report, 1980* (New York: Oxford University Press, 1980), 90; W. D. Lakshman, "Economic Growth and Redistributive Justice as Policy Goals," *Modern Ceylon Studies* 6 (January 1975): 65.

coffee exports and government revenues soared, resulting in a fusion of state and planter interests. The state provided land, imported Indian Tamil workers, and built a modern infrastructure to service the estates. But in 1868 a coffee leaf rust appeared, and by 1895 coffee was dead. In the interim, planters and the state scrabbled for an alternative—and found it in tea, plantings of which increased from 19 acres in 1867 to 384,000 acres by 1900, and to 552,000 acres by the time of independence.[3] The shift to tea changed the nature of the estate sector. Much coffee was estate grown, but because this was a low/low sector, cultivation was open to all. Tea's sharply higher capital and scale requirements, however, led to "the displacement of proprietary planters and partnerships by corporate enterprises financed by capital markets abroad."[4] By the 1920s the sector had assumed its final form: capital-intensive, large-scale estates under corporate ownership, managed by a few interconnected agency houses, and dependent upon foreign markets.

In 1947 Sri Lanka produced 30 percent of the world's tea and the tea industry dominated the political economy. Tea, rubber, and coconuts generated 97 percent of foreign exchange and 37 percent of GDP. Export taxes on them generated 50 percent of government revenues. Most manufacturing took the form of export processing, and commerce, finance, and transport depended on export agriculture. But tea was the key, generating 60 percent of export earnings and 17 percent of GDP. Export duties on tea provided 40 percent of government revenues; the industry employed 20 percent of the work force and indirectly provided jobs for far more.[5]

All seemed to be going well. The war had increased foreign reserves, and a postwar commodities boom boosted export earnings and revenues to record levels. When the boom ended there were few demands for action, for Sri Lanka's "fortunate circumstances . . . hid the structural weaknesses of the economy. Because of apparently limitless tea revenues, leaders were complacent. There was no planning

[3] Weerapurage Fernando, "Continuity and Change in Plantation Agriculture" (Ph.D. diss., University of Wisconsin, 1980), 96.
[4] S. B. D. de Silva, *The Political Economy of Underdevelopment* (London: Routledge and Kegan Paul, 1982), 37.
[5] Premachandra Athukorale, "Export Development," *Economic Review* (July–August 1984), 4; Donald Snodgrass, *Ceylon: An Export Economy in Transition* (Homewood, Ill.: Richard Irwin, 1966), 54, 128; W. D. Lakshman, "The IMF-World Bank Intervention in Sri Lankan Economic Policy," *Social Scientist* (February 1985), 4; Sudatta Ranasinghe, "Tea and Underdevelopment," Sri Lanka Association of Economists, Seminar Paper no. 2/86 (February 1986), 4.

for the future, . . . no sense of a need to diversify. . . . We had no concept of using these resources to invest in other sectors."[6] Still, each government since 1947 has tried to reduce tea dependence and has largely relied on tea taxes to finance growth. Planners preparing for independence warned that "the national income should be wisely distributed between expenditure on consumption and expenditure on development," as has every finance minister since independence.[7] Faced with a growing population, planners have encouraged peasant agriculture and new land development, but they also stress the need for "a structural change in the economy with industry taking the place of agriculture as the leading sector."[8]

But "no steps were taken towards diversifying the export structure," because "no method was ever devised to allocate a sufficient quantity of resources to investment."[9] Foreign reserves "were frittered away in an orgy of unplanned spending"; social programs increased government spending fourfold and the deficit fivefold between 1950 and 1960.[10] Everything hinged on tea, but after tea prices collapsed in 1955 exports stagnated. In the absence of foreign reserves, policy makers believed that ISI was the only hope, and after 1958 they imposed ever tighter exchange controls as well as licensing measures, tariffs, and quotas. Sri Lanka's terms of trade continued to fall 4–5 percent per year through the 1960s, however. Policy failed to "alleviate the structural vulnerability of the economy and resulted in a genuine economic cul-de-sac of high unemployment, internal and external deficits, scarcities, slow growth, and austerity budgets." Controls prevented "the expansion of productive capacity," leaving Sri Lanka "even more dependent on the traditional export sector."[11] Foreign borrowing surged, increasing long-term official debt by 5920 percent from 1960 to 1977, though the ISI firms such borrowing

[6] Sanderatne interview.

[7] Report of the Commission on Social Services, cited in L. A. Wickremeratne, "The Emergence of a Welfare Policy, 1931–1948," in University of Ceylon, *History of Ceylon*, vol. 3 (Colombo: University of Ceylon, 1973), 483–84.

[8] L. A. Wickremeratne, "Planning and Economic Development," in *Sri Lanka: A Survey*, ed. K. M. de Silva (Honolulu: University Press of Hawaii, 1977), 152.

[9] Athukorale, "Export Development," 4; Snodgrass, *Ceylon*, 182.

[10] Jeyaratnam Wilson, "Politics and Political Development since 1948," in *Sri Lanka*, ed. de Silva, 294; H. M. Gunasekera, "Foreign Trade of Sri Lanka," in ibid., 184.

[11] Quotes from Ronald Herring, "An Assessment of the Liberalization Regime in Sri Lanka," paper presented at the Annual Meeting of the Association for Asian Studies (Chicago, March 22–23, 1986), 37–38; Germani Corea, "Aid and Development," *Marga* 1, no. 1 (1971): 30; and Athukorale, "Export Development," 4–10. See also Buddhadasa Hewavitharana, "Recent Trends in the Management of External and Internal Finances in Sri Lanka," *Marga* 2, no. 4 (1975): 1–3.

financed were "a drain on the government budget and national economy" and hurt "future development." Between 1963 and 1975, manufacturing's share of GNP remained unchanged, the ISI effort failed to provide jobs, and open unemployment soared from 14 percent to 37 percent.[12]

By 1977 growth had stopped; Sri Lankans showed they had had enough by voting into office a new United National Party (UNP) government, which took up restructuring. It sought to liberalize trade and exchange rates, stimulate exports, abolish price controls, cut spending, increase investment, and promote private enterprise. The effort brought a flood of foreign aid, investment, and loans. From 1977 to 1985, real economic growth and investment doubled, the annual growth rate of industrial production increased from 1.0 percent to 5.1 percent, per capita income rose 70 percent, and unemployment fell 50 percent.[13] But most of this surge followed the influx of inputs permitted by foreign aid and lending immediately after the UNP victory; after 1983, the numbers show no positive trend. Most investment went to nontraded sectors, which generated 70 percent of GDP growth between 1977 and 1983, compared with 55 percent in the 1970s. After 1983, manufacturing's share of GDP remained unchanged through the late 1980s, and export processing of estate crops still accounted for 75 percent of manufacturing-sector output. "The structure of exports has also not changed," a Central Bank official noted in 1986, export growth has been "disappointing," and Sri Lanka's ability to cover import costs with export earnings has sharply decreased.[14]

[12] Quote from Sanderatne interview. See also Hewavitharana, "Recent Trends," 5; Marshal Fernando, "Foreign Debt of Sri Lanka, 1970–1984," Seminar Paper no. 4/86 (Colombo: Sri Lankan Association of Economists, May 1986), 12–13; N. Balakrishnan, "A Review of the Economy," in *Modern Sri Lanka,* ed. Tissa Fernando and Robert Kearney (Syracuse, N.Y.: Maxwell School of Citizenship and Public Affairs, Syracuse University, 1979), 107; and Balakrishnan, "Industrial Policy and Development since Independence," in *Sri Lanka,* ed. de Silva, 202; Sudatta Ranasinghe, "Unemployment and Job Expectations among Our Youth," *Economic Review* (July 1977), 24.

[13] Ronnie de Mel (minister of finance), "Government's Investment Priorities and Expectations of the Private Sector," *Economic Review* (May–June 1984), 15; National Planning Division, Ministry of Finance and Planning (NPD), *Public Investment, 1986–1990* (Colombo, 1986), 7, 95–98; Athukorale, "Export Development," 10–11.

[14] Quote from Jayamahu interview; NPD, *Public Investment, 1986–1990,* 95; Premachandra Athukorale, "The Impact of 1977 Policy Reforms on Domestic Industry," *Upanathi* 1 (January 1986): 79–80; and Athukorale, "Export Development," 8–11; Export Development Board (EDB), *National Export Development Plan, 1983–1987,* vol. 1 (Colombo, 1983), 2.

Tea, however, is back. Overtaxation, underinvestment, and low prices have depressed production and exports since 1960, but tea still dominates export earnings, employment, GDP, and revenues. Thus, policy makers again believe that "in the short-term the highest priority has to be given to the traditional plantation sector."[15] Sri Lanka, in short, must *reculer pour mieux sauter*—attempt to revitalize tea today in order to restructure the economy tomorrow. But to explain why Sri Lankan leaders face the same situation their predecessors faced in 1947, we must analyze the international tea market and Sri Lanka's place in it.

THE INTERNATIONAL DIMENSION

An industrial plantation is more a factory than a farm. Few crops lend themselves to estate production, but those that do cannot be produced competitively any other way. Such crops demand immediate processing, which must be done on site because of perishability and the need to reduce bulk. An estate's core is thus a factory that may account for 90 percent of capital costs. The resulting high fixed costs require a crop that can be harvested continuously and extensive fields to supply the volume of raw material needed for efficient factory operation. Since field work cannot be mechanized, estates must maintain large labor forces, which may account for 60 percent of operating costs. Capital intensity, scale, and technical complexity make skilled managers and specialized management organizations essential.[16]

Tea is the perfect plantation crop and Sri Lanka is the perfect place to produce it.[17] Plucking demands speed and skill, since tea leaves must be delivered to the factory in a matter of hours. There they lose 75 percent of their weight and 95–97 percent of their moisture. A minimum of 500 acres of tea is needed to support a factory; such an estate requires 750 pickers and a dozen managers. Sri Lanka has a climate that permits continuous plucking, a mix of growing areas that

[15] EDB, *National Export Development Plan,* 1: 18.

[16] Jeffrey Paige, *Agrarian Revolution* (New York: Free Press, 1975), 14–15, 83–85; T. Eden, *Tea* (New York: John Wiley, 1958), 61; P. P. Courtenay, *Plantation Agriculture* (New York: Praeger, 1965), 54–57, 224–25; Goutam Sarkar, *The World Tea Economy* (Delhi: Oxford University Press, 1972), 178–79.

[17] Courtenay, *Plantation Agriculture,* 179–83; Paige, *Agrarian Revolution,* 50–58; G. H. Peiris, "Plantation Agriculture," in *Sri Lanka,* ed. de Silva, 219.

permits its teas to satisfy many tastes, and the finest estate work force and managers in the world.

High capital intensity requirements and economies of scale ensure that a few large corporate players dominate tea production. Starting a new estate requires clearing and terracing the land, planting and nurturing the bushes, building access roads, and then constructing the factory. Even in the 1890s, capital costs ranged from £20 to £100 per cultivated acre in Sri Lanka, and by 1947 they exceeded £1,000 per acre. Thus, the cost of starting an estate of 500 acres to 1,500 acres ranged from £10,000 to £150,000 in the 1890s, and from £500,000 to £1.5 million at independence.[18]

The lumpiness of estate investments and the related market uncertainties amplify the problem of high capital intensity. Large sums must be committed up front, but ten years must elapse before an estate begins to yield and another twenty are necessary to amortize the investment. This "money is irrevocably invested and the assets must either be worked or deteriorate. . . . The owner . . . is therefore 'locked in' to a far greater extent than in almost any other economic activity; few of his assets are movable nor can they be used for any other purpose."[19] Together, high capital requirements, a large sunk investment, and long payback periods make estate investments very risky, thus excluding smallholders and favoring corporations with access to international capital markets.[20]

The minimum efficient scale in tea production is 500 acres—and bigger is better, since the large estates' average yields exceed those of smaller estates by 30 percent. In Sri Lanka, 50 percent of tea acreage is in estates of more than 500 acres and much of the rest is in estates of more than 200 acres.[21] Estate size reflects the need to size leaf pro-

[18] D. M. Forrest, *A Hundred Years of Ceylon Tea* (London: Chatto and Windus, 1967), 144–47; V. D. Wickizer, *Coffee, Tea, and Cocoa* (Stanford: Stanford University Press, 1951), 161–62.

[19] Edgar Graham and Ingrid Floering, *The Modern Plantation in the Third World* (New York: St. Martin's Press, 1984), 51.

[20] Courtenay, *Plantation Agriculture*, 126; Sarkar, *The World Tea Economy*, 7–8; Wickizer, *Coffee, Tea, and Cocoa*, 161, 448–49; Shamsher Singh, Jos de Vries, John Hulley, and Patrick Yeung, *Coffee, Tea, and Cocoa* (Baltimore: Johns Hopkins University Press, 1977), 6–7.

[21] Interview with Ilangakoon; C. R. Harler, *The Culture and Marketing of Tea* (New York: Oxford University Press, 1956), 256; Frederick Hung, "The Tea Plantation System in Ceylon," *Professional Geographer* 20 (September 1968): 323–24; Dias Bandaranaike, "Tea Production in Sri Lanka," Central Bank of Ceylon (CBC), Occasional Paper no. 7 (Colombo, July 1984), 20.

duction to optimize factory throughput. And since an MES factory manufactures 350,000 kgs of made tea per year, estates require at least 350 acres producing 1,200 kgs of made tea per year. Only large estates can achieve such yields, because they alone can employ the required number of workers efficiently; afford to invest in new technology, new plant varieties, soil conservation, and agronomy; and "sustain the specialized and specialist organization" required to manage a modern estate.[22]

Low barriers to entry aggravate the problems posed by high capital and scale requirements. Climate and geography set wide limits to where tea will grow. In fact, the current distribution of production is an artifact of past imperial policy, not a result of natural endowments. Many other countries could grow tea if they so chose.[23] Furthermore, though high, capital intensity and scale requirements are not overwhelming; they may discourage peasant producers, but they deter few others. The sector thus does not offer the safety and rents of an oligopoly. Instead, firms face high competition with hardly any means to control costs or production.

The nature of tea and tea production also makes it hard to match supply and demand. Consumption is inelastic and demand grows proportionately with population—about 3 percent per year. Short-run supply is stable, too, so prices vary little from year to year. The problem is tea's long-run tendency to oversupply and a 2.5 percent annual average decline (constant dollars) in prices since 1955.[24] Tea bushes take ten years to mature; thus plantings begin to yield long after the high prices that encouraged them have passed. This discourages planting, which in the medium term results in price spikes, since supply cannot be increased to meet accumulated demand. Price spikes encourage new plantings, which depress prices, since "with investment costs at about 75 percent of total costs, producers are unlikely to stop plucking unless prices fall to a very low level. They are even more unlikely . . . to actually uproot bushes [as] maintenance costs are less

[22] Quote from Graham and Floering, *The Modern Plantation*, 25–26. See also World Bank, *Staff Appraisal Report: Sri Lanka, Fourth Tree Crops Project*, Report no. 5265-CE (1985), 27; Sarkar, *The World Tea Economy*, 17, 184; Hung, "The Tea Plantation System," 323; S. B. D. de Silva, "Plantations and Underdevelopment," in *Capital and Peasant Production*, ed. Charles Abeysekera (Colombo: Social Science Association, 1985), 23.

[23] Courtenay, *Plantation Agriculture*, 59–66; 179–84.

[24] Wickizer, *Coffee, Tea, and Cocoa*, 160–61; Sarkar, *The World Tea Economy*, 69–73, 91–94, 144; World Bank, *Fourth Tree Crops Project*, 43; Paul Casperezs, "Sri Lanka and the Changing World Tea Economy," *Marga* 3, No. 1 (1976): 14.

than 20 percent of the cost of production." Indeed, "producers attempt to compensate for unfavorable prices by increasing output."[25]

Failure of the International Tea Agreement

Tea producers have long tried to control the tendency to oversupply. But despite temporary success in the 1930s and fifty years of talk, collective efforts to manage supply and prices have failed. In 1986 producers were still "no where near an agreement" because the same factors that make the collective control of excess capacity critical bar its achievement.[26] Unlike mining companies, producers need not worry that higher prices will cut demand; their concern is that other producers will increase production. The large number and small size of competing producers induce free riding. Large numbers of producers and high buyer concentration make it hard to monitor compliance and punish cheaters; low barriers to entry let nonsignatories to agreements capitalize on supply restrictions to increase their market share.[27]

But the main barrier to agreement is that tea-producing countries cannot agree on a proper target price, a way to manage excess capacity, or a fair distribution of future production. The higher the target price, the smaller the export quotas, a restriction that is unacceptable to new, low-cost producers who do not need high prices to turn a profit and see quotas as an attempt by old producers to exclude them. But low prices and new production threaten mature, high-cost producers' ability to maintain big, sunk investments as well as revenues, export earnings, and jobs. The resulting impasse ensures that each "country finds it to its relative advantage to expand rather than contract exports, even though the cumulative result is disaster for them all."[28]

Producers' first attempt to achieve a tea accord, in 1933, worked deceptively well. High prices in the 1920s had encouraged new plantings, causing a supply to surge just as the depression killed demand.

[25] Quotes from D. M. Etherington and R. L. Jones, "The Economic Gains from an International Tea Agreement," *Marga* 3, no. 4 (1976): 27; and Wickizer, *Coffee, Tea, and Cocoa,* 191.

[26] Sambasivam interview.

[27] Sarkar, *The World Tea Economy,* 159–61; Liaqat Ali, "The Regulation of Trade in Tea," *Journal of World Trade Law* 4 (July–August 1970): 582.

[28] Etherington and Jones, "The Economic Gains," 33.

Facing disaster, Ceylon, India, and the Dutch East Indies, which together supplied 97 percent of the tea trade, cut exports, thus increasing prices 125 percent by 1937. But success in reaching agreement resulted from the fact that only three colonial states were involved, each of which had a huge stake in the outcome and could ignore the pain caused by export restrictions. Equally important, British authorities intent on protecting India blocked an increase in exports from East Africa. But decolonization has eliminated these mitigating factors and increased the number of major exporters from three to fifteen as African producers have flourished. Their booming exports have depressed prices and sharply reduced the market share of India and Sri Lanka. Whereas Kenya's share of world tea exports rose from 6.7 percent to 11.6 percent between 1972 and 1983, Sri Lanka's fell from 27 percent to 18 percent, leaving it in the position of "a price taker in a market that is . . . impossible to control."[29]

Under these conditions no identity of interests exists among tea producers. India and Sri Lanka cannot compensate for declining returns with a larger volume of exports because they are still such large exporters that "half of any increase in export volume will be offset by an associated price decline." The corresponding proportion for African producers is less than 10 percent such that for them export expansion pays, especially since low costs make increased production profitable despite low prices.[30] Thus, an international tea agreement offers India and Sri Lanka "the only possibility for . . . raising their income from tea," whereas African producers' interest is in "taking export market share from the Asian producers, rather than in creating and sharing in a high price market for all."[31]

Going It Alone

In the absence of international collaboration, tea producers must make do with individual risk management strategies, the most effective of which has been vertical integration, a course not open to Sri

[29] Quote from Sambasivam interview; Sarkar, *The World Tea Economy*, 159–74; Courtenay, *Plantation Agriculture*, 184–85; Singh et al., *Coffee, Tea, and Cocoa*, 20–22; NPD, *Public Investment, 1986–1990*, 77–78; and "Tea and the Economy," *Economic Review* (September–October 1985), 23.

[30] Quote from Singh et al., *Coffee, Tea, and Cocoa*, 73. See also Etherington and Jones, "Economic Gains," 32; G. P. Tyler, "Recent Developments in the World Tea Economy and the Potential of an ITA," *Marga* 3, no. 4 (1976): 46–48.

[31] Sambasivam interview; Tyler, "Recent Developments," 42.

Lanka. Tea is dominated by vertically integrated MNCs that produce, ship, blend, and retail tea. Indeed, the merger of the Lipton Tea Company, Brooke Bond, and Unilever in the early 1980s gave one firm control of 60 percent of world tea purchases.[32] Such firms can raise capital, marry far-flung producers to consumers, and deploy the sophisticated management practices such operations demand. As both producers and consumers, they can ignore falling prices and offset slim profit margins on their estates with bigger downstream profits. As MNCs, they can diversify their production base to take advantage of new, lower-cost sources and improvements in production technology and planting stocks.

These advantages are disadvantages for Sri Lanka, however. As the tea bushes on older estates reached the end of their productive lives in the 1950s, and the newly independent state raised tea taxes to pay for development, the MNCs decamped to East Africa to start new estates, which they planted with high-yielding clonal varietals and equipped with high-tech factories. The government of Sri Lanka then exaggerated these advantages by nationalizing many of the MNCs' highest-cost estates and assuming the capital costs of replanting and factory renovation necessary to sustain the aging industry. Thus, Sri Lanka's production costs have risen as those of the MNCs have fallen, but as an unintegrated producer, it cannot offset these upstream losses with downstream profits.[33]

Sri Lanka has tried to help itself, but to no avail. It continues efforts begun in the 1880s to link Ceylon tea with quality in consumers' minds. Changes in the tea market have turned this attention to quality against it, however, for consumption of quality tea is down, while demand is up for tea bags and instant teas, which require the low-quality tea produced by the African competition. Sri Lanka is therefore trying to sell blends and tea bags, but these face high tariffs and lack the consumer loyalty enjoyed by MNC brands in established markets; in new markets the MNCs sell below cost to increase market share and exclude newcomers.[34]

Sri Lanka, in short, must restructure. The characteristics of tea production and the risks associated with it, structural disadvantages vis-à-vis the MNC competition, and barriers to collective action with other national producers counsel against continued dependence on

[32] Sambasivam interview.
[33] Ibid.; Peiris, "Plantation Agriculture," 227–28.
[34] Interviews with Sambasivam and Panabokke.

tea. To assess the prospects for restructuring, however, we must shift our focus to the domestic dimension.

THE DOMESTIC DIMENSION: AN INTRACTABLE PROJECT

The restructuring of industrial plantation crop sectors presents intractable problems. Production inflexibility dogs all estate crop producers, tea producers included. Big capital outlays saddle firms with high fixed costs, and efficient factory operation requires full-capacity production, regardless of prices. Even labor is a fixed cost; an army of skilled workers is needed to maintain an estate and must pluck constantly, for even brief production stops impose high restart costs and may permanently damage an estate. Tea producers thus can neither cut production in times of glut nor increase it rapidly to profit from short-term price hikes.

Asset/factor inflexibility darkens the long-term outlook, too. Tea bushes produce only tea, and tea factories have no other uses. The layout of fields required for efficient plucking prohibits intercropping. Tea requires an extensive, dedicated support infrastructure. In fact, since 1927, when the rail lines serving the tea districts were completed, only two miles of track have been added to the Sri Lanka system. Like the road and communications systems, the rail system is poorly located to serve a diversified economy, and it is unprofitable without the traffic provided by tea.[35] The tea sector is also served by specialized banks, agency houses, equipment manufacturers, and research and instructional organizations.

The estates' human assets are also inflexible. Pickers possess specialized, nontransferable skills—and are otherwise unskilled. The estates concentrate 500,000 workers *and* their dependents in a tiny area of the island where they depend solely on estate employment and live solely in estate housing, isolated from the rest of the population, from which they are further separated by language, culture, and religion.[36]

[35] Vidanapathirana, "Recent Trends of Rail Transport in Sri Lanka," CBC *Staff Studies* 6 (September 1976): 126–34; Kumari Jayawardena, *The Rise of the Labor Movement in Ceylon* (Durham, N.C.: Duke University Press, 1972), 6–7; L. A. Wickremeratne, "The Development of Transportation in Ceylon," in University of Ceylon, *History of Ceylon* 3: 304–5.

[36] Sri Lanka is typical. See Ida Greaves, "Plantations in World Economy," in *Plantation Systems of the New World*, Pan American Union, Social Science Monograph no. 7 (Washington, D.C., 1959), 15.

Estate managers, too, have specialized, nontransferable skills, and estates are organized to produce just one product. Further, the industry's traditional management-training system not only provides the necessary skills but inculcates an identity that sets estate managers apart "from the rest of the managerial community in Sri Lanka."[37]

In the short term, production inflexibility means that market downturns inflict immediate, massive blows on export earnings and tax revenues. And since estates cannot adapt to the market, they demand state aid in the form of reduced taxes, tariffs, and so on. This only makes matters worse; for example, estate-sector pressure to limit rates explains the big losses and high state subsidies of the Sri Lankan railroad and the road transport parastatal.[38]

Asset/factor inflexibility has equally nasty implications for restructuring. Tea plantations cover 15 percent of Sri Lanka and 70 percent of the tea districts, but these lands can be converted to other uses only by bulldozing the fields and factories; moreover, no other crop pays better or employs more workers than tea. Abandoning tea would marginalize the rail and road systems, and building new ones would be unthinkably costly.[39] Sri Lanka's industrial and service sectors provide specialized inputs for the estates, few of which could find other markets. Finally, restructuring spells disaster for estate workers and threatens estate managers. The Sinhalese elites in the tea districts and their peasant constituents dread the addition of 500,000 Tamil tea pluckers into the local economy. Asset/factor inflexibility thus means that the state must build the new from scratch, without allies, in the face of opposition from powerful erstwhile allies, and in the midst of fiscal crisis.

Sri Lanka's problems are exaggerated by the "Dutch disease." Since the 1840s, the estate sector has driven the economy, but it gave rise to broad-based demand only for foodstuffs and necessities. Booming exports, an overvalued exchange rate, and low tariffs, however, made even these goods cheaper to import than to produce locally. The flood of imports discouraged manufacturing investment and agricultural intensification. Commerce and trade-related services flourished, and

---

[37] Quote from "Tea and the Economy," 7; interviews with Ilangakoon and Ratnayaka.

[38] S. T. G. Fernando, "Patterns of Investment, Political Stability, and Rates of Growth" (Ph.D. diss., Oxford University, 1966), 347, 399; Sarkar, *The World Tea Economy*, 140–42; Vidanapathirana, "Recent Trends," 128–29.

[39] Fernando, "Continuity and Change," 263–64; NPD, *Public Investment, 1986–1990*, 113.

Sri Lanka developed a financial system geared to providing short-term trade financing, not long-term investment capital.[40]

State policies made things worse. During World War II, colonial officials built state-owned factories which later failed or required subsidies, eventually leading policy makers to accept the World Bank's 1952 advice that industrial policy focus "on the development of numerous small or medium-sized industries."[41] But because few would invest in view of the boom in imports, the state was forced to offer protection and after 1957 "to promote the development of large-scale and basic industries in the public sector." The result of this policy, however, was that small firms were replaced by big, capital-intensive, inefficient ones requiring huge subsidies.[42] Since these firms could neither turn a profit at home nor export, they depended on tea, the ultimate source of state investment funds, subsidies, and foreign exchange. The policy thus increased the state's fixed costs; tied its ability to meet them to tea prices, exaggerating the impact of tea's production inflexibility; and saddled Sri Lanka with an industrial sector that was as asset/factor inflexible as tea.

Sri Lanka is in a bind: its prospects in the international tea market are bleak, but the barriers to exit are high and there are no promising alternatives. The question, however, is whether the state has the autonomy or the capacity to undertake this intractable project.

The Domestic Political Economy of Tea: Absolute Capacity

At independence, Sri Lanka seemed ready to restructure. It had a strong national identity, a working democracy, and a professional, apolitical civil service. Still, the state had only limited absolute capacity, and since 1947 its leaders' actions have undermined many of its initial advantages. To see why, we must look to tea.

[40] Fernando, "Continuity and Change," 22–23; L. A. Wickremeratne, "The Economy in 1948," in *Sri Lanka*, ed. de Silva, 135–36; Balakrishnan, "Industrial Policy," 195–96; Kumari Jayawardena, "The Origins of the Left Movement in Sri Lanka," *Modern Ceylon Studies* 2, no. 2 (1971): 196; John Blackton, "The Private Sector in Sri Lanka since 1977," *Asian Survey* 23 (June 1983): 736–37.
[41] Balakrishnan, "Industrial Policy," 193.
[42] Quote from the State Industrial Corporations Act of 1957, in ibid., 195–203; Wickremeratne, "The Economy in 1948," 135–36; Neil Dias Karunaratne, "A Historical Review of Industrial Development Policy in Sri Lanka," *Asia Profile* 7 (February 1979): 53–56.

Resource Extraction

Tea gave Sri Lanka an enviable revenue base. Colonial authorities limited taxes on the estates, but they raised 75 percent of revenues from duties on imports—most of which were paid for by tea exports. With independence, Sri Lankan leaders increased the revenues extracted from the estates tenfold; an average of 22 percent of GDP has gone into state coffers annually since the mid-1960s.[43] Better still, extracting these revenues was easy, for it involved no intrusive institutional interventions in citizens' lives, and it even won politicians kudos when they made the planters pay. But in Sri Lanka as in Zambia, the tax system is inflexible and presents a barrier to restructuring.

Because Sri Lanka is an island with only two major ports, its customs and excise services could raise revenue easily. The growth of state trading after 1957 and nationalization of the estate sector in 1975 further facilitated revenue collection by giving the state control of 80 percent of total imports and exports. Thus, as direct taxes' share of revenues decreased after 1960, indirect, trade-based taxes remained "the predominant source of revenue," providing most of the 4620 percent increase in revenues between 1947 and 1985.[44] Higher taxes on tea led the way. In the 1930s export duties on tea and coconuts together generated 4 percent of revenues; in 1947 duties on tea alone were raised to provide 17 percent of revenues, and within a decade they provided 24 percent. Tea revenues then leveled off as exports stagnated and prices fell, leading to further increases in the tax rate. By the mid-1960s Sri Lanka's tea taxes were the highest in the world—the equivalent of 23 percent of the average export price—and tapped 80 percent of the estates' before-tax profits. By the 1980s, tea taxes were 35 percent of the average export price.[45]

But the tax effort has increasingly failed to meet revenue needs. Whereas in 1954–55 Sri Lanka raised Rs 173 million more than it

---

[43] Fernando, "Patterns of Investment," 83, 346–47; William Cramner, "Fiscal Policy-Making in Sri Lanka" (Ph.D. diss., University of Wisconsin, 1982), 418; Satchi Pannambalam, *Dependent Capitalism in Crisis* (London: Zed, 1980), 49; W. D. Lakshman, "State Policy in Sri Lanka and Its Economic Impact, 1970–85," *Upanathi* 1 (January 1986): 17.

[44] Quote from Lakshman, "Economic Growth," 72. See also "Management in the Public Sector," *Economic Review* (August–September 1979), 4; Snodgrass, *Ceylon,* 189; CBC, *Review of the Economy, 1984* (Colombo, 1984), Appendix Table 84; Wickremeratne, "The Economy in 1948," 139–40.

[45] Fernando, "Patterns of Investment," 346–47; Fernando, "Continuity and Change," 142–43; Snodgrass, *Ceylon,* 136; World Bank, *Sri Lanka: Institutional and Policy Issues for Agricultural Development,* vol. 1, Report no. 5800-CE (1986), 24.

spent, by 1964–65 it was spending Rs 464 million more than it raised. By 1980 the gap was Rs 14,619 million, or more than 55 percent of total spending.[46] In part, this reflects an inability to control spending; it also reveals two weaknesses in the tax system. The former is due to the link the system forges between revenues and tea prices. When prices escalate, as they did in 1984, revenues do as well. But as the Central Bank of Ceylon noted at the time, "The high buoyancy in revenue experienced during the year . . . constituted a transitory phenomenon rather than a sustainable improvement in the revenue system." Indeed, in mid-1985 the bank reported that falling prices had already produced the "inevitable concomitant deterioration in the government budgetary operations."[47]

The tax system is also inflexible. Having exhausted the possibilities of indirect taxation by the mid-1960s, Sri Lanka needed to increase direct taxes; twenty-five years later, "the mobilization of revenue has not shown much progress."[48] Ironically, the key problem has been the inability to tax such politically *impotent* groups as farmers and small businesses. Thus, "a large and growing sector of the economy re-main(s) largely outside the purview of direct taxation," and the only revenue gains from direct taxes have been from higher taxes on the salaried classes. Tax "evasion . . . is rampant" because of "administrative problems." In fact, in the 1980s higher income tax revenues depended on the growth of big, state-sponsored construction projects, since the large corporations involved had few incentives to evade.[49]

Inflexibility hurts the state and the economy. The vicious cycle of faltering economic performance and rising taxes saps public faith in the state. Dependence on customs duties raises import costs, exaggerating the impact of falling export earnings and the distorting effects of ISI. Tea tax dependence hurts Sri Lanka relative to African producers and reduces its future export-earning potential. High corporate taxes drain the private sector of investable income, leaving the

[46] S. T. G. Fernando, "Challenges and Sacrifices," *Economic Review* (September 1981), 4–5.

[47] CBC, *Review of the Economy, 1984*, 214; CBC, *Economic Performance in the First Half of 1985* (Colombo, n.d.), 1.

[48] Gamini Abeysekara, "The Economic Objectives of the Budget of 1985," *Economic Review* (January 1985), 5.

[49] Quotes from Lakshman, "Economic Growth," 84–85; and N. U. Jayawardena, "Highlights of the 1986 Budget," *Economic Review* (December 1985), 14–15. See also CBC, *Review of the Economy, 1984*, 214–15.

state the sole agent of development. And when they lack revenues, politicians print money and borrow, giving Sri Lanka a perennial inflation problem and raising public debt from 38 percent of GDP in the 1960s to 65 percent by the late 1970s.[50]

Restructuring has suffered, too. Tea dependence led the tax authorities to raise rates so high that costs exceeded earnings in seven of the ten years 1972–82.[51] The resulting losses, however, forced the state to subsidize the Janatha Estates Development Board (JEDB) and the State Plantations Corporation (SPC), reducing net revenues from tea. Even so, subsidies have been "below the levels required to maintain assets and achieve efficient production"; and this cut output, "discouraged activities aimed at increasing productivity and output," and diminished the "sector's long-run revenue potential." But "attempts to design and implement an alternative tax and subsidy system . . . are obviously constrained by the Government's revenue requirements."[52]

Monitoring, Regulating, and Redirecting the Economy

A similar irony haunts Sri Lanka's ability to monitor, regulate, and redirect the economy. The state can run the estate sector. The Ministry of Plantation Industries, SPC, and JEDB control over 60 percent of the tea acreage. The Tea Board oversees the registration of tea lands, the operation of factories, the Colombo Auction, tea storage and shipping, replanting, and compilation of industry statistics. It promotes Ceylon tea, runs Tea Centres overseas, and does tea market research and marketing; its Tea Research Institute offers consultancy services to estates. The state has long managed the estate labor market, and in 1980 it created the National Institute of Plantation Management (NIPM) to train estate managers. The state also owns the transport infrastructure servicing the tea industry. In fact, so many estate-sector institutions had been established by 1984 that the state had to create a National Tree Crop Policy Committee just to manage them.[53]

[50] World Bank, *Institutional and Policy Issues*, 1: 24; Fernando, "Challenges and Sacrifices," 4–6, 12.

[51] Bradman Weerakoon, "The Socio-Economic Environment," in *Aspects of Plantation Management in Sri Lanka*, ed. R. L. Wickremasinghe (Colombo: National Institute of Plantation Management, 1983), 120–22; Bandaranaike, "Tea Production," 23–24, 29; Sambasivam interview.

[52] World Bank, *Institutional and Policy Issues*, 1: 24–25.

[53] World Bank, *Fourth Tree Crops Project*, 9.

These institutions are a liability in restructuring, however. Sri Lanka lacks "the institutional infrastructure required for industrial development," and existing "state institutions . . . and institutional attitudes" are "outdated."[54] Estates can tap state funds, but entrepreneurs depend on a banking system that is "still largely [estate] export oriented" and shows "little interest in providing credit for industrial investment."[55] Except for the NIPM and a school for parastatal managers, Sri Lanka has no business or technical schools to train the personnel new industries need, nor any "organization in the major markets for any kind of promotion and feedback to producers" of nontraditional items.[56]

Sri Lanka has created new agencies to aid alternative sectors but they have failed. In 1966, it set up the Industrial Development Board (IDB), and in 1973 it established an Export Promotion Secretariat because "Sri Lanka had no export promotion machinery except that belonging to the tea industry."[57] In 1979 the secretariat became the Export Development Board (EDB), the executive arm of the Export Development Council of Ministers chaired by the president. The IDB and the EDB have achieved very little, however. The director general of the EDB, contrasting his organization to the Ministry of Plantations Industries, JEDB, SPC, and the Ministry of Industries and Scientific Affairs (MISA), which is the parent ministry of the parastatals, notes that "we are small, have no money, no effective mandate, and no real political constituency."[58] Likewise, the National Planning Division of the Ministry of Finance and Planning lacks the resources and clout "to sustain a policy dialogue within Government over the long run—much less to translate policies into effective investment instruments and projects."[59]

The IDB and the EDB are also under constant attack by those threatened by restructuring. The estate sector has its own minister to protect it and the president chairs the committees that oversee it. The parastatals, too, have MISA to protect their interests as well as its own against restructuring. In 1970, for example, MISA demanded an investigation of the IDB. The Committee of Inquiry, convened by

[54] NPD, *Public Investment, 1986–1990,* 110.

[55] H. N. Karunatilake, "The Public Sector in the National Economy," CBC *Staff Studies* 6 (September 1976): 181.

[56] Quote from EDB, *National Export Development Plan,* 1: 25–26. See also CBC, *Review of the Economy, 1984,* 72; NPD, *Public Investment, 1986–1990,* 120.

[57] Interviews with Kulantunga and Laneroll.

[58] Kulantunga interview.

[59] World Bank, *Institutional and Policy Issues,* 1: 37.

MISA, found that the IDB "detracted from the authority and responsibility of [MISA] by establishing a rival body with overlapping functions." Victory cemented MISA's control of industrial policy, enabling it to defend the ISI policies on which the parastatals depend and to block private-sector development.[60]

Tea and the Other Institutions of State

Sri Lanka's politicized civil service and parastatals also reflect tea's impact on absolute capacity. In each case, today's trials have arisen from past efforts to use tea revenues to achieve political and developmental goals—and the stickiness of the institutions created to do so. These efforts were not dictated by the characteristics of tea, but they would have been impossible without the easily obtained revenues it provided. Today, however, the civil service and the parastatals block restructuring, largely by depriving the state of the necessary funds, and force continued dependence on tea monies.

From the start, politicians sought to expand the civil service, make it more representative, and transform it from an administrative institution to an agent of change. But by the mid-1950s less principled motives prevailed. In a democracy with a stagnating economy, the power to appoint proved irresistible. Not merit, but "a recommendation from a politician of the party in power" became "more or less mandatory for entry into government service." By the early 1960s, all "lower-rung members of the bureaucracy were being appointed under political pressure. . . . [By 1968] political appointees had entered middle-rung positions. . . . By the end of the decade . . . politicization . . . extended to the highest positions," precipitating "the collapse of the bureaucracy as an independent arm of the government."[61]

Politicization "systematically undermined" the civil service and state capacity.[62] It shifted attention from long-term development to short-term party political ends and debased the civil service. Once high entry requirements were discarded in the mid-1950s, and ever since performance appraisal has been "almost totally absent."[63] As quality declined, the government ballooned from 40 departments in 1947 to

[60] Quote from Karunaratne, "Industrial Development Policy," 59; interviews with Dias, Tilakaratna, Fernando, Kulantunga, and Laneroll.

[61] G. H. Pieris, *Basic Needs and the Provision of Government Services in Sri Lanka*, WEP 2-32/WP.35 (Geneva: ILO, 1982), 183; "Management in the Public Sector," 7–8.

[62] Tilakaratna interview.

[63] Quotes from A. S. Amaraskera, "A More Efficient Administrative Service," *Economic Review* (July–August 1984), 28; and "Management in the Public Sector," 9.

150 by 1961; in the same period, the number of bureaucrats doubled and the payroll tripled. In the mid-1980s, 20–40 percent of Sri Lanka's 500,000 public servants were redundant; the cost of the redundancies alone was between 2.6 percent and 5.2 percent of the 1985 national budget. Size itself is a problem. Indeed, there are so many agencies making agricultural policy, for example, that in 1986 150 committees were needed to *coordinate* their activities.[64] In sum, the price of politicization is policy incoherence, increased expense, and administrative paralysis because of a civil service bound to maintenance of the status quo.

The parastatals that dominate the economy suffer similar debilities. They are the product of Sri Lanka's first effort to restructure, undertaken to displace foreign capital and tea, and to cure the Dutch disease by shifting resources away from the estates. But despite huge investments, the parastatals have failed to promote restructuring and are now *the* barrier to it, for they drain the economy and the state coffers, strengthening dependence on tea and inhibiting the development of alternatives.

The parastatal sector is huge. By the mid-1970s, parastatals accounted for 20 percent of fixed capital formation, 75 percent of industrial investment, 60 percent of industrial output, 80 percent of banking activities, 80 percent of exports and imports, and 60 percent of modern-sector employment.[65] And to support the parastatals, Sri Lanka created the National Institute of Business Management, the Academy of Administration, and the National Institute of Management to train parastatal managers and provide consulting services to them.

The scale of parastatal failure is also huge. The parastatals survive only because of subsidies or monopoly control of markets. When the state seized profitable, tax-paying firms, profits turned to losses, subsides offset tax payments, and productivity fell. Capital investment (less losses) in industrial parastatals rose from Rs 1,320 million to Rs 2,964 million from 1970 to 1975, but in 1975 parastatals earned profits of just Rs 69 million. In 1976 *total* parastatal contributions to the state's consolidated revenue fund were Rs 162, compared with Rs 548

[64] A. Ekanayake, "Evolution of the Bureaucracy in Sri Lanka," *Vidyodaya* 13 (January 1985): 17; World Bank figures, *Daily News*, June 6, 1986; World Bank, *Institutional and Policy Issues*, 1: 32.

[65] W. D. Lakshman, "Public Enterprises in the National Economy of Sri Lanka," *Modern Ceylon Studies* 6 (July 1975): 105–11; Il Sakong, "Macro-Economic Aspects of Public Enterprise in Asia" (Seoul: Korean Development Institute, 1979), 63–67; Karunatilake, "The Public Sector," 179–80; "Management in the Public Sector," 3–4.

million in estate-sector export duties alone.[66] Worse, capital invest-ment has depended on borrowing, though the parastatals' sad perfor-mance and inability to export have shifted the burden of debt service to others, and their borrowing has crowded out would-be investors in nontraditional exports. As of the mid-1980s the return on parastatal investment was less than 1 percent. No wonder the permanent secre-tary of the Ministry of Finance and Planning considers parastatal investment "a huge sacrifice."[67]

In part, this failure is the predictable result of implementing ISI policies in a tiny country; it also reflects the corrupting effects of patronage. Parastatal jobs are "an important part of the political spoils" that politicians can hand out, but as a result of such manipulation, by the late 1970s more than 50 percent of public managers had *no* pro-fessional qualifications.[68] Parastatal management is also open to polit-ical demands and disrupted by turnover with every change of govern-ment, thus hampering rational, long-term planning. On the shop floor, parties promise unions jobs and raises in return for support. But since the law forbids firing those hired by previous governments, this means hiring an entirely new, *additional* work force. In 1977 some parastatals had ten times as many workers as were needed.[69] The main problem, however, is that parastatal managers constitute a po-tent pressure group whose jobs depend on maintenance of the status quo. Because they are used to operating without regard to costs or profitability, lack the skills to compete, and head firms that cannot survive without subsidies and monopoly protection, they have every-thing to lose from restructuring and every reason to fight it.

CAPACITY OF BUSINESS AND LABOR FOR COLLECTIVE ACTION

If the characteristics of tea have crippled the state, they have facili-tated collective action by the tea industry and tea workers, and have

[66] G. H. Pieris, "Land Reform and Agrarian Change in Sri Lanka," *Modern Asian Studies* 12, no. 4 (1978): 627; Pannambalam, *Dependent Capitalism*, 103, 126–27; Ka-runatilake, "The Public Sector," 195.

[67] Quote and return on investment figure from Tilakaratna interview; Newton Gun-asinghe, "The Open Economy and Its Impact on Ethnic Relations in Sri Lanka," in *Sri Lanka: The Ethnic Conflict*, ed. Committee for Rational Development (New Dehli: Nav-rang, 1984), 200.

[68] Quote from "Management in the Public Sector," 10, 17; Tilakaratna interview.

[69] P. B. Karandawala, "Problems of Public Enterprise in a Developing Mixed Econ-omy," *Marga* 5, no. 1 (1978): 63; Fernando and Lakshman interviews.

given both incentives to fight restructuring. The small number of big firms facilitates collective action. After 1890, industry concentration increased sharply, as estates passed from private planters to corporate owners who assembled groups of estates under common control. In the 1960s, there were 329 estates of more than 500 hectares and 530 estates of 100–499 hectares, but there were just 150 tea companies, most of them tiny. In fact, before nationalization, three huge corporations—Lipton, Brooke Bond, and Tetley—controlled the industry, and after nationalization only JEDB and SPC did.[70] These firms have such big stakes that they need not worry about free riding by others; furthermore, their small number and knowledge of their own interests permit them to plan, implement, and enforce industry policies.

The agency houses that managed most tea estates prior to 1975 also reduced barriers to collective action. Again, just a few firms dominated. In 1970 six agency houses managed more than 30 percent of Sri Lankan tea lands; they accounted for 40 percent of tea production, 35 percent of export earnings, and 4 percent of the GNP. These firms competed for clients but shared an interest in defending tea, for their profits derived less from the success of any one estate or corporate client than from the overall profitability of the industry. Similarly, estate managers compete to produce quality tea, but the real "competition" is the international tea market. Tea men have thus long cooperated to promote Ceylon tea, since this effort alone could increase demand.[71] Managers of estates and agency houses had a strong, exclusive identity and membership in the "planters' raj" (the highest level of colonial, and now Sri Lankan, society), which strengthened their feeling of solidarity. Indeed, even today JEDB and SPC are "staffed almost exclusively by former private planters" who "maintain a certain identity and culture."[72]

The resources of the tea industry augment its capacity for collective

[70] Forrest, *A Hundred Years,* 146–47; Fernando, "Continuity and Change," 207; Peiris, "Plantation Agriculture," 233.

[71] "The Agency Houses," *Economic Review* (June 1975), 4; Fernando, "Continuity and Change," 135; W. D. Lakshman and Premachandra Athukorale, *A Study of the Structure of Trade Channels in Sri Lankan Foreign Trade* (UNCTC/ESCAP Joint Project on Transnational Corporations in Selected Asian and Pacific Countries, 1982), 9; Forrest, *A Hundred Years,* 170–73, 184–87, 196–200, 226.

[72] Quotes from World Bank, *Fourth Tree Crops Project,* 3; and "Tea and the Economy," 7 and 20. See also R. L. Wickremasinghe, "Basic Principles," in *Aspects of Plantation Management in Sri Lanka,* ed. R. L. Wickremasinghe (Colombo: National Institute of Plantation Management, 1983): 1; Ilangakoon and Ratnayaka interviews.

action. It dominates export earnings, tax revenue, and employment; its talented managers can analyze problems and call on powerful local and international allies for help. Prior to 1975, cross-investment among corporate owners and the agency houses linked the tea industry to international banks and to shipping, insurance, and equipment companies.[73] Domestically, the narrow Sri Lankan political elite has its origins in the estate revolution and includes, besides planters, mostly lawyers and public servants, many of whom now own estates and share an interest in defending the sector.[74]

The agent of collective action is the Planters' Association of Ceylon, founded in 1854. The association pursues planters' interests and has the political power to realize them. It began by seeking a seat on the Legislative Council, and in later years "could literally dictate policy . . . to the Governor."[75] It even acted on behalf of the colonial state, as when it organized the Tea Research Institute, the Ceylon Labor Commission, and the Ceylon Association of London, which still represents Sri Lankan interests in the City. The association also had ties to rubber and coconut planters and to the Low-Country Products Association (LCPA)—which, in turn, linked it to the Bank of Ceylon, founded with LCPA support, and to D. S. Senanayake, the first prime minister and an ex-LCPA chairman. The association had another tie to the political elite: a past president of the Ceylon Chamber of Commerce and member of Parliament became its first Sri Lankan chairman. Since nationalization of the estates in 1975, the Planters' Association has changed itself "from a defender of private plantation interests into a trade union of planter-managers in the state sector"; its members now run JEDB and SPC.[76]

The situation of estate labor is more complex. For a century, estate workers have constituted the largest labor group in Sri Lanka and have produced much of its wealth. They make up more than a quarter of union membership and their unions, especially the Ceylon Workers' Congress (CWC), are the best organized unions in Sri Lanka. Nor are estate workers shy about flexing their muscle: between 1962 and 1984, 6.3 times as many estate workers as other Sri Lankan

[73] "The Agency Houses," 5.
[74] K. M. de Silva, *A History of Sri Lanka* (Delhi: Oxford University Press, 1981), 333–37; James Jupp, *Sri Lanka—Third World Democracy* (London: Frank Cass, 1978), 44; Peiris, "Plantation Agriculture," 217.
[75] Quote from Ilangakoon interview. See also de Silva, *A History of Sri Lanka,* 357–58; Forrest, *A Hundred Years,* 180–81.
[76] Forrest, *A Hundred Years,* 183, 188–91; "Management in the Public Sector," 12.

workers engaged in 4.8 times as many strikes at a cost of 2.7 times more worker days lost than were lost as a result of all other strike activity.[77] Still, until 1977 estate workers lived in squalor because planters squeezed their wages and the state taxed away the profits of their labor to benefit others. Then the CWC's president joined the new UNP government in 1977, and their fortunes soared.

Estates require abundant, cheap, permanent labor, but when the tea boom began in the 1880s there were no landless Sinhalese peasants, and landowning peasants refused to work for the wages offered or to become full-time estate workers. Importing Tamils from India solved both problems: they were cheap and had no job opportunities except those on the estates. By 1931 there were 700,000 Indian Tamils in Sri Lanka. Initially, their circumstances prevented organization. Workers were confined to their estates, further isolated by language barriers, illiteracy, and rudimentary communications. Until the 1920s, most saw themselves as temporary sojourners and would not invest in organization efforts despite bad working conditions. The kangany labor recruiters who supplied labor to the estates brutally suppressed all organization, and the Planters' Association pressured the state to bar unionization. The system, one planter confided in 1908, "is slavery, . . . nothing else."[78]

But by 1920 the barriers to organization were falling. The tea industry had stopped growing and the Indian Tamils constituted a permanent work force living in stable, closed communities. The kangany system had faded "and the ties that kept the worker in bondage to the kangany . . . loosened, making the development of trade unionism feasible."[79] Planters and government officials saw the need for new forms of labor management, and in 1927 the Minimum Wage Ordinance was passed, which set wages and conditions of employment and created Wage Boards to oversee both. Maturation of the industry and the resulting density of estates eased communication among estate workers, and as more of them achieved literacy they had access to politics and union activities. Urban middle-class Indians championed the estate workers and in 1931 helped them form the All-Ceylon

[77] Heidrun Marby, *Tea in Ceylon* (Wiesbaden: Franz Steiner Verlag, 1972), 152–53; CBC, *Review of the Economy, 1984*, Appendix Table 55.

[78] Cited in Jayawardena, *The Rise of the Labor Movement*, 16–23. See also Snodgrass, *Ceylon*, 24–26, 64–65.

[79] Quote from Jayawardena, *The Rise of the Labor Movement*, 333–34. See also de Silva, *A History of Sri Lanka*, 464–65.

Estate Labor Federation, thus laying the base of what would become the most powerful labor movement in Sri Lanka.

The 1931 Donoughmore Constitution enfranchised 100,000 estate workers, giving them a loud voice in the tea districts, where they constituted as much as half of the population. They elected two Indians to represent them, one of whom, Peri Sunderam, became the minister of labor, industry, and commerce. During the depression he and other candidates elected with estate workers' votes defended them against planters who were demanding relief from the minimum wage. Urban trade unionists and members of the Ceylon National Congress, however, used Tamil victories to mobilize Sinhalese support and ultimately to gain passage of the 1948 Ceylon Citizenship Act, which disenfranchised estate workers, thereby permitting politicians to exclude them from the social welfare bonanza they paid for with profits taxed away from tea—profits born of low estate wages.[80]

Estate production offers ideal conditions for labor organization. Estates concentrate large numbers of workers who labor in dispersed gangs with limited supervision and are easily sanctioned if they violate group norms. Skill levels are low, but barriers to new immigration and the peasants' refusal to do estate work give workers leverage; and lacking transferable skills, they have incentives to invest in labor organization. No occupational differentiation divides workers who are bound together in closed communities that reinforce solidarity. Indeed, because they are isolated by language and religion, denied a political voice, and generally excluded from Sri Lankan society, their unions are the sole expression of Indian Tamil–estate worker identity.[81]

Organized estate labor confronts organized planters who have incentives to fight and deal. High labor intensity gives planters incentives to resist unionization. Thus, the Planters' Association and the Ceylon Estates Employers Federation make a determined effort to influence estate labor laws; they ignore work rules, coordinate opposition to labor organization, attack worker representatives, and seek to ensure that labor contracts preserve maximum flexibility. But planters also worry about potentially disastrous work stoppages and about

[80] Jayawardena, *The Rise of the Labor Movement*, 341–42, 350–54; Robert Kearney, *Trade Unions and Politics in Ceylon* (Berkeley: University of California Press, 1971), 24; de Silva, *A History of Sri Lanka*, 422–24; Fernando, "Continuity and Change," 169.

[81] Interviews with Ilangakoon and Devaraj; Ceylon Workers' Congress, "A Statement Adopted by the National Council of the C.W.C. at an Emergency Meeting Held on 14th August 1983" (Colombo, n.d.), 2; Edith Bond, *The State of Tea* (London: War on Want, 1974), 2, 8.

sabotage to factories and fields. The best way to avoid both, they have found, is to deal with a strong union able to control its members.[82]

The CWC's success, especially when compared with that of other unions, reflects the importance of these sectoral factors in facilitating collective action. In fact, the CWC is the dominant union in Sri Lanka today, for unlike other unions, it is a "shop floor" union dedicated to advancing its members' interests as workers. Founded in 1940 as the labor arm of the Ceylon Indian Congress, it established its position by tackling estate workers' primary concerns: wages, working conditions, and gaining citizenship.[83] It flourished: by 1949 it had 118,000 members; by 1951 it had 135,000; by 1967 it had 350,000 (more than a quarter of all union members in Sri Lanka); and by 1971 it had 382,000. Its membership now exceeds 400,000. In fact, the CWC's success is so widely recognized that many Sinhalese unions hire CWC advisers.[84]

The CWC's capacity for collective action makes it a strong force in Sri Lankan politics. Its shop floor focus allows it "to avoid permanent partisan attachments, . . . maintain its freedom to bargain among competing parties," and pressure all politicians to aid estate workers.[85] Though few members can vote, all contribute to the CWC's big political fund, and CWC solidarity means that its president, S. Thondaman, delivers members' votes as a bloc. The weight of this bloc continues to increase, for successive governments have reregistered Indian Tamils in return for CWC support—only to be abandoned at the next election when bigger concessions were offered by the opposition. Indeed, the CWC has a perfect record of electoral vacillation. In 1960 it backed the Sri Lanka Freedom Party (SLFP) for a seat in Parliament. In 1965 it backed the UNP in return for two seats and promises for increased voter registration, only to back the SLFP again in 1970. The SLFP's ties to Sinhalese nationalism and its attacks on estate workers led the CWC to switch again in 1977, giving the UNP the victory and earning Thondaman one of the most secure seats in the cabinet.[86]

The nationalization of the estates in 1975 cemented the CWC's power by making estate workers state employees and so, in effect,

[82] Interviews with Panabokke, Ilangakoon, and Devaraj; Jayawardena, *The Rise of the Labor Movement*, 344–47; Kearney, *Trade Unions*, 18–19, 32–36, 123.

[83] Jupp, *Third World Democracy*, 146.

[84] Kearney, *Trade Unions*, 121–23; Fernando, "Continuity and Change," 171; Devaraj interview.

[85] Kearney, *Trade Unions*, 127.

[86] Ibid., 126–28; Devaraj interview; W. A. Wissa Warnapala and L. Dias Hewagama, *Recent Politics in Sri Lanka* (New Dehli: Navrang, 1983), 121.

moving the union into the heart of the state.[87] To increase industry profits and state revenues, the government tried to squeeze labor costs; to crate jobs for Sinhalese peasants and rid Sri Lanka of Indian Tamils, it pushed repatriation of estate workers. Both policies backfired. Sinhalese peasants lacked the skills necessary to replace experienced Tamil pluckers and few came forward, resulting in labor shortages, declining production, and greater leverage for the CWC.[88] Nationalization also eased the CWC's task by giving all estate workers a single employer, the state; CWC labor actions were now political actions, and the CWC's ability to pressure the planters became a potent political weapon that could be used against the state, which had replaced them.

In particular, the CWC could block restructuring at estate workers' expense.[89] The deal the CWC struck with the UNP in 1977 included a final resolution of the question of estate workers' citizenship, assurance of a political voice for estate workers in the tea districts, and better wages and benefits. The first two enhanced CWC power by undoing the Ceylon Citizenship Act and returning estate workers to the political mainstream. The third locked the state in a losing battle with the CWC over restructuring. Thus, despite the tea industry's flagging performance and the state's need to raise revenues, cut costs, and move monies from tea to other sectors, Thondaman forced an immediate 79 percent increase in estate workers' minimum wages and benefits. When inflation erased these gains, he called for further increases in 1982. A tug-of-war ensued and in April 1984 the CWC took 600,000 estate workers out on strike, shutting down the industry. The strike was, in Thondaman's words, "a great success" and confirmed the CWC's ability to defy state efforts to restructure.[90]

AUTONOMY: CONTROLLING THE CHANNELS OF INTEREST REPRESENTATION

For Sri Lanka, the issue of state autonomy is: Can leaders formulate a restructuring project free from societal pressures? Indeed, do they have an interest in doing so?

[87] Interviews with Ilangakoon, Devaraj, de Silva, and Peiris.

[88] Fernando, "Continuity and Change," 238.

[89] The following discussion is based on interviews with de Silva, Ilangakoon, Peiris, and Devaraj.

[90] Ranasinghe, "Tea and Underdevelopment," 14–15; S. Thondaman, speech to the ICFTU-APRO Executive Board meeting, Pattaya, Thailand, August 28–30, 1985 (mimeographed), 11.

168

Before 1947 planters filled the channels of interest representation. By 1850 they had access to the governor and had their own member on the Legislative Council, thus giving them "an influential voice in the disbursement of the government's contingent expenditure."[91] By the 1890s, industry concentration ensured that the Planters' Association voiced clear policy preferences. For its part, the weak colonial state could not manage the industry and depended on agencies created by the association to do so. Even when they were absorbed by the state, these agencies remained committed to the industry, with which they continuously exchanged information and personnel. The industry also had influential advocates in, for example, the Public Works Department, which was powerful because it maintained the infrastructure that serviced the estates.[92] Finally, planters belonged to the small colonial upper crust and thus had easy, informal access to officials. Indeed, many planters were retired colonial officials who "stayed on."

After 1947 the state temporarily gained more control of the channels of interest representation. Indeed, until 1977 policy makers made tea the main target of revenue extraction and froze estate sector–related public investment. In part, this reflected an ability to use state sovereignty against foreign estate owners. But much of the apparent increase in autonomy was the obverse of the state's *decreased* autonomy from overwhelming societal pressures born of the tea-induced concentration of the national wealth and job opportunities in the state. Then in 1975 nationalization dispelled even the appearance of greater autonomy, for it melded tea industry and state interests, both represented in a single entity headed by the president himself.[93]

Sectoral and Societal Pressures

Intense sectoral and societal pressures help to explain leaders' lack of autonomy. Production inflexibility forces planters to demand state relief when prices fall; asset/factor inflexibility forces planters and workers alike to fight restructuring. But all other Sri Lankans want to penetrate the state, too: it is the funnel through which tea revenues flow; it allocates the national wealth. The state itself has thus become a plantation to be plucked, for outside the estates, it alone promises

[91] de Silva, *A History of Sri Lanka,* 357–58.
[92] Forrest, *A Hundred Years,* 188–90; I. H. vanden Driesen, "Some Trends in the Economic History of Ceylon in the 'Modern' Period," *Ceylon Journal of Historical and Social Studies* 3 (January–June 1960): 8–9, 14–15.
[93] Fernando interview.

power, wealth, and prestige. No wonder a survey of university graduates in the early 1970s found that 94 percent of the respondents wanted government jobs and 76 percent would work for parastatals, but only 1.5 percent would consider working for the private sector.[94]

Pressures to penetrate the state explain the politicization of labor. By the mid-1980s some 45 percent of workers belonged to one of more than 1,100 unions. Virtually all have party affiliations; most are controlled by politicians without shop floor input or organization and depend on parties for money, office space, and staff. Still, despite stagnant per capita real income and high unemployment nationally, the unions increased their members' real wages 150 percent between 1949 and 1978—2 to 3 percent per annum—by combining with politicians to penetrate the state and tap the tea monies.[95]

The labor movement was tied to tea from the start, for an urban working class arose along with development of the industries supporting the estates. But urban Sinhalese workers did not collaborate with estate workers, since higher wages for them turned on tea's profitability and estate workers' continued exploitation. Nor was collaboration in the interest of their middle-class leaders who were also tied to the estate sector.[96] Thus began a cozy rent-sharing relationship: labor gave elite politicians the constituency needed to gain access to the state and its resources; in return, the politicians promoted nonestate labor, higher wages, and social welfare spending financed by tea taxes. As a CWC official put it, "You could allow unions to develop, and political and civil rights, and whatnot *because* you had the productive estates sector where estate workers could be exploited."[97]

The resulting loss of autonomy is conspicuous in the case of public-sector unions. State employees got permission to organize in 1948; by 1963 more than 400,000 belonged to unions. These unions are militant and "particularly prone to partisan alignment," as controlling

[94] R. K. Srivastava, "The Unemployment Problem," *Marga* 2, no. 2 (1974): 57–58.
[95] Robert Kearney, "Militant Public Service Trade Unionism in a New State," *Journal of Asian Studies* 25 (May 1966): 397–98; and Kearney, *Trade Unions*, 16–17, 47–48, 79–83; W. D. Lakshman, "The Sri Lanka Ports Authority," in *Workers' Self-Management and Participation in Practice,* ed. Ales Vahcic and Grobovsek Smole (Ljubljana: International Center for Public Enterprises, 1986), 242; Hewavitharana, "Recent Trends," 27; P. C. Rodrigo, "Wage Behavior in the Sri Lankan Economy, 1949–1978," *Modern Ceylon Studies* 7, nos. 1 and 2 (1976): 180.
[96] Jayawardena, "The Origins of the Left Movement," 196; and Jayawardena, *The Rise of the Labor Movement,* 332–33.
[97] Devaraj interview.

them offers a powerful weapon.[98] But more important, the state is the employer against which they are organized, and their success is measured by the extent to which they influence the policy process. By this metric they are *very* successful, having reversed cuts in social welfare and transfer payments, blocked work rule changes, and toppled prime ministers. Today, these unions are bitterly opposed to restructuring; they continue to fight efforts to increase parastatal efficiency and demand "laxity in adherence to rules for the Government party loyalists."[99]

A glance at Sri Lankan democracy reveals a pernicious pattern similar to that of party politics in Zambia. There are hotly contested elections and regular changes of government, but "the real core of Sri Lankan politics is patronage," initially made possible by seemingly unlimited tea revenues.[100] The exigencies of the electoral system forced politicians to mobilize voters; "mass political parties . . . served as instruments whereby the political elite maintained and rationalized its rule under mass suffrage" by articulating encompassing patronage networks.[101] But once in place, the patronage system had to be fed, and its rising demands choked the state and economy.

The Donoughmore Constitution linked tea and democracy and established the basic pattern of politics that endures to this day. The British retained authority over the Exchequer, police, and judiciary but entrusted the rest of government to elected officials. This "combination of politicians under democratic political pressure to serve the voters and a healthy treasury" led to the rapid growth of a "state-welfarist system," as politicians used state funds to "buy off the masses with welfare" to stay in office and *prevent* calls for changes that would imperil their power.[102] Thus, despite a decline in revenues and total spending, they increased absolute and relative spending on social welfare dramatically—by slashing public investment. An apt appraisal of spending in the 1930s is still accurate: "While the social investment of the period was both socially justifiable and politically expedient, the neglect of complementary real investment in the fields of produc-

[98] Kearney, "Militant Public Service Trade Unionism," 399; and Kearney, *Trade Unions,* 171.

[99] Quote from "Management in the Public Sector," 12; Kearney, "Militant Public Service Trade Unionism," 403–4; and Kearney, *Trade Unions,* 3, 39; Lakshman, "The Sri Lanka Ports Authority," 289–90.

[100] Interview with Kanesalingam.

[101] Jupp, *Third World Democracy,* 96, 119.

[102] de Silva interview.

tive economic activity [blocked] long-term structural and institutional transformation," and consequently left politicians ever more dependent on tea monies.[103]

The problem has worsened since 1947. Government spending rose almost twice as fast as revenues between 1947 and 1965, driven by social welfare spending and transfer payments, which by the mid-1950s accounted for 40 percent of the budget, were more than 50 percent of the budget in 1965, and constituted 69 percent in 1979. These provided "a safety valve" and were "political and psychological compensation for the failure of the government to undertake a successful development plan." They also helped *cause* the failure, preventing future growth by diverting funds from economic services and capital investment, which fell from 19 percent to 14 percent of the budget in the period 1960–75.[104]

Winner-take-all access to the pork barrel also gave rise to a politics of inclusion, not transformation, for politicians fashioned coalitions the sole aim of which was to seize and share in the rents from tea. Victory went to the best coalition-building effort at the price of "ill-conceived policies intended more to settle internal political problems than advance the national welfare." Indeed, "the welfare program . . . formed the centerpiece of government activity" because it permitted "a social consensus across political ideologies," whereas real development programs risked dividing constituents.[105] Falling tea prices and the resulting revenue and foreign exchange crises forced politicians to go further, however.

Each step politicians took damaged the economy. They seized opponents' businesses and rewarded followers with jobs in the new "national" firms, which then lost money. They added services and doled out jobs—repeatedly expanding the school system, for example, to create jobs for "politically correct" teachers—and used land reform to

[103] Fernando, "Patterns of Investment," 129–30.

[104] Ibid., 357–70, 432–33, 481–86; Warnasena Rasaputram, "Changes in the Pattern of Income Inequality in Ceylon," *Marga* 1, no. 4 (1972): 88; Gratien Jayamahu, "The Growth of Public Expenditure in Sri Lanka, 1960–1975," CBC *Staff Studies* 6 (September 1976): 78–81; Godfrey Gunatilleke, "Participatory Development and Dependence," *Marga* 5, no. 3 (1978): 77; Marga Institute, *Welfare and Growth in Sri Lanka*, Marga Research Studies, no. 2 (1974): 19–21; Wickremeratne, "Planning and Economic Development," 150.

[105] Quotes from interview with Canekeratne; and Gunatilleke, "Participatory Development," 77.

reward rural notables and their peasant constituents.[106] Starting in 1958, they also tightened economic controls and distributed the resulting scarcity rents as patronage. In Colombo, access to scarce foreign exchange and import licenses bought the support of the powerful; Village Councils, Rural Development Societies, and District Political Authorities put scarce resources in the hands of rural notables who provided votes for the ruling coalition. And the worse things got, the more people needed such patronage goods, and the greater the political value of continuing the controls that were killing the economy.[107]

Defining State and "National" Interests

Clearly, it is impossible to define a state interest autonomous of sectoral interests. Sri Lanka suffers from the political equivalents of production inflexibility and asset/factor inflexibility. In the short run, the politicization of daily life led voters to view tapping politicians as the only way to get what they needed. Delivering what voters requested earned politicians votes, but as a result "the major political objectives of the government as a whole became almost indistinguishable from the electoral objectives of individual politicians."[108] In the long run, the growth of economic controls gave politicians perverse incentives. Whatever the potential benefits of trade liberalization and deregulation, they threaten politicians' sources of patronage, the value of which increases as the economy declines. Tea remains critical because it is the primary supplier of revenues and foreign exchange.

Policy has thus been distributional, not developmental, because the state lacks the autonomy necessary to resist short-run societal pressure and to invest in long-run restructuring. As the economic crisis has worsened, asset/factor inflexibility and the related lack of alternative sectors have forced politicians to return to defining the interests of the estate sector as their own. Having tapped tea to build a costly,

---

[106] Karandawala, "Problems of Public Enterprise," 55; Gunatilleke, "Participatory Development," 75–77; Pieris, "Land Reform," 623–26; and Pieris, *Basic Needs*, 183–86; Gunasinghe, "The Open Economy," 203–4.

[107] Interview with Lakshman; G. H. Pieris, "Local Level Institutions and Participation in Sri Lanka," in *Employment, Resource Mobilization, and Basic Needs through Local Level Planning* (Bangkok: ILO, 1979), 229.

[108] Godfrey Gunatilleke, "Development and the Elites," *Marga* 1, no. 2 (1971): 56.

unviable parastatal sector and an equally costly state superstructure, and having encouraged high public expectations, they are stuck. They must cover state commitments, but they lack other sources of revenue and foreign exchange, as well as the capacity to develop them. No wonder the government concluded in 1983 that "the recovery and rehabilitation of the Plantation Industries have . . . become an imperative need for Sri Lanka."[109]

NATIONALIZING THE ESTATES

Nationalization of the estates capped Sri Lanka's effort to seize control of the future—and proved that the past holds it in thrall. Early talk of nationalization went nowhere, for as the SLFP prime minister S.W.R.D. Bandaranaike reminded Sri Lankans in the 1950s, "we can't kill the goose that lays the golden eggs."[110] In 1971, however, the People's United Front government, facing problems of land pressure, rural joblessness, and the Jatika Vimukti Peramuna uprising they had stimulated, reopened the discussion. In 1972 the legislature passed the Land Reform Act, which put 563,000 acres, including 139,000 acres of tea, in state hands. The act affected the big tea estates only marginally because it excluded corporate holdings, but it raised such doubts about the future that corporate owners slashed maintenance expenditures and investment, resulting in depressed production and long-term damage to the estates.[111]

In 1975 Sri Lanka nationalized corporate lands as well, seizing 395 estates that comprised 418,000 acres, 240,000 of which were planted with tea. Sri Lanka now controlled 63 percent of the tea lands and the biggest, most productive estates, but at a huge cost.[112] "The aura of plantation wealth led politicians to believe that nationalization would produce a great revenue windfall, a quick fix" that would permit them to "support the hugely inefficient parastatal sector" and to diver-

[109] National Planning Division, Ministry of Finance and Planning, *Medium Term Investment Programme for the State Owned Plantations: Project Identification Report* (Colombo, June 1983), 3.

[110] Cited in Nimal Sanderatne, "The Political Economy of Asian Agrarian Reform" (Ph.D. diss., University of Wisconsin, 1974), p. 431.

[111] Ibid., 417; Fernando, "Continuity and Change," 210–20.

[112] Fernando, "Continuity and Change," 207–8; Balakrishnan, "A Review of the Economy," 113.

sify.[113] But the payment of compensation to foreign owners worsened the foreign exchange crisis, and many of the estates had huge backlogs of deferred maintenance. Thus, whereas the agency houses "were interested in lengthening the life of the [estates] rather than in maximizing their net profit," the state had to maximize current revenues to the detriment of the sector's future viability.[114]

The state also could not manage the estates, which were divided between two weak organizations reporting to different ministries. The acreage supervised by SPC, which was already under attack for bad management, doubled in 1975; JEDB, which was created in 1976, immediately assumed responsibility for 145,000 acres of tea, as well as large areas planted with other crops.[115] Overcentralization and red tape increased costs. There was a constant turnover of managers, and political hacks—some who were bus drivers and barkeepers—took over. The "management level plunged"; the new appointees "destroyed what were . . . the best-managed plantations in the world." Yield and quality fell "like a stone." Whatever profits SPC and JEDB showed reflected the increase in lands under their control, not improved economic performance.[116]

The state's travails with nationalization reveal its lack of autonomy. Nationalization gave politicians with no other options a wealth of patronage to distribute and the perfect sop with which to placate peasants in key tea district constituencies. Thus, they sacrificed the industry for short-term gains—"economics and the national interest be damned!"[117] Most damaging, given the importance of economies of scale in tea production, politicians parceled out bits of estates to smallholders and ignored village encroachments on estate lands. The acreage losses reduced the estates' viability; production on the fragmented lands fell by 40 percent between 1973 and 1982. The

---

[113] Interviews with Ratnayaka, Ilangakoon, and de Silva.

[114] Quote from K. E. Knorr, cited in de Silva, "Plantations and Underdevelopment," 27; de Silva and Ratnayaka interviews.

[115] Fernando, "Continuity and Change," 228–35.

[116] Quotes from Ilangakoon interview. See also Fernando, "Continuity and Change," 245; A. K. M. Masihur Rahman, "Political Economy of Income Distribution" (Ph.D. diss., Fletcher School of Diplomacy, 1980), 185.

[117] Quote from Ilangakoon interview. One report states: "The measures adopted so far have been excessively motivated by a desire, maybe indeliberate, of quick gain in a process where everyone has an eye on the majority vote of the Sinhala villager." "Memorandum of the Coordinating Secretariat for Plantation Areas to the Steering Committee on Estate-Village Integration," mimeographed (Kandy, 1978), 2.

resulting losses constitute the biggest element in the 2.2 million kg per year decline in production during the same period which also drained the export earnings.[118]

The failure of nationalization set the stage for Sri Lanka's second attempt to restructure. By 1977 the economy had hit bottom, and for the first time in decades the costs of *not* restructuring seemed to outweigh the risks of plunging ahead. The 1977 election produced a new government and indicated the voters' rejection of thirty years of economic policy. The IMF and the World Bank promised help, and coincidentally tea and rubber prices surged, giving Sri Lanka its first positive balance of trade in fifteen years and the highest foreign reserves since the Korean War.[119] All did not go well, however.

RELATIVE CAPACITY: TAKING ON THE CRISIS

The UNP program proposed a "shift in public priorities from social consumption to public investment, and from social security to aggregate growth."[120] It sought to remove ISI policies that hindered competition and to liberalize tariffs, eliminate public-sector monopolies as well as subsidies and price controls, end import licensing, free exchange rates, promote exports, induce foreign and private investment, privatize parastatals, reform public management, establish new institutions to carry out the new policies, and reform existing ones.[121]

The new policies sparked changes. Import barriers fell. Investment, aid, and imports poured in, increasing capacity utilization, quintupling the value of industrial production, and boosting manufactures' share of exports from 4 percent to 25 percent in the period 1977–84. Capital spending rose from 28 percent of the budget in 1975–77 to 42 percent in 1981–83. Investment's share of GDP increased from 13 percent to 27–28 percent between 1977 and 1986. In the same period, unemployment fell from 26 percent to 14 percent,

118 Pieris interview; Fernando, "Continuity and Change," 251–52; Bandaranaike, "Tea Production," 12–15, 42.
119 De Silva, *A History of Sri Lanka,* 561; CBC, *Review of the Economy, 1984,* 125.
120 Herring, "An Assessment," 1.
121 Athukorale, "The Impact of 1977 Policy Reforms," 72–78; World Bank, *Sri Lanka and the World Bank,* 8–13, 99–101; EDB, *National Export Development Plan,* vol. 1 passim; Blackton, "The Private Sector"; and "Export Incentives and Other Assistance Provided by the Export Development Board," *Economic Review* (July–August 1984), 16–19.

and the annual growth rate jumped from less than 2 percent (1970–77) to 5.8 percent (1977–86). Some state monopolies were ended, parastatal jobs were cut, efforts were initiated to improve public management, and new export-supporting institutions were created, notably the EDB, the Export Credit Insurance Corporation, and the Greater Colombo Economic Commission.[122]

But problems linger. Revenues still depend on indirect, trade-based taxes and are "quite inadequate." The annual net cash deficit increased from less than 32 percent of revenues in 1970–77 to 95 percent in the early 1980s; the tax effort decreased from 25.7 percent of GDP in 1970–77 to 16.5 percent in 1978–82.[123] Unreformed old institutions stifled entrepreneurship and the new ones failed to divert investment to export production. Two industries, refining and garments, accounted for nearly all the growth in nontraditional exports, and "the export coefficients . . . of the remaining product categories have declined . . . reflecting an increase in domestic market orientation." Moreover, both industries are dominated by foreign firms, are import-intensive, and net little foreign exchange.[124]

The state lacks the autonomy to restructure. The budget is imbalanced because politicians cannot control spending and have *exempted* social welfare spending "from the expenditure pruning exercise."[125] Equally important, parastatal managers and their allies within the state have blocked privatization, efforts to professionalize management, and plans to cut budget-busting subsidies. Indeed, operating subsidies to nonservice parastatals exceeded Rs 40 billion in the period 1978–85, which was Rs 10 billion more than the expected cost of the huge Accelerated Mahavelli Scheme, a massive hydroelectric, infrastructure, and irrigation project and the biggest public investment program ever undertaken by the Sri Lankan government.[126]

---

[122] World Bank, *Sri Lanka and the World Bank*, 11–13, 99–100; CBC, *Review of the Economy, 1984*, Appendix Tables 22–24; Athukorale, "The Impact of 1977 Policy Reforms," 92, 98; EDB, *National Export Development Plan, 1983–1987*, 2: 40–43, 99–106; Lakshman, "State Policy," 12; Tilakaratna and Lakshman interviews; Blackton, "The Private Sector," 738–39.

[123] Quote from Lakshman, "State Policy in Sri Lanka," 16. See also NPD, *Public Investment, 1986–1990*, 15.

[124] Quote from Athukorale, "The Impact of 1977 Policy Reforms," 92; World Bank, *Sri Lanka and the World Bank*, 100; EDB, *National Export Development Plan*, 1: 2, 18–19.

[125] NPD, *Public Investment, 1986–1990*, 4.

[126] Lakshman, "State Policy," 10; Athukorale, "The Impact of 1977 Policy Reforms," 82–83; Ronnie de Mel, "Annual Budget Address" (Colombo, 1985).

Haunted by the Past

Sri Lanka's problem is the double legacy of tea: the consequences of tea dependence and of state actions to counter them. The archaic tax system binds revenue to trade, exposing the state to external shocks, limiting tax returns, and ensuring that efforts to hike current revenue will cut future revenue, deplete national assets, and slow restructuring. In 1978, for example, the UNP program increased revenue needs by 60 percent, 67 percent of which had to be raised by increasing export duties on tea 1800–2540 percent, dealing a blow to modernization efforts. The continued dependence on customs duties also protects domestic producers and tends to reduce exports. Finally, the key business turnover Tax, which is levied at successive stages of production because the tax agency cannot tax value added at different stages, prevents forward and backward linkages in manufacturing.[127]

Institutional stickiness retards restructuring. Cutting infrastructure-related costs, which account for 10–20 percent of the cost of exports, is a key to export competitiveness. But Sri Lanka's infrastructure reflects the estate sector's needs, and reorienting it will cost a fortune: Rs 7.6 billion for power generation, Rs 4.4 billion for communications, Rs 3.5 billion for rail rehabilitation, Rs 1.6 billion to modernize Port Colombo.[128] The state also cannot promote new sectors because existing institutions cannot help exporters "identify and target dynamic comparative advantage situations." Moreover, "credit availability to the export sector has been grossly inadequate" because the banking system is structured to finance the estate sector and short-term, self-liquidating commercial ventures.[129]

Sri Lanka also lacks exporters. Import competition after 1977 bankrupted many small, protection-dependent firms, and because of that competition, most new entrepreneurs have invested in real estate, tourism, and self-liquidating trade ventures. Export promotion has failed to overcome the import substitution bias of tariff, tax, and exchange rate policy.[130] Public firms, too, have failed to meet the import competition and therefore do not export. The state thus has no entrepreneurial allies in the restructuring effort and faces heavy opposition from established producers who cannot compete.[131]

[127] Pannambalam, *Dependent Capitalism,* 153; Bandaranaike, "Tea Production," 39; World Bank, *Sri Lanka and the World Bank,* 34; Blackton, "The Private Sector," 739–41.
[128] EDB, *National Export Development Plan,* 2: 138–45.
[129] Quotes from Ibid., 1: 8–11; and Sanderatne interview.
[130] Interviews with Warnakulasooriya.
[131] Interviews with Tilakaratna, Fernando, Peiris, Kulantunga, Laneroll, Sanderatne,

Sri Lanka has three options, none of them good: depend on foreign direct investment, continue business as usual, or revalorize tea. Since 1977 FDI has escalated, bringing in billions of rupees. In 1985, foreign-invested firms employed 100,000 workers and provided access to inputs, technology, and markets. Despite these firms' declining share of primary exports between 1977 and 1982, their share of exports rose from 21.9 percent to 26.4 percent, and their share of manufactured exports rose from 23.6 percent to 45.5 percent.[132] But to lure investors, Sri Lanka has had to offer generous tax holidays, exemptions from exchange controls and customs duties, and the lowest FTZ wages in Asia, thus limiting FDI's contribution to widening the tax base or increasing personal income. The import-intensive new industries offer few linkages to local firms and net little foreign exchange.[133] Garment industry investments by firms headquartered in Korea, Taiwan, and Hong Kong invited protectionist pressure on the part of OECD countries and denied local firms the traditional first foothold in the manufactures trade. Worse, in 1985 64 percent of foreign-invested firms outside the FTZs exported nothing and were likely crowding out local producers.[134]

The state has also muddled along. Despite the reforms, high effective rates of protection continue to "favor import-substituting industries and raise exporters' costs to uncompetitive levels."[135] Despite devaluations, the real exchange rate appreciated steadily after 1977. By 1986 it was at least 25 percent overvalued, the effect of which was to boost export earnings from tea and to cut debt service, but also to increase imports and kill nontraditional exports. A finance ministry official explains: "You can't [restructure] without hurting somebody—and everybody who might get hurt has access to the gov-

---

and Jayamahu; "Trends in the Open Economy," *Economic Review* (October–November 1982), 29–30; Athukorale, "The Impact of 1977 Policy Reforms," 82, 87–91; CBC, *Economic Performance in the First Half of 1985*, 12.

[132] NPD, *Public Investment, 1986–1990*, 103–8; Gunasinghe, "The Open Economy," 208; Premachandra Athukorale, "Direct Foreign Investment and Manufactured Export Expansion," *Vidyodaya* 12 (February 1984): 32–33; and Athukorale, "The Impact of 1977 Policy Reforms," 96.

[133] EDB, *National Export Development Plan, 1983–1987*, 1: 2, 16–19; Athukorale, "Direct Foreign Investment," 21–23; "Katunayake Industrial Processing Zone," *Economic Review* (June 1982), 8–9; Voice of Women, *Women Workers in the Free Trade Zone of Sri Lanka* (Colombo, 1983), 2, 31; "A Social Profile of Labor at the FTZ," *Economic Review* (June 1982), 16–17; and EDB, *National Export Development Plan*, 2: 45–46.

[134] Lakshman interview; Athukorale, "The Impact of 1977 Policy Reforms," 88.

[135] Quotes from interviews with Tilakaratna, and Kulantunga.

ernment!"[136] Business leaders and parastatal managers lobby for protection, subsidies, and relief from pressure to improve efficiency—and find many officials predisposed to listen. The MISA, for example, believes that Sri Lanka should "build and defend" local industry "even if it produces at less than the international level of efficiency." Even reformist politicians defend the parastatals, which "are too valuable a political resource" to clean up or privatize.[137]

But continuing business as usual solves neither Sri Lanka's problems nor those of its politicians. Foreign debt and imports are soaring, exports are flagging, and so the debt service, balance-of-trade, and balance-of-payments situations are deteriorating. At home, business as usual cannot meet rising public demands and increased patronage needs. Since restructuring is out, the only hope is to retreat to a renewed dependence on tea. No wonder that revitalizing the tea industry has nearly unanimous support both within government and without; the director of national planning comments wryly that it will "provide the resources necessary . . . to carry on as before!"[138]

Back to Tea

Simply restoring the estates posed daunting problems because they had been starved of investment, undermaintained, mismanaged, and plundered for so long. By the early 1980s production had dropped an average of 1.87 million kgs per year since 1968, cutting Sri Lanka's share of world tea exports to less than 20 percent by 1984. Half of its tea bushes are more than seventy years old and many fields produce only a third of what new ones do. Tea factories are "worn out and obsolete." Most are too small to compete with modern MES factories and do not use the type of equipment needed to meet "increasing world demand for small leaf grades for the tea bag trade."[139]

The 1983 Medium Term Investment Program (MTIP) embodies

[136] Quote from Fernando interview; R. M. B. Senanayake, "Maintain Real Exchange Rate," *The Island* (Colombo), June 9, 1986, 9; interviews with Sanderatne, Kulantunga, and Laneroll.

[137] Quotes from Dias and Fernando interviews; World Bank, *Sri Lanka and the World Bank,* 14.

[138] Fernando interview.

[139] Quotes from World Bank, *Fourth Tree Crops Project,* 16–18; and World Bank, *Sri Lanka: Tree Crop Sector Review,* Report no. 48990-CE (1984), 10. See also Bandaranaike, "Tea Production"; Athukorale, "Export Development," 13; NPD, *Medium Term Investment Programme,* 7.

"the main thrust of Government's development strategy to arrest the decline in export earnings and budgetary revenue."[140] The MTIP includes rubber and coconuts, but 75 percent of the investment targets tea in order to restore exports to 1965 levels, and to add $65 million annually to export earnings and $30 million annually to state revenues. It calls for investment in field restoration, factory renovation, and expanded manufacture of teas appropriate for tea bags and instant teas. It also calls for a reduction in tea taxes to raise producer margins, a reorganization of ministerial responsibility, a revamping of JEDB and SPC, and the restoration of the Tea Research Institute to its previous glory.

But the MTIP posed problems. As a finance ministry official notes, "government expenditures have preempted investment funds . . . starving the private sector and closing out would-be investors in . . . new export industries."[141] The Accelerated Mahaveli Scheme and infrastructure rehabilitation are in part to blame, but even when funds are allocated for investment in productive enterprises, tea dominates. In 1983, the EDB projected that by 1987, tea would account for 46 percent of state investment and 34 percent of total investment (including private investment and foreign aid funds) and that the combined estate sector would account for 86 percent and 76 percent, respectively.[142]

The MTIP's tax provisions also threaten state revenues. It is an old problem: revitalization's long-term aim is to hike revenues, but this requires cutting tea taxes today because excessive taxes caused much of the decline that must now be reversed. Sri Lanka's production costs are similar to Kenya's, but taxes reduced Sri Lankan producers' margins to $1.83 in 1968—compared with Kenyans' $16.83—and margins were negative in the period 1979–82, when realized tax rates averaged 38 percent of the f.o.b. value of tea.[143] The short-term benefits to the state can be huge; just the *increase* in tea prices in 1984,

---

[140] Quote from World Bank, *Fourth Tree Crops Project*, 52. The following discussion draws on NPD, *Medium Term Investment Programme;* EDB, *National Export Development Plan*, 2: 5–7; World Bank, *Tree Crop Sector Review;* World Bank, *Institutional and Policy Issues;* and interviews with Sambasivam, Ilangakoon, Fernando, Tilakaratna, and Panabokke.

[141] Quote from Tilakaratna interview; EDB, *National Export Development Plan*, 1: 14.

[142] EDB, *National Export Development Plan*, 34.

[143] Ratnayaka interview; Paul Casperesz, "The Internal Structure and Organization of the Tea Industry," *Marga* 2, no. 4 (1975): 56; World Bank, *Tree Crop Sector Review*, 11–13, 67; and Tyler, "Recent Developments," 38–40.

for example, added Rs 1.5 billion to revenues from ad valorum taxes on tea. But margins must guarantee a *minimum* 10 percent real financial rate of return to induce investment in revitalization—and the tax cuts required to achieve such margins will cut "60 percent to 70 percent of revenues from [estate crops] and about 14 percent . . . of total government revenues."[144]

The tea industry is stronger politically than ever, for it is now part of the state and is the state's sole hope. In 1977 and 1984, when tea prices spiked, JEDB and SPC turned a profit, but when prices fell both went rapidly in the red. To cover their losses, they extracted huge subsidies from the state, thus exaggerating the nasty impact of decreasing tea taxes on revenues. Both borrowed heavily, too, and in 1985, caused much of the big increase in public debt. This borrowing, complains a senior official of the Central Bank of Ceylon, represents a "preemption of credit resources by inefficient, commercially unviable operations" and is proof of the extent to which estate-sector production inflexibility binds the state to international price volatility.[145]

Despite their problems, JEDB and SPC have resisted reform. The key to their problems and to their success is the same: the interpenetration of state and sector. Entrenched bureaucratic interests and the continued importance of patronage and of revenues derived from the estates block reform.[146] Since 1977, however, JEDB and SPC have been restaffed with erstwhile private planters and agency house managers, thus reestablishing the hegemony of the old planters' raj with its ties to the ruling UNP. And the one organizational reform that has gone forward—creation of a single estate-sector policy committee chaired by the president—has given the industry unimpeded access to the state and made the president himself its advocate.[147]

But the final irony of the return to tea is the CWC's rise to political power despite the increasingly ugly Tamil-Sinhalese conflict. Having tipped the electoral balance for the UNP in 1977, the CWC in 1978 won the long delayed implementation of the Sirima-Shastri Pact of 1964, which granted Sri Lankan citizenship to 160,000 Indian Tamils. In the election of 1982, the CWC helped to give President J. R. Jay-

[144] Quote from World Bank, *Tree Crop Sector Review,* 36–41; "Economic Indicators Up to 1988," *Economic Review* (May–June 1984), 6–7.

[145] Sanderatne interview; World Bank, *Fourth Tree Crops Project,* 7; NPD, *Public Investment, 1986–1990,* 24, 84, and "Tea and the Economy," 3; CBC, *Economic Performance in the First Half of 1985,* 2.

[146] World Bank, *Sri Lanka and the World Bank,* 24.

[147] Interviews with Ilangakoon, Peiris, and Ratnayaka; World Bank, *Fourth Tree Crops Project,* 40.

awardene the biggest margin of victory in Sri Lankan history. In return, he put forward a new citizenship act, passed in 1986, which reversed the Ceylon Citizenship Act of 1948 and restored citizenship to the Indian Tamil community. With this, the CWC achieved the political goal of equal citizenship stature on the basis of which it had been organized nearly forty years earlier.[148]

The CWC has also capitalized on revitalization to win benefits for its members, though these gains have gutted the intended benefits for the state. The CWC's efforts increased estate workers' wages from 277 to 394 percent (depending on job classification) between 1977 and 1985. The 1984 contract also guaranteed a minimum of 26 workdays per month, a sharp rise from both the previous minimum of 16 and the average number of days actually worked. These increases cost JEDB and SPC over 1 billion rupees a year and added Rs 6.90 per kg to the production cost of tea.[149] At the time, high prices dulled concern, but the contract let the CWC, not the state, capture much of the windfall they produced. When tea prices fell again in 1985, higher wages and the 26-workday month forced JEDB and SPC to seek state subsidies to cover their now much larger and less flexible wage bill. And when they approached the state, the CWC was their strongest ally, thus making the industry an irresistible force as labor and management teamed up to hog the benefits of revitalization.[150]

We will never know with certainty how the Sri Lankan story would have played out. Just as I completed the research for this chapter, the long-smoldering Sri Lankan civil war burst into flame and still continues unabated as of publication. The evidence is highly suggestive, however; Sri Lanka seems to fit the high/high model. Indeed, what is striking is how clear the parallels are between Sri Lanka and Zambia, despite differences in the timing of their entries into the international economy, as well as in their cultures, colonial experiences, and, of course, sectoral bases—high/high industrial versus high/high agricultural. What, then, about Costa Rica, with a low/low, peasant cash crop leading export sector? Does it, too, fit the model and suggest that our core variables—capital intensity, economies of scale, production flexibility, and asset/factor flexibility—matter more than whether a sector is industrial or agricultural?

---

[148] Warnapala and Hewagama, *Recent Politics in Sri Lanka*, 65–66; Blackton, "The Private Sector," 749; Devaraj interview.

[149] NPD, *Public Investment, 1986–1990*, 85–86.

[150] Interviews with Ilangakoon, Ratnayaka, and Devaraj.

CHAPTER SIX

Costa Rica: The Peasant
Cash Crop Sector

To many, Costa Rica is an exception. In a region known for rule by dictators, it is committed to upholding civil liberties and democracy. In a region mired in poverty and inequality, it has reduced inequality and absolute poverty, and it has implemented effective public health, education, and social security policies. Despite the wars and economic shocks that have shaken Central America, it has kept the peace and restructured the economy without sacrificing social welfare goals. But Costa Rica is not an exception; it is a perfect coffee case, with a political economy based on a "peasant proprietor class" of "yeoman farmers" who form "the backbone of Costa Rican democracy."[1] In this chapter I analyze coffee production, the coffee market, and Costa Rica's tractable restructuring project to explain sectoral actors' weaknesses and the state's autonomy and capacity. I then explore how the state used its capacity to restructure after the "revolution" of 1948, and why this effort slowed but did not bar restructuring in the 1980s.

Coffee is the key to understanding Costa Rica. In the 1940s and 1950s, it provided 35–57 percent of export earnings and 10 percent of national income; since 1960 coffee has provided between 25 percent and 72 percent of export earnings—far more than provided by bananas, Costa Rica's second biggest export. Between 1960 and 1978,

---

[1] George Earl Church, 1895, cited in John Riismandel, "Costa Rica: Self-Image, Land Tenure, and Agrarian Reform" (Ph.D. diss., University of Maryland, 1972), 112; Charles Ameringer, *Democracy in Costa Rica* (New York: Praeger, 1982), 2–3. Bananas have also contributed to exports, jobs, and infrastructure development since the 1880s. But that industry is a pure enclave, whereas coffee is under national control and has influenced life in Costa Rica since the 1820s.

184

the coffee industry also generated 20–27 percent of the agricultural portion of GDP and 4–7 percent of total GDP, and employed 30 percent of the labor force. In the same period, coffee taxes generated 4–13 percent of total revenues; and customs duties on imports bought with coffee earnings have long been the main source of state revenues.[2]

Coffee revolutionized life in Costa Rica, a country that a Spanish governor described in 1719 as "the poorest and most miserable colony in all America."[3] With large areas of open, unsettled land and no indigenous populations to enslave, Costa Rica was at first a nation of widely scattered dirt farmers. At independence in 1821, its leaders cast around for a source of income and exports and chose coffee. They launched an aggressive promotion program, distributing free seedlings and land, then required families to plant coffee in their yards; they also exempted coffee sales from taxes. Plantings increased from zero to 3,000 ha in the 1850s and 14,000 ha in the 1890s. Annual exports jumped from a few bags in 1831 to 4 million kg in the 1850s and 18 million kg in the 1890s. Coffee dominated exports from the start, generating 80 percent of export earnings between 1885 and 1900.[4] By the 1880s Costa Rica was the richest country in Central America, and it has been ever since.

Coffee's distributional consequences have been equally important. Limited labor and unlimited land discouraged haciendas. The rich thus limited their involvement in coffee growing and instead financed, processed, and exported the coffee of others. As coffee production increased and land prices rose, land concentration did, too, producing a class of landless farm workers. But small producers continued to predominate, and labor shortages meant that farm workers could expect wages that were triple the regional average. A visitor wrote in 1858: "The whole Republic breathes a certain air of well

[2] Riismandel, "Costa Rica," 151–52; J. W. F. Rowe, *The World's Coffee* (London: Her Majesty's Stationery Office, 1963), 87–88; Gayle Morris, "An Economic Evaluation of the *Beneficio* System of Coffee Credit Delivery, and the Allocation of National Funds to the Coffee Subsector of Costa Rica" (Ph.D. diss., University of Nebraska, 1981), 38–47, 146.

[3] Cited in Riismandel, "Costa Rica," 47–48.

[4] Mitchell Seligson, *Peasants of Costa Rica and the Development of Agrarian Capitalism* (Madison: University of Wisconsin Press, 1980), 15, 19; Anthony Winson, *Coffee and Democracy in Modern Costa Rica* (New York: St. Martin's Press, 1989), 16; Ciro F. S. Cardoso, "The Formation of the Coffee Estate in 19th-Century Costa Rica," in *Land and Labor in Latin America*, ed. Kenneth Duncan and Ian Rutledge (New York: Cambridge University Press, 1977), 177, 189–92.

being. . . . Prosperity is there a universal fact; pauperism is un-
known."[5]

Coffee transformed the state as well. Costa Rica was so poor before
coffee became the primary export that people used cacao beans as
money. The state had no reserves, and it had annual revenues of just
16,000 pesos in the 1820s, but by 1849 customs duties on imports
bought with coffee earnings totaled 120,000 pesos annually.[6] Costa
Rica became the first, best example of the "liberal oligarchic state"
that prevailed in Central America after the 1870s. It pursued export-
led growth and achieved national integration with export-facilitating
infrastructure investments, as well as with land, tax, trade, and foreign exchange policies. Already by the 1880s, however, Costa Rica
revealed differences from its neighbors, especially in the much greater extent to which successive Costa Rican "governments had begun to
distance themselves from coffee interests and acquire a separate
identity"—reflected, for example, in their use of coffee export taxes
to promote national goals.[7]

Coffee dependence also posed risks, which prompted leaders to
consider restructuring. After reaching a peak in the 1890s, prices
dropped 50 percent in 1900. The crash produced the first talk of the
need to diversify, but such discussion was soon silenced by increases in
export prices and volume. World War I cut coffee sales again, but with
peace, prices spiked—only to crash in the mid-1920s. Banana exports
saved Costa Rica, but even politicians could see "signs of satura-
tion . . . in the coffee and banana sectors [and] the need for diversification." The financial, monetary, and exchange rate reforms they
implemented began "a period of remarkable exchange rate stability
which survived . . . the worst years of the post-1929 depression." The
related growth of exports resulted in increased state revenues and
borrowing power. But diversification went nowhere; "instead the
export-led model based on coffee and bananas was enthusiastically
promoted."[8] One problem was that "the institutional framework de-

[5] Cited in Carlos Joaquin Saenz, "Population Growth, Economic Progress, and Op-
portunities on the Land" (Ph.D. diss., University of Wisconsin, 1969), 32; Seligson,
Peasants of Costa Rica, 23; Cardoso, "The Formation of the Coffee Estate," 170–81;
Victor Bulmer-Thomas, *The Political Economy of Central America since 1920* (New York:
Cambridge University Press, 1987), 21.

[6] Mitchell Seligson, "Agrarian Policies in Dependent Societies: Costa Rica," *Journal of
Interamerican Studies and World Affairs* 19 (May 1977): 210.

[7] Bulmer-Thomas, *The Political Economy*, 22–24, 46–47.

[8] Ibid., 10–11, 26.

veloped around coffee production . . . was inadequate to provide for the needs of those not directly engaged as proprietors in coffee production."[9] The main problem, however, was that coffee demand rose 30 percent *and* prices doubled between 1921 and 1929. In the same period, exports jumped 50 percent, real income increased for all sectors, and state revenues skyrocketed.[10] Politicians gave in to temptation and pushed for still more coffee production, increasing Costa Rica's vulnerability to external shocks.

Then came the depression. Export prices and volume took a nose dive, causing export earnings to decrease 60 percent and GDP to decrease 21 percent by 1932. Unemployment rose and wages fell. Total revenues dropped 35 percent between 1929 and 1932. The government cut investment and "deferred" payment of public employees' wages, but public debt and debt service costs soared. Having no other sectors to turn to, politicians rescued the coffee growers. When recovery finally came in the late 1930s, Costa Rica still lacked "the basis for long-term sustained growth."[11]

The outbreak of World War II marked the beginning of a fifteen-year boom, in which increased coffee production was accompanied by political changes that permitted restructuring. The 1940 Inter-American Coffee Agreement (IACA) opened new American markets and resulted in a price increase of 50 percent in the years 1941–45, despite price controls. It expired in 1945, and by 1954 prices had reached an all-time peak.[12] Surging export earnings and their distribution throughout the economy further committed Costa Rica to export agriculture and created a rich domestic market. They were also sufficient to underwrite the revolution of 1948, which reestablished Costa Rican democracy on a broader, more solid foundation, and created the extensive social welfare system necessary for it to function.

The boom went bust in 1955, however, and politicians decided to pursue two different tacks. One was to promote the intensification of coffee production, soon giving Costa Rica "virtually the highest productivity per hectare of any coffee producing country in the world" by the mid-1960s. As a result, Costa Rica not only increased exports in the late 1950s but, alone in Central America, increased export earn-

[9] Saenz, "Population Growth," 44.
[10] Bulmer-Thomas, *The Political Economy*, 37.
[11] Ibid., 48–49, 55–58, 69 (quote); Winson, *Coffee and Democracy*, 37.
[12] Bulmer-Thomas, *The Political Economy*, 91–92, 109.

ings as well. Equally important, the preponderance of peasant producers meant that intensification benefited a large segment of the
population.[13] Politicians also recognized that in the long run, these
gains depended on the behavior of other states. Thus, in 1957 they
joined other Latin American producers in negotiations that in 1959
produced the first International Coffee Agreement.

Policy makers also pursued restructuring by means of export diversification and a policy of increased openness. They encouraged new
agricultural exports but understood that expanding export agriculture "was neither a desirable nor feasible long-term strategy. Each
government, with increasingly influential pressure from private industrialists, recognized the need for industrial promotion." The state
funded new sources of industrial financing, extended incentives for
extraregional exports, offered training programs to break labor bot-
tlenecks, started parastatals in key industries, and in 1963 joined the
Central American Common Market (CACM).[14]

The effort worked; "Costa Rican industrial performance . . . showed
what could be done when long-term industrial strategies were matched
by consistent state policies."[15] Manufacturing's share of GDP rose
from 11.5 percent to 18.4 percent between 1950 and 1978. Industrial
employment grew from 11.7 percent to 16.0 percent of total employment in the period 1963–78. The number and size of firms increased
rapidly, and the composition of production changed: between 1960
and 1982, consumer goods' share of industrial production fell from
88.0 percent to 70.4 percent; intermediate and capital goods' share
rose from 12.0 percent to 29.6 percent. Manufactured exports rose
from 4 percent to 29 percent of total exports in the years 1963–79.
True, "this was not export-led growth of the East Asian type," for 80
percent went to protected CACM markets.[16] Still, the strategies and
policies did cut Costa Rica's exposure to coffee market volatility.

[13] Quote from Winson, *Coffee and Democracy*, 110. See also Bulmer-Thomas, *The
Political Economy*, 154–55; and Bulmer-Thomas, "Economic Development over the
Long Run," *Journal of Latin American Studies* 15 (November 1983): 288; James
Mwandha, John Nicholls, and Marcolm Sargent, *Coffee: The International Commodity
Agreements* (Brookfield, Vt.: Gower, 1985), 7.

[14] Bulmer-Thomas, *The Political Economy*, 207, 211.

[15] Ibid., 211–12.

[16] Ibid., 210; Hector Brignoli and Yolanda Martinez, "Growth and Crisis in the Central American Economies," *Journal of Latin American Studies* 15 (November 1983): 374–
75; Gary Fields, "Employment and Economic Growth in Costa Rica," *World Development*
16 (December 1988): 1494; Marc Lindenberg and Noel Ramirez, *Managing Adjustment
in Developing Countries* (San Francisco: ICS Press, 1989), 192.

Intensification and diversification paid large dividends. Agriculture's share of total employment and GDP declined from 1949 to 1979, but in the same period intensification increased coffee exports, the diversification of export agriculture increased sugar and beef exports, and domestic agricultural policies boosted food production. The GDP grew 6 percent per year from 1960 to 1978—faster than in any other Latin American country except oil-rich Ecuador and Brazil in its miracle years (1970–78). Inflation averaged 2.3 percent annually between 1960 and 1970 and rose only modestly after the 1973 oil shock; unemployment stayed low despite labor force growth. Per capita income doubled from 1960 to 1979, and because this "growth benefited the labor market and hence the poor," Costa Rica was able to reduce income inequality to the lowest level in Latin America.[17]

But in 1978 Costa Rica suffered "the crisis," an economic shock as overwhelming as the Great Depression. Export prices plunged; import prices and international interest rates soared. Foreign debt and debt service skyrocketed; foreign reserves disappeared. By 1982, the reversal of economic growth had erased all the gains of the 1970s. Unemployment doubled to nearly 24 percent, pushing an additional 12 percent of the population below the poverty line.[18] Costa Rica staggered, but it did not collapse; instead, in 1982 its voters elected a new government to fix things.

Neither the new president, Luis Alberto Monge Alvarez, nor his successor, Oscar Arias Sánchez (1986–90), succeeded entirely. They did, however, stabilize the situation without sacrificing democratic principles or the interests of the poor. Inflation was cut from 100 percent to 12 percent in 1982–84. Unemployment was reduced to pre-crisis levels. The budget deficit was reduced, and the balance-of-payments deficit was almost eliminated. More important for the future, both presidents effected substantial restructuring.[19] But to un-

[17] Quote from Fields, "Employment and Economic Growth," 1491, 1495–97, 1506. See also Lindenberg and Ramirez, *Managing Adjustment,* 258; Bulmer-Thomas, *The Political Economy,* 205–7, 271–72; Mitchell Seligson and Edward Muller, "Democratic Stability and Economic Crisis," *International Studies Quarterly* 31 (September 1987): 309; Juan Diego Trejos, "Costa Rica: Economic Crisis and Public Policy," Occasional Paper no. 11, Latin American and Caribbean Center (Miami: Florida International University, 1985), 3–4; Harold Nelson, ed., *Costa Rica* (Washington, D.C.: American University, Foreign Area Studies, 1984), 133.

[18] Seligson and Muller, "Democratic Stability," 315.

[19] Ibid., 316; Fields, "Employment and Economic Growth," 1504–6; Eugenio Diáz-Bonilla, *Structural Adjustment Programs and Economic Stabilization in Central America,* Economic Development Institute Policy Seminar Report no. 23 (Washington, D.C.: World

derstand how they managed to restructure in the midst of crisis, we must begin with the international coffee market and the restructuring project faced by Costa Rica.

THE INTERNATIONAL DIMENSION

Although peasant cash crops are grown on both large and small farms, smallholders are their most efficient producers.[20] Such production exhibits low capital intensity and small economies of scale, thus requiring limited investment, few specialized skills and little management organization, no permanent work force, and no specialized infrastructure. Self-employment gives peasants unbeatable incentives to practice husbandry and to maximize productivity. The greater efficiency of peasant production and low economic barriers to entry bar MNCs and mean that hacienda production depends on *political* barriers to entry enforced by the state.[21]

Production of peasant cash crops demands little but land and labor.[22] It does not require costly field preparation or equipment; sweat equity is peasants' main investment. Such crops show no economies from specialization. Producers can add incrementally to their crop area, and the absence of special cultivation requirements means they can plant a mix of crops without loss of efficiency. Further, even though cacao, rubber, and coffee trees take years to bear, peasants can "weather the waiting period by interplanting with food crops."[23] Finally, processing can be done on the farm without a big investment, or it can be delayed long enough that production need not be subordinated to the requirements of centralized processing.

Bank, 1990), 14; Marc Edelman and Joanne Kennan, eds., *The Costa Rica Reader* (New York: Grove Weidenfeld, 1989), 189.

[20] Jeffrey Paige, *Agrarian Revolution* (New York: Free Press, 1975), passim.

[21] Ibid., 86; C. F. Marshall, *The World Coffee Trade* (Cambridge: Woodhead-Faulkner, 1983), 4. The Costa Rican coffee crop is produced with peasant labor, so we will ignore the implications of this for now. But countries where hacienda production of peasant cash crops prevails have repressive, unstable domestic political economies. We will return to this subject in Chapter 7 with an analysis of El Salvador.

[22] Paige, *Agrarian Revolution*, 15–16; V. D. Wickizer, *Coffee, Tea, and Cocoa* (Stanford: Stanford University Press, 1951), 47–49; Peggy Barlett, "Agricultural Change in Paso: The Structure of Decision-Making in a Costa Rican Peasant Community" (Ph.D. diss., Columbia University, 1975), 57, 111–12.

[23] V. D. Wickizer, "The Smallholder in Tropical Export Crop Production," *Food Research Institute Studies* 1 (February 1960): 95.

Coffee is the perfect peasant cash crop. Land is *the* capital requirement, and little of it is needed; in Costa Rica even peasants with the least land plant half an acre of coffee trees. Farmers can also invest in coffee a tree at a time. The only tools needed are a machete and a hoe; other inputs are minimal, and there is no need for special expertise that would put peasant producers at a disadvantage.[24] Coffee trees require little care apart from weeding and annual pruning and will yield even without attention. Coffee does demand a worker to every two hectares. This is well within the capacity of peasant families, however, and since labor accounts for 75 percent of variable costs, it again suggests peasants' preference for growing coffee. Coffee is thus "good money and secure," a crop that is risk free and permits producers to adjust the application of labor and other inputs to market prices.[25]

The important role of small growers in Costa Rica is evidence of the low economic barriers to entry. The Land Registry of 1867 and the coffee census of 1935 show the early predominance of small holdings. In 1978–79 Costa Rica had 88,750 registered producers; 89 percent were small farmers who accounted for 35 percent of production, and 10 percent were medium-sized farmers who accounted for 39 percent.[26] The important issue is not size of holdings, however; it is peasant producers' competitiveness. Although average yields in 1973 rose from 3,863 kg/ha for *minifundia* to 5,325 kg/ha for farms of 100–199.9 ha, profit margins are similar when these figures are corrected for the higher fixed costs, inputs costs and labor costs of the higher-yielding big farms.[27] Peasants do not pay a price penalty either; indeed, Costa Rican coffee commands a premium for its quality. Nor has intensification of production hurt peasants; despite a doubling of coffee production between 1952 and 1962, their share of the total did not decrease. Use of herbicides and fertilizers does vary by farm size,

[24] Barlett, "Agricultural Change," 123–31, 182; Luella Dambaugh, *The Coffee Frontier in Brazil* (Gainesville: University of Florida, 1959), 7–8; Richard Smith, "Diversification Alternatives and Inducements in the Colombian Coffee Industry" (Ph.D. diss., University of Texas, 1974), 25–26, 90–95.

[25] Peasant quoted in Barlett, "Agricultural Change," 176. See also Rowe, *The World's Coffee*, 92; Neil Ridler, "Labor Force and Land Distributional Effects of Agricultural Technology," *World Development* 11 (July 1983): 594.

[26] Carolyn Hall, *El Café y el Desarrollo Historico-Geographico de Costa Rica*, 3rd ed. (San José, Costa Rica: Editorial Costa Rica, 1978), 88; Nelson, *Costa Rica*, 147; Morris, "An Economic Evaluation," 6, 48–50, 147.

[27] Figures from Winson, *Coffee and Democracy*, 183; analysis from Rowe, *The World's Coffee*, 100.

but the use of herbicides to cut labor costs matters only to big farmers who are dependent on hired workers, and peasants' lower costs offset the yield gains from fertilizer use.[28]

Costa Rica is not unique. Even in Brazil, big planters constitute just 3 percent of growers and average farm size is less than 9 ha; elsewhere big farms play an even smaller role.[29] In Colombia, the world's second biggest coffee producer, for example, 90 percent of the farms are 10 ha or less and produce more than 50 percent of the crop. Furthermore, productivity is actually *lower* on big farms because of "a lack of vested interest in output by workers," as opposed to peasants' desire to achieve "the highest output . . . and greater willingness to expend the quantity and quality of labor needed to obtain the better yields that are characteristic of [small] holdings."[30] Quality also suffers with increasing farm size. Colombian and Jamaican peasants' coffees, like that of Costa Rican peasants, command price premiums; coffees grown on Brazilian plantations set the price floor. Although all peasants have limited access to the inputs needed for intensification, the problem is not coffee related or insurmountable, as evidenced by successful credit schemes and extension services for coffee smallholders in Costa Rica, Colombia, the Ivory Coast, and Kenya.

Coffee processing is more capital-intensive and exhibits larger economies of scale, but it bears no relation to estate crop processing. Processing involves removing the pulpy "cherry" surrounding the beans, then cleaning and drying the green coffee. Two methods are used. The dry method produces lower-quality coffee but requires no investment. The coffee cherries are spread on the ground to dry; the outer shell and inner parchment are then cracked open by hand or with a simple mill and the beans are separated from the debris by winnowing. The wet method produces better coffee but requires more capital and large amounts of water. The cherries are first fed to a pulping machine that tears off as much of the flesh as possible. The beans are then soaked in an enzyme bath to dissolve any remaining pulp, dried, and milled to remove the parchment.

Coffee processing is organized differently according to local condi-

---

[28] Marshall, *The World Coffee Trade*, 186; Winson, *Coffee and Democracy*, 116–17.

[29] Marshall, *The World Coffee Trade*, 1, 60–69; Richard Lucier, *The International Political Economy of Coffee* (New York: Praeger, 1988), 29.

[30] Figures from Ridler, "Labor Force," 597; quote from Smith, "Diversification Alternatives," 95–100.

tions.[31] At the most simple extreme, growers can use the dry method, thus conserving capital and water (as in Brazil and Uganda). In between, peasants can use home pulpers and fermentation tanks to wet-process their cherries (as do 90 percent of Colombian growers). Most costly, centralized, mechanized wet-process *beneficios* prevail where farm size permits or where good roads permit the collection of peasants' cherries and labor costs make mechanization economical.

Costa Rica's beneficios are at the high end of the range with regard to capital intensity and economies of scale in coffee processing. Most process at least the MES of 2,000 fanegas (3,200 bushels), and some process 20,000–30,000 (32,000–48,000 bushels). Very little of the coffee processed is grown by beneficio owners, however; instead they buy cherries from local farmers (sometimes from thousands of them).[32] Moreover, although many beneficios are privately owned, producer cooperatives own a growing share. In part, this reflects state support for the National Federation of Coffee Cooperatives. But the point is that peasants are not barred from coffee processing, even in Costa Rica where it is as capital-intensive and large-scale as it is anywhere in the world.

Peasant competitiveness has ensured that landownership was never the Costa Rican elite's "defining characteristic or basis of power. . . . The road to wealth led through dominance of the marketplace, not directly through landlording."[33] Further, given the relatively low barriers to entry even into processing, beneficio owners depend less on control of processing than on control of credit, inputs, and export marketing. As late as the mid-1980s, they provided 95 percent of all rural credit and sold growers fertilizer and other inputs on credit against their anticipated crop yield. In short, from the start Costa Rica had a coffee aristocracy of beneficio owners and exporters—an industrial and commercial elite—which, under pressure from below, had strong incentives to diversify.[34]

---

[31] Marshall, *The World Coffee Trade*, 157–58; Rowe, *The World's Coffee*, 25–26, 67–68; Paul Morrison and Thomas Norris, "Coffee Production and Processing on a Large Costa Rican *Finca*," *Papers of the Michigan Academy of Science, Arts and Letters* 39 (1954): 322.

[32] Rowe, *The World's Coffee*, 94–96.

[33] Lowell Gudmundson, "Costa Rica before Coffee," *Journal of Latin American Studies* 15, part 2 (November 1983): 445–46.

[34] Cardoso, "The Formation of the Coffee Estate," 192–93; Morris, "An Economic Evaluation," 53–55, 61–64; Barlett, "Agricultural Change," 129–30; Seligson, *Peasants of Costa Rica*, 32–33, 40–42.

In the international market, coffee states face short-term price volatility and long-term price stagnation. Prices change frequently and fluctuate widely; coffee's price instability index is twice that of tea.[35] Demand is steady, but demand growth is slow and both demand and price are inelastic. The problem is on the supply side, where a grower's yields in good years may be ten times those in bad ones. Because of demand inelasticity, there is sharp price fluctuation; even radical price decreases produce little increase in demand, whereas supply shortfalls produce price spikes. To make matters worse, Brazil, the world's largest coffee producer, is the most prone to disaster, thus exaggerating the boom-bust cycle.[36]

Boom and bust have nasty short- and long-run effects. Growers pick, even during a bust, because of the "wide surplus of the marginal revenue . . . over the marginal cost of harvesting." The short-term price elasticity of supply is thus low and *positive*, for producers offset low prices with more intensive picking, adding to the glut.[37] The aftermath of a boom is even nastier. Because supply is inelastic in the short run, booms last for five to eight years, encouraging new planting. When the new trees begin to bear, supply surges, prices plunge— and remain depressed, for no peasant will stop picking or uproot trees that will continue to produce for a century. The result is an inherent tendency to oversupply.[38]

The structure of the international market poses additional problems. On the production side, coffee is an oligopoly with a competitive fringe.[39] Brazil and Colombia can influence prices by withholding or releasing stockpiled coffee; small producers must sell at the price dictated by supply, demand, and the big two producers. All fifty of the

[35] Vernon Wickizer, "International Collaboration in the World Coffee Market," *Food Research Institute Studies*, 4 (1963/1964): 275; Mwandha et al., *Coffee*, 46–47.

[36] Shamsher Singh, Jos de Vries, John Hulley, and Patrick Yeung, *Coffee, Tea, and Cocoa* (Baltimore: Johns Hopkins University Press, 1977), 19, 37–38; Smith, "Diversification Alternatives," 17–19; G. Lovasky, "The International Coffee Market," *IMF Staff Papers* 9 (1962): 233; Wickizer, "International Collaboration," 275; and Wickizer, *The World Coffee Economy* (Stanford: Food Research Institute, Stanford University, 1943), 4.

[37] Quote from Mwandha et al., *Coffee*, 25. See also Singh et al., *Coffee, Tea, and Cocoa*, 31; Lucier, *The International Political Economy of Coffee*, 31–34.

[38] Christopher Brown, *Primary Commodity Control* (New York: Oxford University Press, 1975), 7–10; Wickizer, *Coffee, Tea, and Cocoa*, 27–29; Paul Streeten and Diane Elson, *Diversification and Development* (New York: Praeger, 1971), 14–16; Lovasky, "The International Coffee Market," 226–31.

[39] Thomas Geer, "Price Formation on the World Coffee Market and Its Implications for the International Coffee Agreement," *Weltwirtschaftliches Archiv* 106, no. 1 (1971).

other producers can expand production, however, free riding on the efforts of the big two to manage supply. Their combined increases negate supply management efforts and exaggerate the tendency to oversupply. On the demand side, producers face high buyer concentration; in 1978 the top four firms controlled 40.1 percent of the processed coffee industry, 59 percent of the roast coffee industry, and 81 percent of the instant coffee industry.[40] The market power imbalance of many small producers versus a few huge buyers does not favor the producers.

Two changes in the coffee market have hurt producers of quality arabicas, including Costa Rica. First, to achieve a brand taste, firms blend a variety of beans, negating the distinctiveness of different coffees. Brand flavors can also be achieved in many ways, thus allowing substitution of different types and qualities of beans to take advantage of price movements in different segments of the market, and limiting the price premium that quality coffees command.[41] Second, instant coffee is the only rapidly growing segment of the market— and it demands robustas and low-quality arabicas. Robustas' share of the coffee market has sharply increased as a result, and demand for high-quality arabicas such as those of Costa Rica has lagged.[42]

Individual producers are stuck. They can cut costs and increase productivity to improve profit margins, but these steps do nothing to manage price volatility. Some have tried to create a kind of brand recognition with promotions such as Colombia's "Juan Valdez" campaign, but again, these do not address price volatility. Long-term contracts guarantee a market but not a price, for if prices fall, buyers are refunded the difference between the contract price and the market price at delivery. Buyer concentration and consumers' brand loyalty block downstream integration and hinder producers' efforts to internalize the market. The exception is instant coffee; some producers have gained access to what is the fastest-growing, highest-value-added market segment. But the investment costs are high and competition is fierce.[43]

[40] Lucier, *The International Political Economy of Coffee*, 56–59.

[41] Wickizer, *The World Coffee Economy*, 25–26.

[42] Singh et al., *Coffee, Tea, and Cocoa*, 24–27; Lucier, *The International Political Economy of Coffee*, 31–32; Marshall, *The World Coffee Trade*, 196.

[43] Singh et al., *Coffee, Tea, and Cocoa*, 39–41; Marshall, *The World Coffee Trade*, 202–4; Michael Sivetz, *Coffee Processing Technology*, vol. 2 (Westport, Conn.: Avi Publishing, 1963), 287–97.

The Failure of International Collaboration

Unable to act alone, coffee producers have sought an international coffee agreement, but this required the cooperation of some fifty states that depend on coffee for export earnings, revenues, and jobs. The coffee market thus resembles a multiplayer Prisoner's Dilemma in which each state faces four possible payoffs: (1) all producers restrict production or exports or both, thus stabilizing or even raising prices (the best alternative from a long-term, collective point of view); (2) other producers restrict production and it does not, but captures market share and big profits by free riding (the best alternative, from its point of view); (3) all producers pursue the latter course, resulting in excess supply and a price collapse (the more likely choice of all producers); and (4) the state restricts but other producers do not, resulting in lost earnings and market share (the worst option for it).[44]

Three barriers bar escape from this dilemma. First, there is the knotty issue of price, market share, and quotas. Higher-cost, established producers seek quotas based on historical market share to freeze low-cost newcomers out of the market and to peg supply at a level that protects their profit margins. New, low-cost producers seek quotas that peg supply at a higher level, since they prefer to trade profits for market share.[45] Second, states will comply only if they are assured that cheating will be punished. But the ease with which coffee's origins can be disguised makes detection difficult, and sanctioning sovereign states is always problematic. Third, to endure, an agreement must promote diversification, for as long as excess capacity exists, the more effective an agreement, the more incentives there are for even "honest" states to cheat, lest they lose market share to the unscrupulous. Unfortunately, the more successful an agreement is in the short run, the fewer incentives there are to diversify.[46]

The difficulties in negotiating an international agreement, its anticipated ineffectiveness, and its ultimate failure attest to the intractability of producers' collective-action problem. Indeed, even the limited success that has been achieved has depended on exogenous factors. The 1940 IACA, for example, began with an American desire

[44] I owe thanks to my student Bill Robinson for this neat summary.

[45] Elwood Vanderslice, Jr., "The International Coffee Organization and the Control of Coffee Overproduction" (Ph.D. diss., University of Michigan, 1971), 45, 61–62; Geer, "Price Formation," 144–45; Marshall, *The World Coffee Trade*, 108, 123–25.

[46] Christopher Brown, *The Political and Social Economy of Commodity Control* (New York: Praeger, 1980), 25.

to ensure hemispheric solidarity against the Nazis and worked because the United States enforced quotas at American ports. The IACA expired in 1948, and surging coffee prices led to an 80 percent increase in world production from 1948 to 1958. In 1957, with coffee prices falling, coffee stocks increasing, and new competition from Africa, Latin American producers reopened talks, hoping to negotiate a treaty that would offer stable, higher prices supported by coffee-consuming countries, protection against lower-cost African producers, and limits on exclusionary ties between the Africans and the European Community (EC).[47] But Latin American producers' efforts failed until American worries about revolution in Latin America, and French and British concern about peaceful decolonization in Africa, led them to agree to a joint producer-consumer pact in 1963. The resulting International Coffee Agreement (ICA) stabilized prices in the short run, but the producers' failure to resolve the collective-action problem killed the agreement when these special external conditions disappeared.

The 1963 ICA had problems from the start.[48] Signatories had ignored overproduction and had based the agreement on export quotas alone. And since these states had refused to accept quotas lower than the current volume of exports, the ICA froze existing excess capacity in place. Worse, to the extent that it raised prices, the ICA prompted increased production. In the absence of diversification, these surpluses represented most signatories' sole hope for development. Thus, the lack of production controls gave states the means to cheat, and the more effective the ICA was, the greater their incentives to do so. The allocation of export quotas also pitted the big, established Latin American producers against the new, low-cost African producers, which viewed quotas as a barrier to growth. Further, coffee-consuming countries opposed high prices and could make their opposition stick because they enforced the quota system. Finally, the International Coffee Organization, the secretariat charged with administering the ICA, never achieved the legitimacy or the authority necessary to mediate effectively.

These problems persisted throughout the renegotiations of the

---

[47] Lucier, *The International Political Economy of Coffee*, 120–27; Karen Mingst, "The Process of International Policy-Making in Regulation of Tropical Agricultural Products" (Ph.D. diss., University of Wisconsin, 1974), 87–90, 103–7; Brown, *Commodity Control*, 25–29.

[48] Mingst, "The Process of International Policy-Making," 109–11, 212–14.

ICA in 1968, 1976, and 1983. True, the international agreements seem to have reduced price instability, and the 1968 ICA cut world coffee stocks (though Brazilian frosts in 1969 and 1972 helped). But from the start, higher prices resulted in higher production and serious cheating. The 1968 ICA also created a Diversification Fund but left implementation to the ICA signatories who did nothing as long as favorable prices prevailed.[49] Other problems surfaced in 1972 when talks began on a new accord. Producers and consumers split over prices; producers split over quotas and allowable stocks. Not until 1975 did both groups reach an agreement—by eliminating production controls, recalculating quotas in a way that gave states "incentives . . . to increase exports immediately," and appeasing the consuming countries.[50] The 1983 ICA extended this agreement, and the entire system collapsed in 1989 when efforts to enforce quotas were abandoned.

THE DOMESTIC DIMENSION: A TRACTABLE PROJECT

Costa Rica is a competitive producer of quality coffee with a steady demand for its product, but it confronts a volatile market. It has two options: it can continue efforts to intensify production and cut costs to increase profits in booms and minimize losses in busts; or it can restructure. Luckily, the domestic political economy of peasant cash crops makes achieving the latter relatively easy.

Peasant producers are production-flexible. Coffee trees are fixed assets, but since sweat equity is peasants' main investment, few are saddled with high fixed costs. Farmers incur coffee-related debts when buying inputs but settle them at harvest time. In bad years inputs can be cut, for coffee yields without the use of fertilizer, and weeding by family members can replace herbicides. Indeed, coffee can be ignored without ceasing to yield or risk to long-term productivity. Thus, farmers can even reduce labor costs by minimizing care

---

[49] Ibid., 187–88, 227–33, 313–14; Lucier, *The International Political Economy of Coffee*, 129–35, 147–57; Mwandha et al., *Coffee*, 99–101, 113–14; Vanderslice, "The International Coffee Organization," 123–34, 150, 156–57, 162–64; Brown, *Commodity Control*, 29–33. Thomas Galloway, "The International Coffee Agreement," *Journal of World Trade Law* 7 (May–June 1973): 362–65.

[50] Quote from Lucier, *The International Political Economy of Coffee*, 148–52. See also Mingst, "The Process of International Policy-Making," 262–70; Vanderslice, "The International Coffee Organization," 18; Brown, *Commodity Control*, 33–35.

or working harder themselves. (Commented a Costa Rican farmer when prices fell in the 1980s: "We do our own work now. It's cheaper.")[51] Farmers can also change their crop mix seasonally to adjust for coffee prices.

Coffee processing presents a more complex picture. If it takes place on the farm, processing costs add little to production costs and do not reduce flexibility. Centralized beneficios such as those in Costa Rica are affected by price changes, since they get a fixed percentage of the sale price of their coffee. But just as producers can offset lower prices with closer picking, processors can make up with volume what they lose as a result of reduced prices.

Coffee production is moderately asset/factor flexible, and mitigating factors offset the rigidities. Again, the problem is that coffee trees are fixed assets. Nothing else related to coffee production is coffee-specific, however. Even big Costa Rican coffee farms grow a mix of crops, using general-purpose equipment (hoes, machetes, pesticide sprayers). The farmers, too, are generalists, not coffee specialists; they change their crop mix in accordance with market signals, and their unskilled laborers are no more bound to coffee than they are.[52] In sum, coffee farms are also Costa Rica's alternative agricultural sector.

Asset/factor flexibility prevails beyond the farm. The geographical dispersion of coffee farms demands a wide network of general-purpose roads, not a specialized infrastructure like the railroads built by the banana companies to service their plantations. This extensive road system has not only facilitated coffee production but has sparked the growth of a national market and has expanded peasants' economic opportunities.[53] Coffee also requires no special handling, storage, or port facilities. Finally, though Costa Rica has coffee-specific state agencies, growers' needs as general farmers ensure that even these organizations serve all farmers.

Flexibility benefits the state. In the short run, producers' ability to offset price drops insulates the state from sharp declines in export earnings and revenues. Coffee prices fell 32 percent from 1979–80 to

[51] Cited in Leslie Anderson, "Alternative Action in Costa Rica," *Journal of Latin American Studies* 22 (February 1990): 97; Barlett, "Agricultural Change," 57, 111–12, 197; Wickizer, *World Coffee Economy*, 39–40; Gordon Wrigley, *Coffee* (New York: John Wiley, 1988), 204–5, 227–28; Carolyn Hall, *Costa Rica* (Boulder, Colo.: Westview Press, 1985), 160–61.

[52] See Barlett, "Agricultural Change," passim.

[53] Ibid., 230–31; Hall, *Costa Rica*, 129–30, 263; Nelson, *Costa Rica*, 167–74.

1980–81, for example, but farmers increased production by 34 percent. As a result, coffee export earnings decreased just 9.3 percent, not the 32 percent they would have, had coffee exports stayed level.[54] Volume increases also insulate processors, thus limiting the intensity of their demands on the state for help. Similarly, peasants' ability to alter their crop mix eases the suffering caused by shocks. Indeed, "the predominance of peasant producers" helps explain "why the Depression did not produce as much disruption . . . as it did in countries where large capitalist haciendas dominated." Today a similar shift to food crops helps explain Costa Rica's successful adjustment to foreign exchange shortages.[55] Such evasive action reduces the intensity of rural demands for state help, too, limiting pressure on a budget hurt by lower revenues.

These benefits are most evident in the evolution of Costa Rican politics. Whereas elsewhere in Central America, coffee elites depended on force to seize and hold huge haciendas and to control a landless work force, the Costa Rican elite did not need an army to survive or to prosper. In fact, because the elite's wealth depended on the level of economic activity in Costa Rica, its members soon recognized that their interests were best served not by repression but by progress. They thus built schools, not an army, for they saw education as the key to labor productivity, economic growth, and stability. Unthreatened, they pursued a democratic politics of inclusion, permitting a rapid expansion of the electorate after 1910, which, in turn, legitimated the state still controlled by the elite.[56]

The political and economic wiggle room that asset/factor flexibility gave the coffee elite is also evident in early responses to restructuring. By the 1930s, all the Central American coffee republics needed to restructure.[57] In El Salvador, where commercial haciendas dominated, coffee elites violently opposed restructuring; they murdered 30,000 peasants to defend the status quo and created an enduring system of repression. Costa Rica's coffee barons, however, were processor-exporters whose wealth derived from capital, not land, and

[54] Ameringer, *Democracy in Costa Rica,* 95.

[55] Quote from Winson, *Coffee and Democracy,* 38–39. See also Bulmer-Thomas, *The Political Economy,* 57.

[56] Héctor Pérez Brignoli, "Reckoning with the Central American Past," in *The Costa Rica Reader,* ed. Edelman and Kennan, 38–40; José Vega Carballo, "The Dynamics of Early Militarism," in ibid., 47–48; Samuel Stone, "Aspects of Power Distribution in Costa Rica," in ibid., 25–26; Ameringer, *Democracy in Costa Rica,* 21.

[57] Bulmer-Thomas, *The Political Economy,* 125–26, 279–80.

they were already diversifying. Initially, they had diversified because coffee is "particularly vulnerable to taxation" and because limited landholdings required that they find other businesses for their sons. Some of their offspring pursued law and medicine, but many went into commerce, banking, shipping, and light manufacturing. Therefore, by 1920 Costa Rica had a true middle class that could trace its origins to the coffee elite but had different interests.[58] After 1929, family and business ties to this thriving middle class ensured that the remaining coffee barons found diversification possible and profitable. They thus did not oppose restructuring but sought to control "the reform potential of the state" so that restructuring favored their interests.[59]

The revolution of 1948 is proof of this effort. It created conditions favoring "the diversification of agricultural exports and industrialization," recommitted Costa Rica to democracy, and "[won] over a politically important sector of smallholders."[60] The revolution pitted the remnants of the old elite against the victorious coalition headed by a populist party, the Partido Liberación Nacional (PLN), which was founded by erstwhile members of the old elite and "enthusiastically backed" by "the smallholding peasantry, especially in the central coffee-growing regions," and "the new class . . . the professionals, entrepreneurs, and budding manufacturers." The winners created a new, more autonomous state "to institutionalize social reform" and adopted "a new form of state capitalism that would guarantee them power, enable them to expand economically beyond the parameters of the traditional coffee economy, and lay the groundwork for industrialization."[61]

Progress was made. Booming coffee prices until 1954 and rising productivity yielded a bonanza of export earnings and profits for the coffee sector that were far in excess of its investment needs, thus providing a big budget surplus. The state devoted huge sums to economic infrastructure investments and nontraditional investment lending. High prices inflated the banana and coffee industries' share

[58] Quote from Stone, "Aspects of Power Distribution," 23–24. See also Ameringer, *Democracy in Costa Rica*, 18; Winson, *Coffee and Democracy*, 23.

[59] Quote from Mark Rosenberg, "Social Reform in Costa Rica," in *The Costa Rica Reader*, ed. Edelman and Kennan, 95. See also Winson, *Coffee and Democracy*, 40–41.

[60] Quotes from Marc Edelman, "Recent Literature on Costa Rica's Crisis," *Latin American Research Review* 18, no. 2 (1983): 169; and Winson, *Coffee and Democracy*, 7.

[61] Quotes from Edelman and Kennan, *The Costa Rica Reader*, 88, 169. See also Ameringer, *Democracy in Costa Rica*, 32–33.

of export earnings and their economic activity, but the statistics disguise ample diversification. Beef and sugar exports rose rapidly, cutting the coffee and banana industries' share of exports by the 1960s. Domestic agriculture fared less well but also received considerable new financing. Industrial promotion efforts culminated in the 1959 Law of Industrial Production and Development, and manufacturing activity sharply increased thereafter.[62]

Although the state successfully completed its restructuring program, the policies it implemented had nasty long-term effects. Intensification of coffee production kept the industry competitive and provided the surplus to fund diversification, but it deepened the economy's coffee dependence. Justified as the temporary price of transforming the economy, this emphasis on coffee permitted an industrial policy that reflected the desire of the "new class" to escape the vagaries of international markets by industrializing "under the protective umbrella of tariffs, special duty exemptions, and fiscal abatements." The new industrial economy was thus inefficient and import-intensive but internationally uncompetitive, and so depended on the continued vigor of the coffee economy.[63] High fixed costs, import dependence, and policy-induced capital intensity also made the industrial sector far less flexible than the coffee sector.

These problems went critical after Costa Rica joined the CACM in 1963. Formation of the CACM removed the main barrier to industrialization in Central America—small domestic markets—because a single market was created for goods originating in member states protected by a common external tariff. As a result, Costa Rican manufacturing grew an average of 10.6 percent a year from 1961 to 1971, and 7.0 percent a year from 1973 to 1977. Manufactured exports (80 percent of which went to CACM countries) increased from 4 percent to 30 percent of total exports between 1960 and 1978. To achieve these gains, Costa Rica encouraged foreign investment, offered liberal tax exemptions, and waived customs duties.[64] But protected markets, subsidized capital, and cheap imports also gave Costa Rica "a distorted form of industrialization: very capital-intensive, biased to-

[62] Bulmer-Thomas, *The Political Economy*, 110, 123–25, 160–64, 188–90.

[63] Quote from Eduardo Lizano, "Costa Rica and the Central American Common Market," in *The Costa Rica Reader*, ed. Edelman and Kennan, 145, 147–48. See also Edelman, "Recent Literature," 174–75.

[64] Nelson, *Costa Rica*, 159; Dennis Gayle, *The Small Developing State* (Brookfield, Vt.: Gower, 1986), 79; Clark Joel, "Tax Incentives in Central American Development," *Economic Development and Cultural Change* 19 (January 1971): 229–33.

wards consumer goods, heavily dependent on imports and offering little opportunity for backward linkages because of the preference built into the system for assembly of imported components over the manufacture and processing of local raw materials."[65]

Restructuring created a costly and fragile hybrid: a hothouse industrial sector grafted onto—and dependent upon—a well-rooted traditional export agriculture sector. Industrial development responded to the needs of outside investors, and Costa Rica's dependence on foreign capital placed it in competition with the rest of the Third World for funds. The tax exemptions, investment allowances, and accelerated depreciation schedules that were established to attract investors were so generous, however, that such sums could not be recouped even if the new firms flourished. (By 1965, import duty exemptions alone equaled 15 percent of total tax revenues.) The resulting shortfalls added to a growing budget deficit, cut into public investment, and made necessary an increase in domestic taxes.[66]

The final irony of this first attempt to restructure is that it *increased* vulnerability to foreign market shocks and dependence on traditional exports. The extreme, inflexible dependence on imports left industry vulnerable to the cost pressures that were a consequence of rising oil prices and world inflation. The resulting "squeeze on industrial profits . . . reduced the opportunities for funding investment through self-finance and made access to outside sources of finance much more important." It also increased industrial concentration by savaging small-scale firms, potentially the most competitive part of manufacturing.[67] Huge investments in public firms gave the illusion of structural change. But the firms "that emerged . . . were highly protected and . . . not competitive in broader international markets," thus requiring heavy subsidies from export agriculture.[68] In 1970, 77 percent of Costa Rica's industrial raw materials and 99 percent of its capital goods originated outside the CACM; they accounted for 55 percent of total non-CACM imports and used up 74 percent of non-CACM export earnings—but less than 20 percent of its manufactured

[65] Bulmer-Thomas, *The Political Economy*, 194.

[66] Ibid., 175–76, 185–86, 190–92; Joel, "Tax Incentives," 242–44.

[67] Bulmer-Thomas, *The Political Economy*, 209.

[68] Quote from Joan Nelson, "Crisis Management, Economic Reform, and Costa Rican Democracy," in *Debt and Democracy in Latin America*, ed. Barbara Stallings and Robert Kaufman (Boulder, Colo.: Westview Press, 1989), 151–52. See also Juan M. del Aguila, "The Limits of Reform Development in Contemporary Costa Rica," *Journal of Interamerican Studies and World Affairs* 24 (August 1982): 370–71.

exports found buyers outside the CACM. In 1978, when commodity prices crashed, shattering the hothouse, Costa Rica was still as dependent on coffee and bananas as it had been in 1970, and it still lacked export alternatives.[69] Before we turn to "the crisis" and Costa Rica's second attempt to restructure, however, let us look at the domestic political economy of coffee.

THE DOMESTIC POLITICAL ECONOMY OF COFFEE: ABSOLUTE CAPACITY

Costa Rica had three crucial advantages in its restructuring effort: a dedication to education and a growing middle class gave the state a readily available pool of talented help; democracy gave it legitimacy; and the revolution of 1948 gave it a mandate to restructure. In addition, the sectoral characteristics of coffee gave the state a relatively high absolute capacity and considerable autonomy.

Resource Extraction

Coffee offered two easily tapped sources of income, thus encouraging the development of specialized and inflexible fiscal institutions and discouraging the development of an institutional capacity to tax other sectors. Customs duties have long been the main source of state revenues (they provided 30–50 percent of the total revenue from 1940 to 1978), and their collection requires only a small customs service. Taxes on coffee have also brought in large sums—and they, too, require little effort to collect. Peasant production spreads coffee income widely, but this dispersion does not require the establishment of deeply penetrating institutions to tax peasants throughout the country. Instead, Costa Rica levies taxes at three key venues and on three small, easily monitored groups—beneficio owners, domestic wholesalers, and exporters—on the basis of volume (the unprocessed coffee tax), weight (the domestic tax and the certificate of origin tax), and price (the ad valorem tax on processed coffee, the fixed-rate tax on exported coffee, and the ad valorem tax on exported coffee).[70]

By 1945, the common perception was that "fiscal reform was . . .

---

[69] Bulmer-Thomas, *The Political Economy*, 192–96, 201–3; Nelson, *Costa Rica*, 158.
[70] Seligson, *Peasants of Costa Rica*, 44–47; Riismandel, "Costa Rica," 152, n. 66; Morris, "An Economic Evaluation," 41, 144–45.

long overdue" because restructuring necessitated higher public expenditures. The antiquated tariff system, however, prevented customs revenues from increasing "in line with the value of imports," and all trade-related revenues followed coffee prices.[71] Costa Rica implemented tariff reforms that "improved the elasticity of import taxes," increased the revenue from export taxes, initiated a tax on the banana companies, and increased direct taxes. As a result, total revenues increased after the late 1940s, but they did not "grow at a rate to match the increase in public expenditure" or provide the resources necessary for restructuring.[72]

Costa Rica lacked the institutional capacity to tap new or alternative sources of income. It sought to achieve economic growth and diversification, for example, by offering tariff "exonerations" to foreign firms. These exemptions sharply reduced customs collections, and even processing them meant assigning "a large proportion of scarce, qualified personnel to the tedious task of studying, classifying and processing hundreds of applications." This cost the state "the additional tax revenue that could have been collected if this administrative personnel had been permitted to perform its traditional function of assessing and collecting taxes."[73] Worse, despite rising investment and increased economic growth, "administrative weakness, coupled with widespread tax evasion, made it clear that the yield from direct taxes was not going to rise sufficiently fast to compensate for the falls in import duties provoked by the formation of the CACM."[74]

The effects of this situation were all bad. Total revenue as a proportion of GDP remained flat, forcing the state to borrow increasingly heavily to finance the increase in public spending, and pushing the annual budget deficit from CA\$2.6 million in 1960 to CA\$100.5 million in 1978–79.[75] The inability to raise revenue from traditional sources or from new direct taxes also forced the state to pursue administratively feasible, but regressive, distortionary alternatives. It imposed high sales taxes (on such things as alcohol, soft drinks, and gasoline) that could be collected from a few wholesalers, and it offset lost customs duties by raising tariffs and increasing export taxes, thus

[71] Bulmer-Thomas, *The Political Economy*, 121–22, 169–70.
[72] Ibid., 170, 183.
[73] Joel, "Tax Incentives," 246.
[74] Bulmer-Thomas, *The Political Economy*, 183.
[75] Ibid., 183–85; Benjamin Villanueva, "Changing Relations between the State and the Economy in Central America," Occasional Paper no. 9, Latin American and Caribbean Center (Miami: Florida International University, 1985), 73.

exaggerating the bias for import substitution and against export-ing.[76] The tax system's inability to tap new sources of income gives politicians incentives to maintain the old, but the distortions intro-duced in the effort to raise revenues favor the powerful import-substituting and CACM-oriented industrialists.

Monitoring, Regulating, and Redirecting the Economy

Luckily, the coffee sector's characteristics have had more positive consequences for the state's capacity to monitor, regulate, and pro-mote economic activity. Costa Rica has institutions to manage both the coffee industry as a whole and the activities of the smallest grower. The first of these was the Coffee Office (OFICAF), a consolidation of two agencies that were created to cope with the depression: the Coffee Settlement Board, charged with setting minimum producer prices and the maximum net profits beneficios could earn; and the National Institute for the Defense of Coffee, charged with promoting Costa Rican coffee. In 1948 OFICAF assumed these agencies' functions and added new ones; in 1963 it assumed responsibility for Costa Rica's obligations under the ICA. It also administers the Center for Investi-gations in Coffee, which conducts coffee research, provides extension services, and oversees the many services provided by the beneficios and cooperatives. Finally, OFICAF provides the state with a means to force diversification, as it did from 1970 to 77 by cutting the coffee industry's share of total credit by 73 percent and the actual amount of credit coffee producers received by 52 percent, in order to shift funds to the production of other crops.[77]

But the state's institutional ability extends beyond the coffee sector for two coffee-related reasons. First, most coffee growers are general farmers producing several crops; their problems as general farmers are therefore the same as those they face as coffee growers. Thus, although OFICAF serves the coffee industry, it has a wider impact because of its deeply penetrating reach, its resources, and its exper-tise. As a result, too, the state has long had incentives to support

[76] Bulmer-Thomas, *The Political Economy*, 183, 280–81; Michael Best, "Political Power and Tax Revenues in Central America," *Journal of Development Economics* 3 (1976): 51–53; Joel, "Tax Incentives," 247; Gayle, *The Small Developing State*, 79, 81.

[77] Seligson, *Peasants of Costa Rica*, 36; Barlett, "Agricultural Change," 132–33; Wins-on, *Coffee and Democracy*, 106–7; Morris, "An Economic Evaluation," 55–56, 98–101, 120–31.

small-scale agriculture. Hence, in 1937 it created the *Juntas Rurales de Crédito Agrícola* to provide credit to small farmers. By 1960, forty-nine juntas were dispensing 40 million colones annually and had become a critical, accessible source of financing and technical assistance for small farmers. In 1943 Costa Rica also organized the National Production Council (CNP) to provide credit, extension services, and price supports for small producers of food crops.[78] The state's investments in dams, drainage, and soil conservation serve all farmers, as do the roads built to service the coffee industry; and the agencies that plan, build, and maintain this general-purpose infrastructure are no more wedded to coffee than is the infrastructure itself.

Second, after the revolution of 1948 brought to power the "new class" born of the old elite's flight from coffee, Costa Rica created a vast array of state and "autonomous" agencies to monitor, regulate, and promote alternative sectors.[79] By the late 1970s, 180 *autónomos* were engaged in everything from refining petroleum to combating alcoholism. The National Council for Scientific and Technological Research and the National Institute of Vocational Training provide services to assist in diversification; the National Economic Council, the National Industrial Council, the Interinstitutional Committee of Small Industry and Crafts, and the Costa Rican Development Corporation (CODESA) promote it. Supporting these autónomos are such state agencies as the Office of National Planning and Economic Policy, and the Ministry of Economy, Industry, and Trade.

Costa Rica's institutional capacity to promote alternative sectors is most evident in the successful push to industrialize. Early initiatives such as the New Industry Law passed in the 1940s and the Law of Industrial Production and Development encouraged the importation of industrial equipment and the use of local raw materials by industry; they were supplemented by the creation of autónomos to promote industrialization and the making of large investments in economic infrastructure. Later initiatives included the Exports Promotion Law of 1972, the creation of CODESA in 1973 and the National Committee for the Coordination of Industrial Development in 1975, the founding of a stock exchange, the adoption of pro-industry lending policies by the Bank of Costa Rica, and the establishment of the Ministry of Exportation in 1983. These measures increased manufactur-

[78] Riismandel, "Costa Rica," 154–56; Seligson, *Peasants of Costa Rica,* 123–24; Bulmer-Thomas, *The Political Economy,* 113, 164–65.
[79] Anderson, "Alternative Action," 49; Ameringer, *Democracy in Costa Rica,* 41–44.

ing's share of GDP from 13 percent to 22 percent (1961–79), doubled manufacturing's value added (1970–80), and explain why Costa Rican efforts far surpassed those of its neighbors, which lacked the capacity to promote alternative sectors.[80]

Coffee and the Other Institutions of State

The quality of Costa Rica's other institutions of state makes them a key determinant of its success; their size, cost, and stickiness make them a barrier to restructuring. The Costa Rican bureaucracy is non-partisan and competent, but also huge; the public sector has grown from 10 ministries and 8 autónomos in 1955 to 12 ministries and 180 autónomos in the mid-1980s. Public employment increased sixfold in the same period, or twice as fast as the working population, making the state the biggest employer after agriculture. Costa Rica's bureaucracy is one of the largest in the world relative to population.[81] Job security and advancement opportunities give public employees an incentive to organize and their geographical concentration facilitates it. Whereas in the mid-1980s just 7.1 percent of private-sector workers were unionized, 56.2 percent of public-sector employees belonged to unions such as the National Educators Association (22,000 members) and the National Union of Public Employees (13,000 members).[82]

Two coffee-related factors help explain this growth and the quality of Costa Rican public servants. First, in the years after the revolution of 1948, during which the PLN created the institutions intended to transform Costa Rica, coffee prices boomed and the budget showed a surplus.[83] Second, many of those who made the revolution of 1948—and who filled the new state jobs—were members of the old coffee elite who had taken public-sector jobs because of the absence of jobs

[80] Saenz, "Population Growth," pp. 76–78; Nelson, *Costa Rica,* 158–60; Gayle, *The Small Developing State,* 80; Bulmer-Thomas, *The Political Economy,* 211–12.

[81] Richard Kearney, "Political Responsiveness and Neutral Competence in the Developing Countries," *Review of Public Personnel Administration* 8 (Spring 1988): 75; Luis Garita, "The Bureaucratization of the Costa Rican State," in *The Costa Rica Reader,* ed. Edelman and Kennan, 139–40; Seligson, *Peasants of Costa Rica,* 47; Nelson, *Costa Rica,* 202; Trejos, "Costa Rica," 2–3.

[82] Ralph Russomando, "Structures of Integration and Labor Relations in Costa Rica" (Ph.D. diss., University of Massachusetts, 1982), 107, 131; Elisa Donato and Manuel Bolaños, "Problems and Prospects of the Costa Rican Trade Unions," in *The Costa Rica Reader,* ed. Edelman and Kennan, 155.

[83] Winson, *Coffee and Democracy,* 70–71.

not related to coffee. As a result, since its creation in 1949, the civil service has been staffed by well-educated individuals from socially and politically prominent families. After 1960, public-sector growth accelerated as this "new political-bureaucratic oligarchy" really settled in.[84]

Today the public sector stymies restructuring. In the 1980s, public-sector pay absorbed 28 percent of the national income; the state now borrows to pay public employees rather than tangle with their powerful unions. Indeed, the size, strength, and strategic position of these unions give them the power to extract wages double those in the private sector, block manpower cuts that threaten their members, and bar the reallocation of state spending to more productive purposes. The drain on the budget "cannot be brought under control without a major bureaucratic restructuring. [But] given the political influence of organized middle class and professional interests—the main beneficiaries of bureaucratic growth and publicly financed welfare and social services—reorganization will prove difficult."[85] Currently, government spending on wages depletes the capital budget, increases the deficit, and increases the cost of loans for public and private investment. Further, because middle-class public employees are heavy consumers of imports, there is a reduction in the foreign exchange available for productive uses. Finally, high public-sector wages and comprehensive benefits force private employers to compete with the state for skilled labor. As a result, these employers face serious shortages of skilled manpower; whereas by the mid-1980s 26 percent of all wage earners worked for the state, 74 percent of salaried professionals and 80 percent of technicians did.[86]

In sum, coffee's legacy for the state is mixed. Coffee provided the liberal state with the limited revenues it required at low cost. But as revenue needs grew, Costa Rica's revenue-collecting institutions failed to meet them. Today these institutions need an overhaul if they are to

[84] José Vega cited in Edelman, "Recent Literature," 179; Ameringer, *Democracy in Costa Rica*, 46; Charles Denton, "Bureaucracy in an Immobilist Society," *Administrative Science Quarterly* 14 (September 1969): 420.

[85] Quote from del Aguila, "The Limits of Development Reform," 369; Ameringer, *Democracy in Costa Rica*, 94–95; Gayle, *The Small Developing State*, 73; Fields, "Employment and Economic Growth," 1498; Gary Fields and Henry Wan, Jr., "Wage Setting Institutions and Economic Development," *World Development* 17 (September 1989): 1472–73.

[86] Saenz, "Population Growth," 85–88; Fields and Wan, "Wage Setting Institutions," 1473; Kearney, "Political Responsiveness," 74.

extract the funds required for restructuring. Peasant production, however, has resulted in the establishment of deeply penetrating, flexible institutions able to aid all farmers and to promote agricultural diversification. Equally important, pressure on members of the coffee elite to diversify led them to establish institutions to promote manufacturing. The related rapid growth of the public sector gave the state important strengths, but today the public sector hinders restructuring. Luckily for the state, these liabilities are offset by sectoral actors' incapacity for collective action.

INCAPACITY OF SECTORAL ACTORS FOR COLLECTIVE ACTION

The production characteristics of coffee stymie collective action by sectoral actors. Costa Rica has been a coffee economy for a hundred years, but coffee producers as a group have been unable to defend their interests since 1945. Until the 1920s "wealthy coffee industrialists" dominated society, the economy, and politics, and despite occasional squabbles, they could usually "unite to advance their own interests through various forms of government action."[87] Indeed, their interests and those of state leaders were often identical, for many politicians grew coffee, too. In the 1930s the coffee barons, joined by many small growers, formed the *Asociación Nacional de Productores de Café* to lobby the state for help and were rewarded with OFICAF's precursors. But even as they were organizing, many began to abandon coffee for safer havens.[88] Coffee's peasant cash crop character then came to the fore, as did the associated barriers to collective action.

And the barriers are high. There are nearly 90,000 registered producers in Costa Rica, few of whom have any contact with others beyond their villages. Furthermore, coffee is grown by self-reliant farmers working in isolation, an isolation reinforced by competition among growers even in the same village. Success permits the winners to expand, and to expand winners buy land from losers forced to sell to survive. In Costa Rica, which has the highest rural population density in Latin America and where 60 percent of the rural population is landless, the fear of failure is intense, as is the resulting compe-

[87] Nelson, *Costa Rica,* 99.

[88] Bulmer-Thomas, *The Political Economy,* 37–38, 58–60; Winson, *Coffee and Democracy,* 21–22, 41; Seligson, *Peasants of Costa Rica,* 33–34.

tition.[89] Growers have no incentive to cooperate either, since given their number, any one producer's return from collaboration will be vanishingly small. As peasants, they also lack both the financial clout to make themselves felt (despite their huge aggregate contribution to the economy) and the information and skills necessary to articulate or lobby for their collective interests. They also lack ties to bankers, lawyers, and other professionals whose expertise and influence could offset their weaknesses.

The evidence of coffee growers' incapacity for collective action is striking. In 1973 small coffee growers owned 73 percent of the coffee farms and accounted for 43.3 percent of coffee production, 40.0 percent of coffee's contribution to the economy, and 14.2 percent of export earnings. Nevertheless, during the 1970s and 1980s, the state systematically—and without effective resistance—limited their access to credit, paid them lower prices than those prevailing abroad, and used export taxes and an overvalued exchange rate to extract resources in order to invest in other sectors.[90] One expert notes "the distinctive [political] quiescence of the Costa Rican peasant in the post-1948 period," because peasants lack the external allies necessary to help them overcome their collective-action problem. Or, rather, the problem is that the PLN and the state "got there first," preempting organization by the Church or by unions that might have helped farmers articulate interests distinct from those of the state.[91]

Growers' problems are most evident in their largely unsuccessful efforts after 1978 to organize unions to lobby for reductions in interest rates, taxes, and import duties on inputs.[92] Most were short-lived and consisted of little more than spontaneous actions such as road blockades. Even in cases where they have lasted, such as UPANacional (the National Union of Small Agriculturists), the returns have been small, and have followed a pattern common to the whole movement: "the organization wins concessions for some members, divisions arise

[89] Seligson, *Peasants of Costa Rica*, 23–25; Barlett, "Agricultural Change," 22, 59; Leslie Anderson, "Mixed Blessings: Disruption and Organization among Peasant Unions in Costa Rica," *Latin American Research Review* 26, no. 1 (1991): 116.

[90] Winson, *Coffee and Democracy*, 182–83; Morris, "An Economic Evaluation," 144; Lindenberg and Ramirez, *Managing Adjustment*, 261–62.

[91] Douglas Kincaid, "Costa Rica Peasants and the Politics of Quiescence," in *The Costa Rica Reader*, ed. Edelman and Kennan, 179, 182–84; Ameringer, *Democracy in Costa Rica*, 72–73.

[92] The following discussion is based on Anderson, "Alternative Action" and "Mixed Blessings," but comes to different conclusions.

within the group, and those who have received nothing lose organizational support and the sympathetic attention of those who have already won." If they quit, the union dies; if they stay, they are further disadvantaged by membership.[93] The tension within the unions replicates the competition that divides smallholders and that bars collective action, dooming them as effective organizations. Put differently, the state can easily co-opt key segments of the rural population by giving them small concessions, increasing the probability that the unions' internal tensions will tear them apart.

Conditions facing coffee workers pose even higher barriers to collective action. Initially, the high wages paid to coffee workers set Costa Rica apart from other coffee republics. This anomaly, however, merely reflected the chronic labor shortage that prevailed until the 1940s.[94] As rural population density and landlessness increased, labor market conditions reversed, forcing wages down. But despite their desperate plight and common interest in survival, coffee workers' efforts to organize have failed.

Coffee workers are disadvantaged in every way. They are unskilled. Employers have no investment in them. Nothing positive distinguishes them from the many others with whom they compete for work. They have no long-term employment or advancement prospects to induce them to invest in organization. Many tend their own minifundia and dare not risk losing their coffee income because without it they might lose their land. Coffee workers often labor in isolation, making it hard to organize them, punish those who break ranks, or bar scabs; but on small farms, supervision is constant. Migrant seasonal workers' ties to their home villages kill interest in organizing; and local coffee workers get no support from their communities, which mix landowners, *minifundistas,* and the landless and are stratified along the same lines. Finally, growers oppose anything that raises labor costs or impairs their own flexibility. In sum, labor organization threatens neither coffee growers nor the state, the state requires no sector-specific labor management capacity, and political parties have no incentive to champion coffee workers' interests.

Coffee workers have not organized, but they have joined peasant unions or attempted self-help through land invasions. In the first case, they have gained the least of what little the peasant unions deliver. Land invasions, however, now figure prominently in rural life.

[93] Anderson, "Mixed Blessings," 137.
[94] Winson, *Coffee and Democracy,* 14–15; Riismandel, "Costa Rica," 147–48.

Indeed, between 1963 and 1982, the Institute of Agrarian Development, Costa Rica's land reform agency, dealt with more than 1,000 cases involving 15,600 families and more than 10 percent of all farm land.[95] But the aim of land invasions is private, not collective, for peasants grab to achieve self-sufficiency. Furthermore, land invasions only seldom involve coffee workers; most are staged by organizations associated with the banana industry or by migrant banana workers who have brought organizational experience home from "the [banana] zone."[96]

Nothing reveals the limits on collective action in coffee more clearly than comparison with the banana industry. Costa Rican bananas are grown on industrial plantations, which provide the huge, steady flow of bananas needed to run costly packing plants, dedicated rail lines, and specialized ports. The plantations are located in the unpopulated lowlands and operate year around, requiring a permanent work force. The industry thus gives large numbers of workers long-term employment and ample reason to organize; it also provides ideal conditions for doing so by concentrating them in isolated, homogeneous communities and employing them in big, dispersed work gangs. Moreover, high fixed costs, large economies of scale, and the resulting need for high-capacity utilization give firms reason to support a union; and as vertically integrated MNCs profiting from an oligopolistic world price structure, they can afford to negotiate.[97]

Banana workers are therefore the best organized and most militant workers in Costa Rica. They staged their first strike in 1934 and won their first collective agreement with the companies in 1938. Many strikes have taken place since then; the banana unions, joined in the Federation of Banana Workers and Unions, and allied with the *Confederación General de Trabajadores Costarricenses* (CGTC), have fought for higher wages, job safety, better living conditions, health care, and pensions. The results are striking: whereas coffee workers are not unionized, by the late 1930s most banana workers were—and were earning ten times as much as coffee workers. The wage gap has since narrowed, but banana workers' working and living conditions remain far better than those of coffee workers. Coffee workers con-

[95] Anderson, "Mixed Blessings," 116, 137; Kincaid, "Politics of Quiescence," 179.
[96] Seligson, *Peasants of Costa Rica*, 106; Marc Edelman, "When They Took the 'Muni': Political Culture and Anti-Austerity Protest in Rural Northwestern Costa Rica," *American Ethnologist* 17 (November 1990): 742–43.
[97] Seligson, *Peasants of Costa Rica*, 94.

tinue to do nothing on the labor front; but the CGTC is responsible for a big proportion of total strike activity and collective agreements, making it an economic and political force.[98]

Outside the banana industry and the public sector, unions are small, fragmented, and weak. Prior to the start of industrialization, most nonfarm jobs were located in tiny artisanal workshops. Indeed, as late as 1958 "there were 6,000 establishments operating in manufacturing, mining and agricultural services; but total employment . . . amounted to only 32,000 [and] only eighty firms employed more than fifty persons." Firm size and unionization have increased since, but so has the number of unions. By 1975 Costa Rica had 258 unions, 46 percent of which had fewer than 50 members and 65 percent of which had fewer than 100 members.[99] Individually, such unions carry no weight with the state, but together their number and their divergent interests bar collection action.

Labor's incapacity for collective action facilitates restructuring. Coffee workers cannot resist resource reallocation; industrial workers cannot resist trade liberalization. Furthermore, though banana workers are organized and their unions' rhetoric is radical, their targets are the MNCs and their aim is to secure more of the rents. It is thus "neither expedient nor necessary for a political party in Costa Rica to seek the support of labor unions."[100] This, in turn, permits the state to dictate to labor rather than accommodate it.[101] In sum, labor's incapacity for collective action increases both the state's flexibility and the tractability of the restructuring project.

AUTONOMY: CONTROLLING THE CHANNELS OF INTEREST REPRESENTATION

At first glance, Costa Rican democracy would appear to limit autonomy. Indeed, the liberal oligarchic state was conceived to support coffee-led growth, and ties between the state and the coffee sector were so strong that "only during the 1930s depression did coffee

[98] Ibid., 70–74, 93–94; Russomando, "Structures of Integration," 37–38, 87–88, 113–15, 137–38, 222–23.

[99] Quote from Joseph McGovern, "The Costa Rican Labor Movement," *Public and International Affairs* 4 (Spring 1966): 97–98. See also Bulmer-Thomas, *The Political Economy*, 191; Russomando, "Structures of Integration," 111.

[100] McGovern, "The Costa Rican Labor Movement," 106.

[101] Russomando, "Structures of Integration," 196.

interests feel obliged to establish formal associations to press the government for policy changes in their favor."[102] But appearances are misleading. In fact, the sectoral characteristics of coffee facilitate state control of the channels of interest representation.

Policy makers easily maintain their autonomy from small growers. The latter are peasants whose number, wide geographical dispersion, and mutual distrust prevent them from exerting heavy, sustained pressure on the state. They also lack allies within the state, for the broad mandate of even the coffee-sector agencies means that they are no one's "client." Moreover, the state does not depend on the industry for expertise or expert personnel; instead, information flows down to the industry from the state via extension workers and other state experts. Finally, smallholders do not travel in the same social circles as officials and are as unwelcome in their clubs as in their offices.

State autonomy from the coffee barons is more limited, because their power "in national, regional and local affairs weighs heavy in contrast to the unorganized and comparatively powerless small operators."[103] Their number is small and has decreased as concentration in the processing and exporting segments of the industry has increased. They are among the best-educated, most sophisticated business leaders in Costa Rica; indeed, they long *were* the business community. Further, their ties to powerful allies in banking, law, and commerce have added to their clout. They also furnish so many OFICAF officials that frequently "the regulated end up doing the regulating."[104] Within the tiny Costa Rican elite, the coffee barons and politicians are family. The barons have access to the policy process; nevertheless, there are limits, which the state has increased since 1948.

The state's growing autonomy is clear in the battle over coffee taxes that took place in the 1950s.[105] The junta and, subsequently, the administration of Otilio Ulate Blanco needed more money to realize their ambitious plans. First they tried a tax on wealth, but the tax system could not collect it. Seeking a tax that revenue authorities could collect, they settled on a coffee tax since, in the midst of the Korean War price boom the revenue potential of coffee seemed un-

---

[102] Bulmer-Thomas, *The Political Economy*, 276.

[103] Thomas Norris, "Decision-Making in Relation to Property on a Costa Rican Coffee Estate" (Ph.D. diss., Michigan State University, 1952), 21.

[104] Seligson, *Peasants of Costa Rica*, 41.

[105] The discussion in the following paragraphs draws extensively on Winson, *Coffee and Democracy*, 78–86.

limited, existing taxes were small, and collection posed no problems. In March 1950 the government proposed a 4.5 percent ad valorem tax on coffee delivered to beneficios in the first year, 2.25 percent thereafter. The proposal unleashed a storm of protest, led by the *Cámara de Cafetaleros,* the coffee barons' organ.

The Cámara's campaign forced revisions in the tax proposal, but its victory had required the mobilization of smallholders and ultimately undercut the barons' power. As first proposed, the new tax fell on producers, giving thousands of peasants common cause with the big producer-processors. The Cámara gave them access to the press and OFICAF, as well as the organizational resources they needed to overcome their collective-action problems. This gave the Cámara the popular support necessary to force a compromise. But the resulting settlement shifted the tax burden from producers to processors by reducing to 9 percent the 16 percent profit margin beneficios were previously permitted, and allocating the difference to the state. When the compromise became law in 1952, "the Government announced a major program to develop rural infrastructure . . . to be financed in part by revenues provided by the new *ad valorem* tax."[106] In short, it rewarded peasants with monies extracted from the barons, a clear indication of the source of the critical pressure in the compromise process. Put differently, the coffee barons could not control a state that had other constituencies to turn to for support.

In general, three related developments since 1948 have increased state autonomy. First, smallholders constitute a large constituency that politicians can mobilize, inter alia, to counter the barons, but that cannot mobilize against them when ignored. The politicians thus passed campaign funding laws that provide public financing for campaigns based on party performance in the preceding election, freeing themselves from dependence on the elite, while blocking new opposition parties attempting to tap peasant anger.[107] Second, diversification has divided the barons to such an extent that even if they have access to policy makers, they are sending increasingly mixed messages. Third, industrialization and the diversification of export agriculture have yielded new interest groups that "in the 1970s . . . combined to form powerful associations capable of articulating their . . . sectoral interests and confident of their ability to influence public policy in their

---

[106] Ibid., 86.
[107] Ameringer, *Democracy in Costa Rica,* 51–52, 61.

favor."[108] The result has been greater state autonomy because these groups offset both the coffee barons and each other.

Sectoral and Societal Pressures

Societal pressures do challenge state autonomy. These pressures do not originate in the rural areas, despite widespread landlessness and grinding poverty. The predominance of peasant production and the desire of the landless only to own enough land to be self-sufficient mean that much of the population is *not* fixated on the state. Moreover, given this interest in self-sufficiency and the existence of high barriers to collective action, the state can ignore the rural majority, or appease them with minor concessions.

The same cannot be said for the rapidly growing middle class. Greater access to education and economic diversification have created a large group of white-collar professionals in need of jobs. Unlike rural Costa Ricans, they both see the state as the key to satisfying their wants and are positioned to pressure politicians. The result, as noted earlier, has been the rapid expansion of the public sector—proof of the intensity of societal pressures resulting from the insufficiency of job growth and the belief that the state is a vast cornucopia.[109] It also suggests the limits to policy makers' ability to formulate policy autonomously.

RELATIVE CAPACITY: TAKING ON "THE CRISIS"

In 1978 an economic shock wave nearly flattened Costa Rica. The state leadership failed to grasp the depth of the crisis and then made things worse. Facing disaster, Costa Ricans elected a new president in 1982 whose policies stabilized the economy and who began a restructuring program that would be carried on by his successors. Recovery and restructuring have proceeded slowly, but Costa Rica *has* made progress, especially when compared with its neighbors. The question is, how?

The economic crisis of 1978–82 rivaled that of the 1930s. Coffee prices, having risen sixfold from 1975 to 1977, collapsed in 1978.

---

[108] Bulmer-Thomas, *The Political Economy*, 200–201.
[109] Fields and Wan, Jr., "Wage Setting Institutions," 1473; Ameringer, *Democracy in Costa Rica*, 97.

Then oil prices doubled, international interest rates and inflation shot up and export markets shrank. Costa Rica's terms of trade and foreign reserves tumbled, and the current account deficit ballooned.[110] By 1982, the GDP had fallen 14 percent, inflation had soared from single digits to more than 100 percent, tax revenues were stalled, and the fiscal deficit reached 14 percent of GDP. Debt service costs had risen to 90 percent of exports, because by 1982 Costa Rica owed more than $3 billion, making it one of the most indebted countries per capita in the world. Costa Ricans saw all they had gained in the 1970s wiped out as unemployment doubled and wages decreased by 40 percent.[111]

But from 1978 to 1982 the administration of Rodrigo Carazo Odio, supported by big coffee and sugar processors and by protected industrialists, implemented policies that aggravated Costa Rica's problems. One such policy increased the volume of lending to export agriculture to increase export earnings—and thus permit continued support for ISI industries. The administration's main response to the crisis, however, was to increase spending without increasing revenues. When the budget deficit and foreign debt reached impossible levels in 1980, Carazo signed a standby credit agreement with the IMF, but he refused to implement the required controls on spending and tax reforms. The IMF canceled the agreement, precipitating the collapse of the colón, which further reduced imports and revenues from trade. Debt service costs escalated and Carazo declared a repayment moratorium in 1981, leading creditors to refuse further loans. Chaos prevailed until the 1982 election.[112]

In 1982 Luis Alberto Monge Alvarez swept into office. He launched a tough stabilization program intended to damp exchange rate fluctuations, cut inflation, "reestablish the overall equilibrium of the balance of payments," and "reestablish the country's foreign credit."[113] He resumed debt payments and attacked the deficit, cutting subsidies, raising charges for government goods and services, and selling un-

---

[110] Bulmer-Thomas, *The Political Economy*, 237–40, 291–92; Nelson, *Costa Rica*, 134–35, 178–79; William Loehr, "Current Account Balances in Central America, 1974–1984," *Journal of Latin American Studies* 19 (May 1987): 92.

[111] Nelson, "Crisis Management," 143, 146; Díaz-Bonilla, *Structural Adjustment Programs*, 14; Trejos, "Costa Rica," 18–19; Lindenberg and Ramirez, *Managing Adjustment*, 87.

[112] Morris, "An Economic Evaluation," 95–97, 123–24; Nelson, "Crisis Management," 144–45; Bulmer-Thomas, *The Political Economy*, 244–46.

[113] Lindenberg and Ramirez, *Managing Adjustment*, 72.

profitable CODESA subsidiaries. He also sought to increase revenues without hurting exports or imports, though to do so he had to raise nontrade taxes, especially sales and income taxes. Monge stuck with the flexible exchange rate system adopted in 1981, without which stabilization could not have succeeded.[114]

And succeed it did. Costa Rica exceeded IMF guidelines for spending and failed to cut public-sector jobs. But real growth in GDP resumed, rising from 2.3 percent in 1983 to 6.3 percent in 1984, slowing to 2.0 percent in 1985 and rising again to 3.0 percent in 1986. Inflation fell from 100 percent to 12 percent between 1982 and 1984. The budget deficit declined because the increase in the rate of spending was cut to half of the inflation rate and tax revenues were increased more than 70 percent. The balance-of-payments deficit improved from 14.5 percent of the GDP to 6 percent between 1980 and 1984, as a result of a lower volume of imports and an 11 percent growth in real exports. Unemployment fell to pre-crisis levels.[115] These indicators fail to show how much Costa Ricans are still hurting: incomes are down; poverty rates are up and social services are more limited. But conditions are improving and are far better than those existing elsewhere in Central America; Costa Rican democracy is intact, and peace prevails.

The real key to success, policy makers had realized by 1984, was to escape the bonds of the old coffee economy *and* those imposed by Costa Rica's first attempt to restructure. Their program thus combined continued stabilization with a structural adjustment program sponsored by the World Bank. The aim of stabilization was to restore state finances, attract foreign aid and loans, and provide a supportive macroeconomic setting for restructuring.[116] The aim of restructuring was to create a diversified, less vulnerable export economy by increasing agricultural exports to finance internationally competitive, nontraditional export industries selling to non-CACM markets. To stimu-

[114] See the "Letter of Intent" signed by the IMF and the Costa Rican government on March 20, 1984, published in Lindenberg and Ramirez, *Managing Adjustment*, 79–80; Trejos, "Costa Rica," 24–25; Loehr, "Current Account Balances," 101.

[115] Fields, "Employment and Economic Growth," 1504–6; Nelson, *Costa Rica*, xxvii; Diáz-Bonilla, *Structural Adjustment Programs*, 14; Edelman and Kennan, *The Costa Rica Reader*, 189; Seligson and Muller, "Democratic Stability," 316.

[116] Trejos, "Costa Rica," 17. For details of the stabilization program, see the March 1984 Letter of Intent submitted to the IMF by Costa Rica, the 1985 Contingency Agreement between the IMF and Costa Rica, and the May 1988 Letter of Intent, in Lindenberg and Ramirez, *Managing Adjustment*, 79–81, 270–71.

late agricultural exports, the combined program called for changes in the exchange rate, prices, subsidies and tariffs, and more state support in the areas of marketing, credit, and extension services. To stimulate competitiveness, the program cut effective rates of protection from 50–1,600 percent to 50–150 percent. To expand nontraditional exports, it reduced export taxes and taxes on income from nontraditional exports, allowed duty exemptions on the inputs used in them, lowered the interest rates charged exporters, offered marketing help, allowed firms to offset their tax liability by an amount equal to one-third of their export earnings, and opened export credit-processing facilities.[117]

Implementation of this program forced policy makers to face the weakness of the tax system. Stabilization required higher revenues, but restructuring demanded cuts in tariffs and export taxes, which together generated 30 percent of annual revenues in 1980. Given the institutional limits, the only solution in the short term was to take more from exporters; indeed, "two-thirds of the increase in 1982 tax revenues was paid by the export sector."[118] Export taxes, already equal to 38 percent of the f.o.b. value of exports and a big "export disincentive," were raised again in 1983, and firms were hit with corporate income taxes as high as 50 percent and a "temporary surcharge" equal to 30 percent of the base income tax. Such high taxes dealt a blow to exports, forcing the government to eliminate the exchange rate differential tax and to cut tariffs and export taxes—but this step reduced annual revenues by more than 1 billion colones.[119]

Tariff cuts presented policy makers with serious political problems as well. They provoked agonized protests from once-protected industries and the Chamber of Industry. The loss in trade revenues had to be offset with spending cuts or tax increases elsewhere, and both options aroused widespread opposition. In the years 1982–87, for example, reductions in spending for public services provoked 19.4 percent of the protests against economic adjustment measures; public-sector layoffs and wage restrictions provoked 41.7 percent, and cuts in consumer subsidies were responsible for 20.8 percent.[120] Tax increases fared no better. Sales taxes were increased, but their regressive nature posed problems for a democratic government. Property and income

[117] Lindenberg and Ramirez, *Managing Adjustment,* 74–77, 193–94. See the 1985 Letter of Intent between Costa Rica and the World Bank, and Costa Rica's 1988 structural adjustment loan application, in ibid., 82, 267–70.

[118] Luis Liberman, cited in ibid., 75.

[119] Ibid., 75–76.

[120] Ibid., 12, 74; Gayle, *The Small Developing State,* 80; Joel, "Tax Incentives," 247–48.

taxes had more potential, but they strained the tax authorities' assessment and collection capabilities and fell on those best able to protest—high-income members of the elite.[121]

Similar problems faced policy makers when they tried to trim the public sector. Although CODESA and the many parastatals it operates were widely viewed as inefficient, CODESA's "original social democratic rationale remained convincing to many . . . legislators and much of the public." Likewise, though they are of most benefit to big producers, the subsidies administered by the CNP embody the guarantee of social welfare that is the basis of Costa Rican democracy. Thus, efforts to downsize the CNP aroused the opposition of powerful lobbying groups representing big producers and backed by peasants and urban consumers.[122] Public employees, who *are* much of the budget problem, adamantly oppose any attempt to shrink the state bureaucracy. In part, their opposition is principled, for many are so committed to state-led growth that the "issue engages fundamental ideological conflicts regarding the role of the state." But the state also employs them for twice what they could earn elsewhere—if there were jobs. Furthermore, public employment is their kids' future, too, for it "is the best hope for the growing numbers of secondary school and university graduates produced each year."[123] State employees therefore vociferously protested cut-backs, and to good effect. Thus, for example, though President Monge sought to eliminate 30,000 public-sector jobs to reduce the deficit, he had to *add* 6,000 new jobs in the midst of the crisis. Public-sector employees accounted for one-third of the protests against economic adjustment between 1982 and 1987—a far higher proportion than any other group.[124]

Measuring the Success

Still, despite the difficulties, stabilization has succeeded and restructuring is progressing slowly. As Monge explained in 1984, "I am not contending that we have surmounted the crisis. But . . . after two years during which we had to adopt bitter and hard decisions to heal a

[121] Best, "Political Power and Tax Revenues," 53–56; Bulmer-Thomas, *The Political Economy,* 212–13.

[122] Quote from Nelson, "Crisis Management," 147, 154. See also Ameringer, *Democracy in Costa Rica,* 48.

[123] Nelson, "Crisis Management," 154.

[124] Lowell Gudmundson, "Costa Rica: The Conflict over Stabilization and Neutrality, 1983–84," Occasional Paper no. 36, Latin American and Caribbean Center (Miami: Florida International University, 1984), p. 6; Lindenberg and Ramirez, *Managing Adjustment,* 49.

seriously ill and almost bankrupt economy, we have . . . drawn away from the precipice."[125] The budget deficit and inflation are under control. The exchange rate is realistic and stable. The tax system has been "overhauled . . . in the direction of greater equity and efficiency," and total revenues are up despite cuts in tariffs and export taxes.[126] Costa Rica's huge debt hurt, but did not stop, the restructuring effort. Real growth in GDP slowed in 1985, barely increased in 1986, and took off only in 1987, for despite rescheduling and foreign aid, "the debt overhang meant Costa Rica suffered large net financial outflows in 1983, 1984 and 1985." The resulting resource drain reduced gross domestic investment in 1983–86 to less than 75 percent of the 1980 figure. But restructuring did continue, and by 1987 gross domestic investment exceeded pre-crisis levels and dramatic changes were evident in the economy.[127]

The extent of restructuring is impressive. Although initially, agriculture increased in importance as other sectors contracted and the state sought a short-term increase in traditional exports to tide itself over, restructuring reduced agriculture's share of GDP from 20.5 percent to 17.9 percent between 1984 and 1987. Although traditional exports rose 18.7 percent from 1980 to 1984, they fell 1.7 percent from 1984 to 1987, while nontraditional agricultural exports rose 12.0 percent, thus generating most of the 10.4 percent gain in agricultural exports recorded in that period.[128] But the key success was in nontraditional, nonagricultural exports to non-CACM markets, which in 1986 generated one-third of export earnings and whose earnings in 1987 exceeded those from coffee. The production and export of shirts and blue jeans, for example, increased from nil in the early 1980s to 400,000 dozen and 825,000 dozen, respectively, in 1986, putting 40,000 people to work and earning $18.5 million to $23.5 million per year. Such exports now more than offset those lost because of the old CACM's demise, a remarkable feat, given the protection once accorded CACM exports.[129]

[125] Cited in Lindenberg and Ramirez, *Managing Adjustment,* 73.

[126] Quote from Bulmer-Thomas, *The Political Economy,* 281. See also Nelson, "Crisis Management," 151.

[127] Quote from Nelson, "Crisis Management," 151. See also Marc Lindenberg, "Central America's Elusive Recovery," *World Development* 16, no. 2 (1988): 238.

[128] Lindenberg and Ramirez, *Managing Adjustment,* 257–59.

[129] Nelson, "Crisis Management," 151; Lowell Gudmundson, "Costa Rica's Arias at Midterm," *Current History* (December 1987), 418–19 and n. 10; Díáz-Bonilla, *Structural Adjustment Programs,* 14.

In part, Costa Rica's success can be explained in simple economic terms. In 1982 the economy had a light manufacturing base and industries ready to export once antiexport biases were removed. An abundance of high-quality, low-cost labor, competitive utility rates, and good transportation facilities also made production in Costa Rica more profitable than it was elsewhere in the region, and the country's political stability made it a foreign investor's dream.[130]

What is also striking is how easily and peacefully stabilization and restructuring have been effected. In part, "the certain prospect of elections" and the possibility of changing governments give Costa Ricans "an important safety valve"; and their belief in the legitimacy of the governments they elect gives the state room for maneuver.[131] Heedful of the majority's views, leaders have also balanced tough policies with negotiated concessions that have given those hurt some satisfaction. In 1982, for example, Monge froze public-sector wages, lengthened the workday, and threatened to fire strikers, but met the subsequent protest by partially indexing wages. Politicians' respect for the ballot box ensured that "concern for social equity influenced the design of the program as a whole." Tax and utility price hikes fell hardest on businesses and large agricultural interests, wage increases favored lower-paid workers, and a safety net was maintained, convincing people "that Monge was making a serious effort to allocate the costs of adjustment equitably and to shield the most vulnerable groups."[132] But although democracy clearly matters, it is not the sole explanation.

The keys to Costa Rican success are the tractability of the restructuring project, the absolute capacity of the state, societal actors' incapacity for collective action, and the resulting high relative capacity of the state. In short, the sectoral characteristics of the old coffee economy have conspired to ease the challenge confronting Costa Rica. Thus, asset/factor flexibility limits the barriers to exit, reduces growers' resistance to change, and even encourages diversification and efforts to get the state to *promote* it. Despite a weak tax system and the weight of the public sector, coffee's sectoral characteristics ensure that Costa Rica has little invested in sector-specific institutions and has the institutional capacity to promote and support new sectors.

Although restructuring has hurt many groups in the private sector,

[130] Lindenberg and Ramirez, *Managing Adjustment,* 151, 201.
[131] Nelson, "Crisis Management," 149.
[132] Ibid.

none is capable of sustained opposition; differences among them bar collaboration; and the diversity of interest groups ensures that the state has organized supporters for its programs.[133] Although farmers were hurt by low coffee prices in the late 1980s, the reallocation of resources away from traditional exports, and cuts in agricultural subsidies, no politically salient rural opposition has emerged. Further, policy makers found that many of the farmers' demands could be met without compromising the government's program. Indeed, devaluation and cuts in export taxes and tariffs actually reduced farmers' input costs, increased their returns, and dulled their opposition.[134]

Nor do elites pose a serious challenge, for though they are organized and expert at lobbying, their interests are often those of the state. True, old agricultural elites opposed reallocating resources to new sectors, but they also profited from devaluation and from cuts in tariffs and export taxes. The elite itself has been diversifying into manufacturing and other potentially competitive export activities for more than thirty years. Some of its members fear lower protection, but many, represented by the free-market-oriented National Association for Economic Development and the Costa Rican Chamber of Commerce, welcome restructuring and are a key constituency for reform-minded politicians. Of the protests against tax increases and changes in trade and tariff policies that were staged between 1982 and 1987, just 4.2 percent were in opposition to economic adjustment measures; actions by business organizations were responsible for just 8 percent.[135] Indeed, the real irony is that the only sustained opposition to stabilization and restructuring came from industrialists and public employees who had participated in ISI—that is, from groups that owed their existence to past state efforts to restructure.

The Costa Rican experience seems to confirm the validity of sectoral analysis—and to raise serious questions. Like the previous three cases, the Costa Rican case seems consistent with the model. The

[133] A survey concerning the protests against economic adjustment measures that were staged between 1982 and 1987 indicates that 90.3 percent of such protests were mounted by a single sectoral organization, that two or more organizations in the same sector collaborated only 5.6 percent of the time, and that multisectoral coalitions mounted only 4.2 percent of total protests. Lindenberg and Ramirez, *Managing Adjustment*, 50.

[134] Ibid., 254; Anderson, "Mixed Blessings," 114.

[135] Figures from Lindenberg and Ramirez, *Managing Adjustment*, 44, 47. See also Nelson, *Costa Rica*, 218; Gayle, *The Small Developing State*, 80.

contrasts between high/high Sri Lanka and low/low Costa Rica could not be clearer and are exactly what sectoral analysis leads us to expect. Although Costa Rica is not comparable with Korea, it clearly fits the more general low/low template, despite the glaring differences that separate Korea and Costa Rica in every other possible dimension. But simple geography makes it hard to ignore the radically different experience of Costa Rica's neighboring coffee republic, El Salvador. If peasant cash crop sectors are supposed to give rise to yeoman farmers and tractable restructuring projects, and to be associated with flexible states and democratic politics, how do we explain El Salvador with its long history of hacienda agriculture, oligarchy, repression, governmental inflexibility, and failed reform?

CHAPTER SEVEN

Conclusion

With the main outlines of sectoral analysis now clear, three tasks remain. We must assay the extent of, and analyze the reasons for, *intra*sectoral variation; relate sectoral analysis to other, established analytic approaches; and explore a research agenda for the future.

VARIATIONS ON A THEME, OR?

The obvious way to test intrasectoral variation is to study many cases. I lack the patience to tackle even one more major study, however, so here I limit myself to merely suggestive treatments of three high-value cases: (1) El Salvador, which seems to defy all expectations of coffee as a low/low peasant cash crop; (2) the petro-states, which would be expected to have the greatest potential to escape the sad fate of high/high mining states; and (3) Taiwan, which is a revealing case of variation on a theme.

El Salvador: Different Starting Point, Same Logic

El Salvador seems to falsify claims that the Costa Rican case can be generalized. Although they have the same leading export and trade in the same international market, Costa Rica and El Salvador could not have more different domestic political economies or political histories. What, then, of the two core contentions of sectoral analysis—that sectors have an optimal economic organization that poses distinctive economic challenges to all producers and states, and that states with

226

similar sectoral bases face similar political constraints when they address these challenges, do so from similar institutional positions, and arrive at similar policy outcomes?

Costa Rica is a near perfect peasant cash crop case. Quality coffee is grown efficiently on small and medium-sized farms. The coffee sector is flexible—witness the history of adjustment to changing market conditions and the easy exit of big growers and processors for other sectors. Restructuring has proved to be relatively tractable. The state has a relatively high degree of absolute capacity and autonomy, and it confronts relatively weak societal actors, especially in the coffee sector. It thus has ample relative capacity, as evidenced by the restructuring effort after the revolution of 1948 and the crisis of 1978. And despite the Great Depression, the revolution of 1948, the crisis of 1978, and the wars that have raged around Costa Rica, democracy endures and Costa Ricans take pride in their ability to find nonviolent, noncoercive ways of settling differences. El Salvador is the near perfect opposite.

In El Salvador, as in Costa Rica, coffee lies at the heart of the political economy, but there the similarity ends. Coffee came to El Salvador in the 1840s and by 1870 was its leading export. Coffee generated 80–90 percent of El Salvador's export earnings between 1880 and 1970, and today it still accounts for 45 percent of total exports. El Salvador is the largest Central American coffee exporter and the fifth largest coffee producer in the world.[1] In El Salvador, however, coffee is grown mostly on huge haciendas; 80 percent is grown on farms of 3,000–6,000 acres owned by the so-called fourteen families that have run the country since the nineteenth century.[2] The countryside is thus marked by extreme concentration of ownership and the poverty of the vast majority, who are landless or near landless agricultural workers.

Restructuring poses intractable problems for a Salvadoran state that lacks capacity and autonomy and that faces strong societal actors. The haciendas' high fixed costs, large work forces, and strict maintenance requirements make adaptation to market shocks difficult; the

[1] Robert West and John Augelli, *Middle America* (Englewood Cliffs, N.J.: Prentice-Hall, 1976), 423–24; General Accounting Office, *Coffee: Production and Marketing Systems*, Report to Congress, ID-77-54 (Washington, D.C., 1977), 75; Bradford Burns, "The Modernization of Underdevelopment," *Journal of Developing Areas* 18 (April 1984): 305–6.
[2] Anthony Winson, *Coffee and Democracy in Modern Costa Rica* (New York: St. Martin's Press, 1989), 94–96; West and Augelli, *Middle America*, p. 424.

big growers' investment in land planted with coffee "right to the last inch" makes exit still harder.[3] Restructuring threatens their very existence and they will fight it by any means, including mass murder. The state has ample coercive capabilities but little capacity to manage the noncoffee economy; revenues depend on coffee export taxes and customs duties, since the state cannot tap other sectors. Through the National Coffee Department and the El Salvador Coffee Company it services big coffee, but it cannot monitor, regulate, or promote other sectors.[4] The coffee oligarchs are organized to pressure the state, which has never been autonomous of them. The concentration of landless workers around the haciendas has permitted limited labor organization in the coffee areas, though not elsewhere, despite unbridled attacks by growers and the state.

Lacking relative capacity, the state has failed to restructure, a failure reflected in El Salvador's violent history. Restructuring requires that the state have autonomy from *elites* with a vested interest in the status quo and the capacity to force *them* to reallocate resources. But the Salvadoran state's relative *in*capacity made it merely the means by which the elite preyed on the nation. The "magic square" of oligarchic rule consisted of control of production, export, finance, and land— all of which demanded control of the state.[5] Thus, the original liberal oligarchic state defined a tiny political community and secured its interests by seizing communal lands, enforcing repressive labor laws, and suppressing opposition. When the depression overwhelmed the state's capacity to keep the lid on, the elite handed the state over to the military, which, with the elite's "wholehearted support," killed 30,000 peasants and preserved the magic square.[6] Repression worked for forty years, but when elite intransigence quashed all hope of reform in 1970s, the lid came off again. A decade of bestiality by both sides followed—bloody testimony to the intractability of the restructuring project facing El Salvador.

What explains this extreme intrasectoral variation, and can sectoral

[3] GAO, *Coffee*, 76.

[4] Ibid., 24–26, 75–79; Burns, "The Modernization of Underdevelopment," 303; Jeffrey Davis, "The Economic Effects of Windfall Gains in Export Earnings," *World Development* 11, no. 2 (1983): 126.

[5] Luis de Sebatián, cited in Enrique Baloyra-Herp, "Reactionary Despotism in Central America," *Journal of Latin American Studies* 15 (November 1983): 311.

[6] Burns, "The Modernization of Underdevelopment," 302–3; Victor Bulmer-Thomas, *The Political Economy of Central America since 1920* (New York: Cambridge University Press, 1987), 21–22, 62–63; Robert Elam, "Appeal to Arms: The Army and Politics in El Salvador, 1931–1964" (Ph.D. diss., University of New Mexico, 1968), 42.

analysis encompass it? Reference to these two countries' radically different starting points provides part of the answer to the first question. A complete answer, however, requires analysis of the underlying logic of sectors, which will answer the second.

The existence of different initial conditions explains the different organization of the coffee sectors of Costa Rica and El Salvador. When colonized, Costa Rica had no exploitable Indian population and was thus a labor-poor nation of small farmers ideally suited for growing coffee when it arrived in the 1830s. In El Salvador, however, an Indian population permitted the establishment of haciendas, and when coffee arrived, the newly independent state was already controlled by the owners of the huge haciendas that dominated the economy. The lure of coffee wealth led them to seize *tierras communales* (common lands) and to dispossess the *ejiodos* (communal villages) and smallholders to increase their holdings and create a pool of landless laborers to work them. By 1880 the coffee sector had assumed its fatal aspect. Around it the increase in population made things worse, and by 1980 El Salvador had "the highest ratio of landless families to total population, as well as the highest ratio of tenant farmers to the population, of any country in Latin America."[7]

Although El Salvador's starting point explains the existence of haciendas, it does not explain why El Salvador developed differently from Costa Rica. After all, estate crop systems exhibit equally skewed patterns of land ownership but do not have the institutionalized repression that has characterized El Salvador. The explanation is sectoral: El Salvador's bloody history is the result of the oligarchy's effort to maintain an unstable, suboptimal hacienda system for the production of a peasant cash crop. In contrast to estate crop systems, hacienda systems have neither capital requirements nor scale requirements that would prevent peasants from growing coffee efficiently. All they need is land. In the absence of economic barriers to entry, therefore, El Salvador's haciendas and grossly skewed distribution of land must be maintained by force. "This fact," notes Jeffery Paige, "transforms economic conflicts over the division of the proceeds from agriculture into political conflicts over the ultimate instruments of control in the society."[8]

[7] Quote from Roy Prosterman and Jeffrey Riedinger, *Land Reform and Democratic Development* (Baltimore: Johns Hopkins University Press, 1987), 143–45; Burns, "The Modernization of Underdevelopment," 296–300; Baloyra-Herp, "Reactionary Despotism," 298–303.

[8] Jeffery Paige, *Agrarian Revolution* (New York: Free Press, 1975), 86.

This conflict is zero-sum and molds actors' interests and organizations, including those of the state.[9] For the rural poor, land is the sole concern. On Sri Lankan tea plantations, year-round plucking and the impossibility of self-employment focus workers' efforts on improving their lot as wage laborers. On Salvadoran haciendas, however, the seasonal nature of employment and the absence of economic barriers to entry into the coffee sector focus peasants' hopes on getting land. But holding on to that land is the oligarchy's main concern. Land is their base of power, and the profitable use of land to grow coffee (unlike that used to grow tea) requires the dependent labor force that widespread landlessness creates, since the less efficient haciendas would not be able to compete for labor in a free market where peasants had the option of growing their own coffee. Retaining the haciendas thus required control of the state to repress opposition and *block* restructuring, since restructuring means eliminating haciendas and thus the oligarchy. This dependence on state power, however, also made the state the target of peasant attacks aimed at overthrowing the political system in order to end the oligarchy's control of the land.

In sum, the case of El Salvador suggests two conclusions. First, it is a reminder of the importance of initial conditions, exogenous variables, and the oddities that make countries unique. El Salvador is different from Costa Rica and from the neat package that sectoral analysis predicts. Who held power and under what conditions when coffee arrived made and continues to make a difference, measured—literally—in terms of human lives. Second, El Salvador is an exception that proves the rule in the proper sense of the phrase. It is a case that seems to violate expectations, but on closer examination, it reveals the workings of a sectoral logic despite the impact of exogenous variables, thus allowing us to explore its consequences in altered situations.[10] Put differently, the conditions that initially prevailed in El Salvador matter, but we need sectoral analysis to explain *how* and *why* they matter—in and of themselves, in a comparison of El Salvador with Costa Rica, or with other countries that do not produce peasant cash crops.

Petro-States: No Escaping the Curse

If the Costa Rica–El Salvador comparison reveals the power of sectoral analysis despite different initial conditions, what about varia-

[9] See ibid., 16–24, 41–45, and 82–86.
[10] Stephen Jay Gould, *The Panda's Thumb* (New York: Norton, 1980), 71.

tions born of differences in the products of different industries in the same sector?[11] Specifically, do the black gold–producing high-fliers of OPEC face the same limits and bleak prospects as the pedestrian producers of base metals? The short answer is yes.[12] Indeed, the seemingly blessed oil-producing states are the perfect exemplars of the high/high ideal type and they suffer—in exaggerated form—all the same debilities that plague the less flashy producers of industrial minerals.

It is hard to imagine lumping Zambia with any member of OPEC. Unlike sorry CIPEC, OPEC challenged the international power hierarchy. OPEC members seized billions of dollars' worth of assets from MNCs richer than most countries, redirected a king's ransom into their own coffers, and stomped on Western nations' political interests with impunity. Furthermore, the oil bonanza dwarfed any copper boom. The quadrupling of oil prices in 1973–74 netted more money, said Hector Hurtado, Venezuela's finance minister, "than we ever in our wildest dreams thought possible," increasing OPEC members' revenues *elevenfold* in one year (2). According to Terry Lynn Karl, for most OPEC states, "the transfer of wealth in 1974 and again in 1980 represented greater revenues than those available to them *over the entire past century*" (42). They invested 50 percent of the windfall and borrowed more against future revenues in order to "sow the petroleum." Certainly they seemed to have the funds necessary to diversify their economies and improve their standings in the world economy without having to make the hard allocative decisions that defeated the Zambians.

Petroleum's promise is matched only by the disaster it caused. As an OPEC spokesman noted bitterly, history will show that oil exporters "have gained the least or lost the most from the discovery and development of their resources" (42). By the 1980s, OPEC no longer dominated a tight international oil market but was increasingly a residual supplier of one awash in oil. As prices fell, revenues plunged; by 1986 Indonesia's oil revenues, for example, were a quarter of its 1976 revenues, and Nigeria's and Venezuela's had decreased by half. Plunging revenues and huge debts reversed economic growth. Worse, the oil bonanza strengthened, rather than reduced, oil dependence as huge

---

[11] For a somewhat crude answer to this question, see D. Michael Shafer, "Undermined: The Implications of Mineral Export Dependence for State Formation in Africa," *Third World Quarterly* 8 (July 1986): 916–952.

[12] For the definitive answer, see Terry Lynn Karl, *The Paradox of Plenty: Oil Booms and Petro-States* (Berkeley: University of California Press, forthcoming). Karl's in-depth study of oil's impact in Venezuela includes a comparison of its impact in Algeria, Indonesia, Mexico, Nigeria, Norway, and Iran. This entire section is based on Karl's book. Page citations referring to Karl's manuscript appear in parentheses.

foreign exchange earnings, overvalued exchange rates, and surging demand sucked in imports, swamped other sectors, and drowned agriculture. So bad was the damage that overall growth rates were *lower* than they would have been had states merely continued their pre-boom progress *and* lower than the LDC average over the same period (62–68). The resulting tensions broke many of the states that in 1973 had confidently proclaimed the millennium. "All in all," says Sheik Ahmed Yamani, former Saudi Arabian oil minister, "I wish we had discovered water" (478).

What explains the fall? The "similar disappointing macro-economic and political outcomes observed in nations as widely disparate as Iran and Venezuela," argues Karl, "can best be understood as the result of a common condition created by the interaction of commodities, booms and states." Indeed, although "dependence upon minerals produces a bundle of characteristics which, when taken together, are unique to mining countries, . . . these characteristics are present in an exaggerated form in all petro-states, which makes them a special subset of mining states" (23–24, 93–94).

Oil exaggerates mining states' problems in international markets. Oil marks the high end of capital intensity and economies of scale. The market is potentially extremely volatile which, given extreme capital intensity and large economies of scale, can have potentially serious consequences for firms. This puts a premium on risk management for firms and on oligopoly management for the industry. The Seven Sisters invented many of the risk management tricks used in high/high sectors and co-managed one of the most durable cartels in the world. OPEC members' national firms have been ineffective at individual risk management, however. Furthermore, collective-action problems lead OPEC members to price-gouge when the market is tight, thus encouraging conservation, substitution, alternative technologies, and new suppliers, and to bar production limits intended to support prices when the market is soft. The resulting, exaggerated boom-and-bust tendency, combined with long periods of oversupply and low prices, spells disaster for oil states, which, on average, depend on oil exports even more than mining states depend on mineral exports (94, 101–6). No wonder that oil states take restructuring even more seriously than do other mining states.

At home, too, oil exaggerates the problems plaguing mining states. Extreme capital intensity and large economies of scale make oil inflexible, rendering intractable the restructuring project faced by these states. Oil also impairs absolute capacity. Although oil delivers revenues, it leads politicians to eschew politically costly broad-based taxes, thus tying total revenues to oil prices. States can monitor, regulate, and promote oil, but its boom-exaggerated dominance kills any incentives to develop similar capacities for other sectors. Sectoral actors are united in an "oil-based social contract"; therefore, restructuring confronts opposition from "powerful countervailing social classes and groups that support a petro-led development model" (125, 130). Moreover, state control of oil revenues makes penetrating it *everyone's* aim. The resulting relative *in*capacity of the state thus gives politicians "overwhelming incentives to sustain existing development trajectories—despite what purely economic logic might dictate" (24).

Like the case of El Salvador, this brief analysis of the oil states suggests two conclusions. First, oil states fit the high/high model well. In fact, the fantastic rents that seem to distinguish oil states exaggerate the underlying sectoral logic, making them the best available approximation of the high/high ideal type discussed in Chapter 2.

Second, the variation *among* oil states is informative. Although Algeria, Indonesia, Iran, Mexico, Nigeria, Norway, and Venezuela are "variations on the theme of the petro-state," Indonesia and Norway have fared better than the rest (524). In part, both suffered a smaller "oil boom effect" than the others—that is, the relevant sectoral variables were weaker. But Norway also suffered less because it had a strong state before oil. Does this nullify sectoral analysis? Karl says no, arguing that even Norway offers "a powerful testament to the 'overwhelmingness' of booms," since it failed to resist "the tremendous incentives to spend more than it should" or to manage "interests vested in rapid oil development." She points out that "conflicts over the use of oil revenues, the appropriate level of extraction, and the relationship with other structural problems" complicate political debate, and "a new oil-related debt burden and an enhanced need for [restructuring] constrain future freedom of action in economic policy." Oil may not define the political economy as it does in countries where oil preceded the establishment of a strong state, but "the choices for the future have narrowed considerably and the task of adjustment become more difficult" (525–35).

Taiwan versus Korea: Sectors and Strategic Choices

The most problematic case of intrasectoral variation is one that is the least expected. Few nonexperts distinguish between Taiwan and Korea, the big two of the East Asian "little dragons." And the countries *do* have much in common, beginning with the economic success that will make them as rich as Britain and Italy by the twentieth century's end. Taiwan's real GNP grew an average of 8.8 percent between 1953 and 1986, advancing it from 85th to 38th in world ranking by per capita GNP (1962–86). In the same period, Taiwan cut unemployment to less than 2 percent, increased literacy and life expectancy rates faster than any other LDC with the exception of Hong Kong, and sustained one of the most equal income distributions in the world.[13] Taiwan, like Korea, "governed the market"; they intervened in similar fashion when facing virtually identical geopolitical and external market conditions to promote economic development and export competitiveness. Taiwan also had the same need to restructure by focusing on industrial deepening. Taiwan increased manufacturing's share of GDP from 22 percent to 29 percent (1960–83), chemicals' and machinery's share of industrial output from 22.2 percent to 47.2 percent (1965–82), and heavy industry's share of manufacturing output from 49.8 percent to 58.5 percent (1965–84).[14]

But there is a key difference: Taiwan and Korea are differentiated by firm size and degree of economic concentration. In 1981 "Korea had 10 firms in *Fortune*'s 500 biggest industrial firms outside the United States, while Taiwan had only 2. Only 176 firms in Taiwan had more than 1,000 employees in 1976 [and] over 80 percent . . . had fewer than 20 employees," not many less than in 1966. The industrial structure has deepened, but firm size has not increased accordingly. In contrast to Korea, where from 1966 to 1976, the number of firms increased 10 percent and firm size doubled, in Taiwan the number of firms increased 250 percent but firm size increased only 29 percent in the same period. Even "in 1985 firms with less than 300 employees accounted for 65 percent of manufactured exports." Politically more important, Taiwan's business groups are smaller than the jae-bul. In 1983, for example, the Formosa Plastics Group, Taiwan's largest business group, had annual sales that were one-fifth those of Hyundai and employed less than one-quarter as many people. Overall, "only 40

[13] Robert Wade, *Governing the Market* (Princeton: Princeton University Press, 1990), 34–39.

[14] Ibid., 44–45. The equivalent figures for Korea are: manufacturing's share of GDP increased from 14 percent to 30 percent (1960–83); chemicals' and machinery's share of industrial output increased from 19.5 percent to 40.4 percent (1965–82); and heavy industry's share of manufacturing output increased from 38.2 percent to 56.8 percent (1965–84). The discussion in the remainder of this section draws on *Governing the Market*. Page citations appear in parentheses.

percent of the 500 largest manufacturing firms belong to business groups, and most Taiwan enterprises remain single-unit operations" (66–70).

There is an easy explanation for this divergence between Taiwan and Korea that is consistent with sectoral analysis: their leaders chose different policies to effect restructuring. Policy makers in both countries could make and implement these choices because both countries had light manufacturing political economies; and therefore, the project was tractable, societal actors were weak, and the state was capable and autonomous. Once made, however, their choices fundamentally altered their countries' political economies, resulting not merely in divergent forms of industrial organization but, for example, in different prospects for democratization. Korean policy makers chose to restructure by implementing policies that encouraged economic concentration in order to build national industrial champions. These policies catapulted Korean steel, automobiles, ships, and chips to international competitiveness, but they reduced the relative capacity of the state, resulted in creation of the jae-bul, empowered big labor, and unleashed an overwhelming, society-driven push for democracy. Taiwan chose a different path.

Recognizing the threat posed by economic concentration, Taiwanese leaders picked policies that fostered restructuring but minimized reductions in relative capacity. Such policies

> encouraged the widest possible accumulation of industrial capital and untrammeled use of that capital, provided it remains small. . . . This is the industrial equivalent of the land reform strategy. Indeed, the land reform, coupled with what some contemporary critics called overinvestment in rural electricity supply, directly helped small-scale industrial investment. The low . . . ceiling on land ownership prevented reinvestment in land assets as a household expanded, . . . thereby encouraging it to look to industrial or service activity for additional income, the establishment of which was aided by abundant electricity. Permitting untrammeled use of small-scale property avoided resentment from those who would have found the restrictions irksome, . . . freed the government to concentrate on preventing big business from organizing in ways that threatened the regime [and created] labor conditions whose only check is competition between firms for workers. (268)

Even where restructuring seems to require larger-scale operations, the state seeks to minimize the threat to relative capacity. In Taiwan, as

235

in Korea, the state promotes mergers to save troubled firms or to foster expansion, but far less often. A more typical effort is the Program for Promoting Center-Satellite Factory Systems, which links final-assembly factories and parts suppliers, and material suppliers and downstream buyers (186–87). This system cuts transaction costs, maintains the benefits of specialization, and captures many of the benefits of scale, while retaining a base of small, dispersed firms. It thus averts the growth of economically and politically powerful large firms and reinforces barriers to collective action by business and labor.

The impact of such policies is evident in key comparisons of Taiwan with Korea. Unlike jae-bul workers, Taiwanese workers are widely dispersed in small factories and cannot organize; a tightly controlled labor regime still ensures "the powerlessness of labor unions" (267). Unlike the jae-bul and the FKI, business cannot organize to lobby government; "even an association like the Taiwan Shipbuilders Association . . . has never been asked to give its views on what appropriate policies for the industry should be" (282).[15] The impact of policy choices is most evident, however, in the different evolutions of Taiwanese and Korean politics in the 1980s. True, in Taiwan "development, urbanization, and the growth of industry have created a 'new middle class'" interested in politics, and groups have formed to press their interests, including Taiwan's first opposition party (289). But the state remains in control, and nothing about this process remotely resembles the democratic explosion that remade Korea during the same period.

Again, this example of intrasectoral variation suggests two conclusions. First, sectoral analysis is valid for these cases. Taiwan and Korea had the autonomy and capacity to restructure. Further, the consequences of the policy choices their leaders made are best understood as reflecting the resulting organization of industry and confirming the recursive relationship between state action, the changing structure of the economy, and its implications for future state action. This comparison confirms a point made in Chapter 1 about sectors, determinism, and choice. As the divergent restructuring programs undertaken by Taiwan and Korea make clear, what their common sectoral

---

[15] Later Wade comments that "if economic corporatism means that only those economic interest groups sanctioned by the state get access to the state, then Taiwan is an extreme example of the genre" (294–95).

starting point conferred was the capacity and autonomy to implement restructuring. But though this common starting point informed policy makers' choice of targets, it did not determine the policies pursued. Taiwanese policy makers did take sectoral variables into account, however, for they sought to restructure without suffering the consequences of moving in the high/high direction.

A second conclusion suggests a need for more research. Taiwan's ability to deepen its industrial structure without ending up like Korea suggests that there are limits to the contention that sectors have an optimal organization. It is important not to exaggerate this point, for Taiwan's chemical complexes are as big and as capital-intensive as Korea's, and statistics suggest that "in upstream, basic industries Taiwan has a more concentrated industrial structure than Korea" (69). Still, the facts that the Taiwanese economy as a whole is less concentrated and that state policies are responsible suggest that efficient factor substitution, organizational innovation, and state support can extend the bounds of optimality. Put differently, if optimal organization is more a matter of nurture than of nature, then the Taiwan case suggests there should be a more central role for politics and policy choice in the "making" of sectors and sectoral political economies than that permitted by the rudimentary argument with which this book began.

This observation suggests that sectoral analysis must be refined and extended. We must ask where and under what conditions factor substitution, organizational innovation, and state support are efficient. Specifically, we must explore where and under what conditions policy can nurture different sectoral forms that are *stable* and *internationally competitive,* for it is only in these cases that policy choice independently alters the rules of the game as defined in sectoral analysis. After all, although Taiwan succeeded in this regard, the industrial equivalents of El Salvador's coffee haciendas are far more common. Consider, for example, the effects of ISI as pursued in Latin American and African countries, and those of central planning in the former Soviet Union and the countries of Eastern Europe. In these cases policy, not technical necessity, produced huge, capital-intensive firms—none of which is internationally competitive and all of which compromise these states' relative capacity. These countries' travails constitute perverse proof of the validity of sectoral analysis—a sort of sectors' revenge.

237

CONCLUSION

DIFFERENTIATING SECTORAL ANALYSIS

If *inter*sectoral differences are big and *intra*sectoral variations small, then sectoral analysis is a powerful tool with implications for many other approaches. I do not want to engage in a long literature review here, however. Rather, I focus on a few comparisons with methological ramifications. I shall first examine the implications of low intrasectoral variation for particularistic explanations of development and then locate sectoral analysis in relation to other general explanations.

The Limits of Particularism

A finding of low intrasectoral variation suggests that many popular explanations are too narrow. Most vulnerable are area-based explanations that make geographical proximity a causal variable. Then there are explanations that give primacy to culture, colonial heritage, geopolitics, or regime type. None of these explanations can contain the compelling commonalities that link mining and oil states, for example, which range from Algeria to Zambia and include Bolivia, Indonesia, and Norway—states from the Middle East, Africa, Latin America, Asia, and Europe. They have no cultural affinities; every possible colonial heritage; divergent geopolitical positions; and regimes ranging from strong, multiparty democracy to shaky, one-party democracy, to weak authoritarian rule, to entrenched one-man rule.

All particularistic explanations evade the question, Compared with what? As revealed by the comparison between Costa Rica and El Salvador, different inheritances from the colonial period matter, but understanding why and how they matter, requires more. Costa Rica and El Salvador also have different regimes, but creating the category "oligarchic despotism" to describe El Salvador's regime does not explain why El Salvador's regime fits the description and Costa Rica's does not, or how either will evolve. Similarly, Norway's strong democracy helped moderate oil's impact, but to grasp what Norway had to cope with and how Norwegian politics have changed as a result, we must understand the "theme" on which Norway's experience is a variation.

The question Compared with what? and the notion of "variations on a theme" suggest an analogy to regression analysis. Regression draws a trend line in relation to which cases are more or less typical and establishes how strong the trend is. If we imagine sectoral analysis

238

in these terms, the sharp *inter*sectoral variation found in Chapters 3–6 indicates a big regression coefficient (a strong trend). Our analysis of *intra*sectoral variation then suggests, first, that states and industries of one sectoral type cluster with little variation up or down the trend line on either side of the norm. Second, it suggests that the scatter above or below the trend line is also small. Finally, the cross-continent, cross-cultural, cross-colonial heritage, cross-regime sectoral groupings of states suggest that if we analyzed the residuals (the scatter off the trend line), we would find no variable that covaries systematically with our dependent variable. These particularistic variables may explain what makes a case unique, but only in relation to the sectoral trend. We could control for those variables and the trend line would not change; adding them to the explanation buys nothing.

Sectoral Analysis in Context

This book echoes the growing consensus that states' economic policies shape how countries develop and how fast they do so. This consensus is superficial, however, for it conceals very different views concerning why a given state (or class of states) is where it is in the international division of labor. We can imagine a continuum of analytic alternatives extending from those approaches that aim the causal arrow from the international sphere inward, at the state and society, to those that aim it from society outward, at the state and beyond. Each offers a different assessment of the state's role, the balance of international and domestic forces that influence the state's behavior, the relationship between economic power and political power, the identities of the political actors, and the prospects for state action. But none of the alternatives is fully satisfying; let us assay them and find out what sectoral analysis can add.

At one extreme are the world system, dependency, and liberal arguments, which give explanatory primacy to the international system and deny Third World states an independent role. World system and dependency analysts assert the existence of a single world system of domination with a hierarchical international division of labor based on a universal principle of unequal exchange. Third World states and their political economies are shaped by their structural position in the periphery or semiperiphery of this world system. The effect of this integration into the international economy, according to such arguments, has been to make Third World states weak and malleable (so they will not impede plundering by the states at the core) or strong and repressive (so they can serve as partners in the plundering process). Either way, they cannot alter their place in the international division of labor or pursue autonomous, as opposed to "dependent," development.[16]

Liberal arguments reflect these claims through the glass darkly. For liberals, international market engagement is the "engine of growth" and more is better, "regardless of a state's position in the international division of labor." In fact, greater engagement promotes *relative* gains in a state's international position.[17] Liberals also argue that international market engagement improves efficiency, growth, and individual welfare at home. Thus liberals, like world system and dependency analysts, view the state with a jaundiced eye, though not because it cannot regulate international economic integration but because it ought not. Indeed, they argue, the state's only positive functions should be to provide public goods such as defense and to facilitate the functioning of the market; otherwise it should, in effect, make itself invisible.[18]

These approaches are subject to attack on three grounds because none offers a theory of domestic politics that can explain states' divergent responses to international integration. First, contrary to the world system and dependency claims, the East Asian NICs are more integrated into the world economy than other Third World states but have done best economically; contrary to liberal claims, the state has "governed the market" in all of the NICs.[19] Second, states respond differently to similar degrees of international integration. This con-

[16] Johan Galtung, "A Structural Theory of Imperialism," *Journal of Peace Research* 8 (1971): 81–117; André Gunder Frank, *Lumpenbourgeoisie, Lumpendevelopment* (New York: Monthly Review Press, 1972); Volker Bornschier, "Dependent Industrialization in the World Economy," *Journal of Conflict Resolution* 25 (September 1981): 371–400; Fernando Henrique Cardoso and Enzo Faletto, *Dependency and Development in Latin America* (Berkeley: University of California Press, 1979); Peter Evans, *Dependent Development* (Princeton: Princeton University Press, 1979).

[17] Geoffrey Garrett and Peter Lange, "Performance in a Hostile World," *World Politics* 38 (July 1986): 524–55. See also Bela Balassa, *Development Strategies in Semi-Industrial Economies* (Baltimore: Johns Hopkins University Press, 1982); Jagdish Bhagwati, *Anatomy and Consequences of Exchange Control Regimes* (New York: National Bureau of Economic Research, 1978): Anne Krueger, *Foreign Trade Regimes and Economic Development* (New York: National Bureau of Economic Research, 1978).

[18] T. N. Srinivasan, "Neoclassical Political Economy, the State, and Economic Development," *Asian Development Review* 3, no. 38 (1985): 41.

[19] Wade, *Governing the Market;* Alice Amsden, *Asia's Next Giant* (New York: Oxford University Press, 1989); Jung-en Woo, *Race to the Swift* (New York: Columbia University Press, 1991).

tradicts the world system and dependency claims that states' structural positions in the world economy determine their policy choice. It also destroys the liberal faith in uninhibited policy choice, for if policy choice is all, why is it that the NICs almost always choose right and other states almost always choose wrong?[20] Third, international integration itself is variable. Contrary to world system and dependency claims, what matters is not a universal law of unequal exchange but the varied effects of engagement in specific markets; liberal analysts often ignore systematic differences in the severity and tractability of the crises states face.

Sectoral analysis may complement or supersede such approaches. By specifying different types of international engagement, their domestic effects, and the logic linking them, it may refine the world system and dependency arguments. It may also refine the liberal argument by attributing deviations from market-conforming behavior to sectorally determined rigidities that delay adjustment. It may go further. Sectoral analysis suggests that the problems discerned by world system and dependency analysts result not from international integration but from integration via high/high sectors.[21] These theories' homogenizing tendencies may overgeneralize from one set of cases, thus obscuring the process of differentiation in the Third World that this book seeks to explain. Dependency may be but one outcome of many, produced by prior sectoral processes that explain not only dependency but the variety of other observed outcomes. There also may be reason to prefer sectoral analysis to liberal arguments to explain change and the diverging trajectories of Third World states. For if sectoral analysis is right, the crises states face and the institutions and actors upon which they act—and that must respond—are shaped by the leading export sector.

At the opposite extreme of our continuum are Marxist, pluralist, and other society-centered approaches that explain policy as the outcome of battles among interested societal actors. To explain who mobilizes, some focus on the distribution of power among interest groups or classes that seek to influence state action; others focus on

[20] Robert Bates, *Toward a Political Economy of Development* (Berkeley: University of California Press, 1988), 1.

[21] All of the best dependency studies are of countries tied to the world economy via high/high sectors or saddled with their ISI-induced equivalents. See, for example, Gary Gereffi, *The Pharmaceutical Industry and Dependency in the Third World* (Princeton: Princeton University Press, 1983); Douglas Bennett and Kenneth Sharpe, *Transnational Corporations versus the State* (Princeton: Princeton University Press, 1985).

the nature of the issues and the resulting division of costs and benefits among groups or classes. All view the state as unimportant. It is the arena in which mobilized interests do battle and its institutions implement policy, but its leaders lack the ability to make autonomous choices and to restructure society in keeping with them.[22] Such approaches also discount the importance of international variables as such, assuming that they, too, shape outcomes according to their impact on the existing social structure or on the division of costs and benefits that responding to them entails.

Such approaches cannot explain states' variable but patterned ability to restructure. Because they treat shocks as being exogenous, they cannot explain the nature or origins of the shocks different types of states face. They are also theories of motivation not results, for the link between group desires and outcomes is assumed to be unproblematic. But restructuring may be antithetical to elite interests, thus requiring an explanation of the elite's *in*ability to defend the status quo. This raises the issue of state autonomy and capacity, and points to such arguments' lack of a positive theory of state action. Restructuring demands an independent state interest and leadership role; "institutional innovation will come from rulers rather than constituents since the latter would always face the free rider problem."[23] Finally, there is the stickiness problem, for if state institutions merely reflect interest groups' desires, they ought to change as those desires change. Institutions do not change easily and instantly, however, demanding explanation of why they do not, of their independent impact on outcomes, and of systematic, cross-national variation in institutional stickiness.

Again, sectoral analysis may complement or supplant such approaches in explaining systematic variations in states' abilities to restructure. By specifying the origins and nature of the shocks states face, sectoral analysis predicts the required restructuring policies and thus the structure of costs and benefits confronted by interest groups. It may do more, however; for sectoral characteristics affect both the existing pattern of interest groups in a society rocked by external shocks and their respective capacities for collective action. Further, sectoral analysis offers a positive theory of the state, which explains

[22] Stephen Krasner, "Sovereignty," *Comparative Political Studies* 21 (April 1988): 68–71.

[23] Douglass North, cited in Stephan Haggard, "The Institutional Foundations of Hegemony," *International Organization* 42 (Winter 1988): 32.

how shocks impose a policy agenda on state leaders that is inconsistent with societal actors' interests, and the patterned variation in leaders' autonomy, as well as their absolute and relative capacities to formulate and implement restructuring policies.

Between the extremes are approaches that focus on the state itself. They explain policy outcomes as reflecting past decisions embodied in institutions, since "capabilities and preferences, that is, the very nature of the actors, cannot be understood except as part of some larger institutional framework"; moreover, "the possible options available . . . are constrained by available institutional capabilities [that] are themselves the product of choices made during some earlier period."[24] Although international and domestic events set the scene, politicians in office and bureaucrats in state agencies are viewed as deciding policy according to institutionally defined rules, on the basis of internal information, and within the limits of existing institutional capabilities.

Such approaches help explain states' varied ties to international markets and varied capacities for restructuring. Advocates of such approaches do not assume that the state has no interests that are independent of international or societal forces, or that it is perfectly flexible in adapting to changing market forces or in accommodating interest group demands. Rather, they contend that state autonomy permits leaders to try to restructure the state's ties to the international economy or reallocate domestic resources, but that to do so they must use existing institutions, which may be unsuited to present needs. An explanation of states' relations to international markets and societal actors thus requires reference not only to environmental incentives, both domestic and international, but to the state itself. Change is possible, but it is difficult and suboptimal because adjustment is limited by the available institutional stock from which new arrangements can be fashioned. Change, in short, is path dependent.

By themselves, such arguments lack content and are indeterminate. They often evade the question of policy innovation, since the substance of policy cannot be deduced from institutional configuration. Path dependency can also imply that outcomes are unique and cases incomparable. Stephen Krasner even suggests that "explanation rather than prediction ought to be the primary objective of science." He claims that this does not imply "that history . . . can only be a collec-

[24] Krasner, "Sovereignty," 72.

243

tion of individual stories. It is possible to delineate general principles and regularities that underlie . . . unique responses."[25] But to do so requires identification of further variables, which challenges both the assumption regarding the priority of institutional variables and the uniqueness assumption. Most analysts thus offer grab bags of circumstances in which, for example, the state is more or less autonomous.[26] These are not explanations, however, but categories to be filled with the historical details of each case.

Two fine examples of statist analysis upon which I have drawn heavily highlight these problems. Alice Amsden and Robert Wade put the state at the core of their explanations of the East Asian economic miracles. Amsden stresses "the crucial role of government . . . in subsidizing certain industries to stimulate growth [and of] government discipline over business."[27] Wade stresses "hard" states sharing an "almost unequivocal commitment . . . to build up the international competitiveness of domestic industry" by serving as "gatekeeper for the national economy . . . scrutiniz[ing] inflows and outflows and affect[ing] the terms of transactions in line with national objectives."[28] Both detail the nature and capabilities of these states' policy-making and policy-implementing institutions, the policies they pursued, and how and why those policies had the impacts they did. And neither leaves any doubt that the character of East Asian states and their policy choices explain why Korea and Taiwan will soon be as rich as Britain.

But the method of Amsden and Wade prevents them from helping to answer the important question: What determines which states, under what conditions, will be able to do how much to further development and improve their standing in the international division of labor? Like dependency analysts who start with the losers in international competition, find out what those states share, and from it establish the descriptive category "dependent state," Amsden and Wade begin with the East Asian winners, find out what *they* share, and from it establish the descriptive category "developmentalist state." But be-

---

[25] Ibid., 80.

[26] See, for example, Eric Nordlinger, "Critique of 'Return to the State,'" *American Political Science Review* 82 (September 1988): 882–83; or Dietrich Rueschemeyer and Peter Evans, "The State and Economic Transformation," in *Bringing the State Back In*, ed. Peter Evans, Dietrich Rueschemeyer, and Theda Skocpol (New York: Cambridge University Press, 1985), 64–65.

[27] Amsden, *Asia's Next Giant*, v–vi.

[28] Wade, *Governing the Market*, 7, 157.

cause their cases—like the Latin American cases of dependency theorists—share so much, it is impossible to make comparisons to states outside East Asia. It is impossible to tell whether others' failings result from their failure to have the right kind of state, or from their lack of antecedent factors as a result of which they fail to have the right kind of state.

This problem can be traced further, however, to the bigger issue of the comparative method itself. Although the arguments in which Amsden and Wade connect states and policy choices to outcomes are rigorous, neither offers a generalizable answer to the question, Why here and not elsewhere in the Third World? (to be fair, neither seeks to either). To explain the origins of East Asia's developmentalist states, Amsden refers to "historical and cultural factors," and Wade refers to "situational, ideological and organizational factors" and "Confucian culture."[29] These explanations may be descriptively accurate, but they are of little help analytically. The problem is that having begun with a descriptive category rather than an analytically motivated one, Amsden and Wade cannot offer a general explanation of why the states of East Asia developed as they did and can act as they do. Both therefore lack a common metric permitting comparisons between East Asian states and other states, or justifying the related claim that the states of East Asia "can serve as a useful model from which other aspiring industrializing countries can learn."[30]

In light of these limitations, we can again make an argument in support of sectoral analysis, because it *does* offer a common metric. By providing a theoretically motivated typology for classifying states and distinguishing the types of international and domestic influences that act on them, sectoral analysis offers a way to understand the "regularities that underlie a variety of unique responses." It also gives content and explanatory bite to the "general principles" that account for these regularities. Indeed, in addition to making comparison possible and being merely "post-dictive," it can be partially predictive, explaining the shocks to which international market forces subject states, and describing the institutional capabilities with which their leaders must respond. Sectoral analysis, in short, permits us not only to trace the recursive interaction of environment and institutional endowment over time but to predict its future course.

[29] Amsden, *Asia's Next Giant*, vi; Wade, *Governing the Market*, 229–31, 337–42.

[30] Amsden, *Asia's Next Giant*, vi. In Wade, *Governing the Market*, see the prescriptions in chap. 11, "Lessons from East Asia."

Sectoral Analysis and Other Sectoral Approaches

What about the relationship of sectoral analysis to other sectoral approaches? To answer this question, we must first recognize that these approaches form a broad and ill-defined category. Still, most who say they use sectoral approaches will likely point to the same motley crew of intellectual forebears: Alexander Gerschenkron, Raymond Vernon, Robert Gilpin, James Kurth, A. G. Hopkins, H. A. Innis, M. H. Watkins, George Beckford, and Robert Brenner.[31] I will focus on just four exemplary works, however—by Jeffery Paige, Terry Lynn Karl, Jeffry Frieden, and Peter Gourevitch.[32] Each is provocative, but none does what this book was intended to do.

Paige gives a sectoral explanation of the patterned variation in agrarian social movements. He offers "a theory of rural class conflict which defines these recurring patterns of conflict in terms of interactions between the economic and political behavior of cultivators and that of noncultivators and predicts the circumstances under which these conflicts lead to cultivator social movements in general and agrarian revolution in particular."[33] He argues that cultivators' and noncultivators' interests and capacities for collective action—and the likely form of conflict between them—are shaped by the sectoral organization of the export crop they are engaged in producing: commercial hacienda, sharecropping/migratory labor, small holding, or plantation.

Anyone familiar with *Agrarian Revolution* will recognize that I owe much to this book. Paige ignores many key issues, however. Although *Agrarian Revolution* is about export agriculture, he ignores international markets, failing to account for intersectoral variation in the

---

[31] Alexander Gerschenkron, *Economic Backwardness in Historical Perspective* (Cambridge: Harvard University Press, 1962); Raymond Vernon, *Sovereignty at Bay* (New York: Basic Books, 1971); Robert Gilpin, *U.S. Power and the Multinational Corporation* (New York: Basic Books, 1975); James Kurth, "The Political Consequences of the Product Cycle," *International Organization* 33 (Winter 1979): 1–34; A. G. Hopkins, *An Economic History of West Africa* (New York: Columbia University Press, 1973); H. A. Innis, *Essays in Canadian Economic History* (Toronto: University of Toronto Press, 1956); M. H. Watkins, "A Staple Theory of Economic Growth," *Canadian Journal of Economics and Political Science* 29 (May 1963): 141–58; George Beckford, *Persistent Poverty* (New York: Oxford University Press, 1972); and Robert Brenner, "The Origins of Capitalist Development," *New Left Review* (August 1977): 25–92.

[32] Paige, *Agrarian Revolution;* Karl, *The Paradox of Plenty;* Jeffry Frieden, *Debt, Development, and Democracy* (Princeton: Princeton University Press, 1991); Peter Gourevitch, *Politics in Hard Times* (Ithaca: Cornell University Press, 1986).

[33] Paige, *Agrarian Revolution,* 10.

nature of the competition and of the market shocks producers face, and in production flexibility, all of which affect cultivator-noncultivator conflict. He also ignores the political, social, and economic context of export agriculture—failing, for example, to link intersectoral variation in export agriculture with variations in state autonomy and capacity. And he fails to consider industrial sectors. In sum, *Agrarian Revolution* is a fine start, but tackling my question requires an overarching explanation that locates agricultural sectors in the international and domestic political economies *and* permits analysis of industrial sectors.

In *The Paradox of Plenty,* Karl offers an in-depth sectoral analysis of Venezuela and a comparative analysis of petro-states as a type. Again, the problem is the lack of a general theory. She presents petro-states as the limiting case of the mining state type but fails to delineate the sectors' underlying causal dynamics or to establish a common metric permitting cross-sectoral comparisons. She uses the Dutch disease literature on the effects of booming export staple sectors to explain "the paradox of plenty," for example. But as shown by the experience of Costa Rica, export booms in low/low sectors have different effects because peasant production spreads the wealth to growers rather than concentrating it in the state; because state institutions are different; and because societal actors have different interests and different capacities to realize them. Thus Karl, like Paige, offers a wealth of ideas and data—and encouragement to supply the missing overarching argument.

In *Debt, Development, and Democracy,* Frieden attempts to do so. Seeking to determine why five Latin American countries responded differently to similar external conditions in the 1970s and 1980s, he finds that the divergence reflects policy variations that

are the result of choices made by social groups [whose] economic interests . . . are central to their political choices. . . . The causal arrows are straightforward: economic interests lead groups to engage in political behavior that affects the evolution of national politics. . . . Policymakers provided more resources to those who exerted more pressure on them and . . . economic interest groups exerted pressure on policymakers in direct proportion to what they had to gain or lose from policy and to the ease with which they could mobilize.[34]

[34] Frieden, *Debt, Development, and Democracy,* 7–8.

247

CONCLUSION

Frieden offers a sectoral explanation of the groups' different interests and capacities for collective action. What matters are the asset-specificity and concentration of the sectors in which the groups are located: the more asset-specific a sector, the more interested sectoral actors are in government policy; the more concentrated the sector is, the easier it is for them to mobilize politically.

But Frieden's argument has the limits common to all society-centered explanations. His economic actors have autonomous interests, but his politicians are merely responsive; the economic actors' interests and capacity for action vary by sector, but state interests, absolute capacity, and autonomy do not.[35] Thus, Frieden argues that in order to explain outcomes, the analyst should follow a four-step program, in which the tie between group desires and outcomes is assumed to be unproblematic and the state to be perfectly flexible:

> Identify the policy preferences of individuals and firms. . . . Determine how they are grouped into politically relevant social forces. . . . Trace the aggregation of organized interests in the context of existing institutions, as they seek to obtain their preferred policies. . . . Determine and trace pressures for institutional change [that produce] new government policies and political institutions.[36]

But as sectoral analysis predicts and the cases show, stateness varies. In high/high cases, societal actors' desires become policy in part, as Frieden says, because of the intensity of actors' interests and the extent of their ability to mobilize, but also because the *inflexibility* of state institutions gives politicians a *state* interest in defending the status quo. In low/low cases, societal actors are less interested in state policy and less capable of molding it, but such states' greater autonomy and absolute capacity also permit their leaders to restructure—to deny the requests of elites and to pursue policies that promote the national welfare, though they do not yet have a constituency. The cases thus suggest that we need an explanation *with* and *of* structures *and* agents, with institutions *and* interested individuals.

Gourevitch attempts to derive such an explanation in *Politics in Hard Times* by first exploring the divergent responses of Britain, France, Germany, Sweden and the United States to economic crises after 1873, 1929, and 1973. He identifies five policy packages among

[35] Ibid., 26–27, 38.
[36] Ibid., 28.

248

which states can choose when facing external shocks, and seeks "to map out the patterns of support which have formed around the various programs" in order "to trace, across countries and within particular countries, how alliances among social actors form, crumble, and reform" before "the stress of international competition on different 'branches' or 'sectors' of the modern economy."[37] On the basis of this effort, he then assesses "the vast universe of theories provided by modern social science," which he simplifies "into five families of argument": production profile, intermediate associations, state structure, economic ideology, and international system explanations.[38]

Like other sectoral approaches, however, the one provided by Gourevitch is incomplete for my purposes. He tells a good story about "why countries chose particular policies" and shows why the alternative explanations are underdetermining: actors' desires are no indication of their power; intermediate associations arguments, like the associations themselves, merely mediate between society and the state; explanations based on state structure are context-specific; ideological explanations say little about periods of rapid change; and explanations centering on the international system seldom specify "how and through what mechanisms" international forces shape politics.[39] But Gourevitch also recognizes that the key is to establish the relationship among approaches, though the method of testing alternative explanations and specifying their relative weights, as a hard scientist might, is out "because satisfying the conditions of experimentation is impossible."[40] Instead, he offers an aggregation of explanations, revealing the virtues of each in a detailed comparison. Thus, though he builds his argument, layer by layer, from sectoral bases, he is ultimately bound by the limits of existing approaches and unable to go beyond them.

That is why I began this book with the assertion that we need a new approach. And I would claim that sectoral analysis meets the basic requirements I established for a new approach. It links the international and domestic arenas with a single logic. It explains the interests of public and private individuals, their prospects for collective action, the effects of the organizations they form when they can collaborate, and the effects of the absence of such organizations when they can-

[37] Gourevitch, *Politics in Hard Times*, 10–11, 20.
[38] Ibid., 54–66.
[39] Ibid., 54–66, quotes on 35, 65.
[40] Ibid., 66.

not. It enables us to categorize states' ties to international markets, and so specify the restructuring project they must undertake and gauge its difficulty. It lets us judge states' autonomy and capacity to make the needed changes, the resources available to them, and the location and potency of resistance. Finally, it permits cross-sectional and longitudinal comparisons because it explains change (or stasis) within and among states.

What Next? A Research Agenda for Sectoral Analysis

This book is just a start. There are several important lines of inquiry to be pursued if sectoral analysis is to be more than simply an interesting possibility. Analytically, I am still bothered by the imprecision of the high/high and low/low ideal types and the whole question, carefully evaded here, of what lies in between. Sectoral analysis will be useful only if it says interesting things about the majority of cases that lie between black and white, but until we better understand "what variables are doing the theoretical work," as Stephan Haggard puts it, the shades of gray will be indistinguishable. Sectoral analysis also does fine with technologically and organizationally stable sectors such as mining and estate crops, but it will need refining if it is to embrace the computer, telecommunications, and biotechnology industries, as well as other rapidly changing industries at the cutting edge.[41]

Further empirical research should extend in at least two directions. First, since sectoral analysis stands or falls on whether *intra*sectoral variation is low, we need more country cases and intrasectoral, comparative studies of the type Terry Karl has done of Venezuela and the petro-states. We also need intrasectoral, comparative studies of unions, business organizations, and tax authorities. And we need intrasectoral, comparative studies that investigate if, where, and under what conditions factor substitution, organizational innovation, and state support can nurture different sectoral forms that are stable and internationally competitive. Second, we need to examine how, and to what effect, different sectoral political economies interact. Although single-sector Third World countries are the norm, the major players

[41] With apologies to Gourevitch, see Kenneth Gilmore, "Politics in Hard Drives: Comparative Responses to Technological Crises in the Computer Industry" (Ph.D. dissertation in progress, Rutgers University); and Herbert Kitschelt, "Industrial Governance Structures," *International Organization* 45 (Autumn 1991): 453–93.

in the international economy—Brazil, China, India, and the advanced industrial countries—are multisectoral.[42]

Whether further research will bear me out is uncertain, but I have done my best to provide a logically consistent argument and to apply it as honestly as possible to real world cases. As you reflect on my work, therefore, I again request that you ask both How well do the facts of the cases fit the sectoral model? *and* Is there an alternative that provides a more accurate, more general, more parsimonious explanation to account for this breadth of cases and materials? If you find my argument sound, I hope you will extend it. If you find sectoral analysis wanting, I hope you will offer your own answer to the big question: What determines which states, under what conditions, will be able to do how much to further development and improve their standing in the international division of labor?

[42] For a marvelous example of such interaction, see Richard Bensel, *The Political Economy of American Industrialization, 1877–1900* (Princeton: Princeton University Press, forthcoming).

Interviewees

KOREA (MARCH–MAY 1986, MAY 1988)

Bae Ie-Dong, Deputy Director, International Department, Federation of Korean Industries

Cha Sang-Pil, Executive Vice-President, Korean Chamber of Commerce and Industry

Cho Kyu-Ha, Senior Managing Director, Federation of Korean Industries (previously with Bank of Korea)

Choi Jang-Jip, Assistant Professor, Department of Political Science, Korea University

Chung Jai Suk, Dean, Graduate School of Management Information Systems, Hankuk University of Foreign Studies (previously with the Bank of Korea and the Ministry of Reconstruction; first Director of the Economic Planning Board; Minister of Commerce and Industry)

Han Jae-Yeul, Executive Vice-President, Korean Federation of Small Business

Kim Kihwan, President and Chairman, Ilhae Foundation (previously Vice-Minister of Trade and Industry)

Lee Kuy-uch, Senior Fellow, Korean Development Institute

Lim Dong Sung, Managing Director, Korean Traders Association (previously with the Bank of Korea)

Minn Choong-Kee, Director, International Affairs Department, Korean Chamber of Commerce and Industry

Minn Wan-Kee, Director, Marketing Department, Korean Chamber of Commerce and Industry

Sung H. J., General Manager, Trade Cooperation Department, Korean Traders Association

Whang In-Joung, Senior Fellow, Korean Development Institute

SRI LANKA (MAY–JUNE 1986)

B.E.S.J. Bastiampillai, Dean of the Arts Faculty and Professor of History, University of Colombo

Nihal Canekeratne, Professor, Department of Politics, University of Colombo

P. Devaraj, Director, Congress Labor Foundation (Ceylon Workers' Congress)

A. A. Justin Dias, Permanent Secretary, Ministry of Industries and Scientific Affairs; Chairman, Sri Lanka Standards Institute; Managing Director of the Sri Lanka Tire Corporation, the State Fertilizer Corporation, and Sri Lanka United Motors (previously with the Central Bank of Ceylon)

L. Fernando, Director of National Planning, Ministry of Finance and Planning

Serala Ilangakoon, Secretary General of the Planters' Association of Ceylon, Ceylon Planters' Provident Society, Estate Staffs' Provident Society, Planters' Benevolent Fund of Ceylon, and Sri Lankan Planters' Benevolent Fund

Ranee Jayamahu, Deputy Director of Economic Research, Central Bank of Ceylon

V. Kanesalingam, Associate Director, International Studies, Marga Institute (Sri Lanka Centre for Development Studies)

S. Kulantunga, Director General, Sri Lanka Export Development Board (previously with the Department of Agriculture, the Ministry of Communications, the Academy of Administrative Studies, and the Export Promotion Secretariat)

W. D. Lakshman, Head, Department of Economics, University of Colombo

S. Laneroll, Chairman, Sri Lanka Export Development Board (previously with Unilever and the Ministry of Planning; organizer of the Export Promotion Secretariat; United Nations International Trade Center)

Patrick Panabokke, Superintendent, Geragama Estate, Pilimatalawa

Gerald Peiris, Professor, Department of Politics, Peridiniya University, Kandy

Kolitha Ratnayaka, General Manager, Janatha Estates Development Board

T. Sambasivam, Deputy Director General, Sri Lanka Tea Board

Nimal Sanderatne, Director of Economic Research, Central Bank of Ceylon (previously with the Ministry of Trade and Commerce and Assistant Director, South East Asian Central Banks Training Center)

Colvin de Silva, retired, formerly Minister of State Plantations

W. M. Tilakaratna, Permanent Secretary, Ministry of Finance and Planning (previously with the Central Bank of Ceylon and the International Monetary Fund)

Dayasiri Warnakulasooriya, founder, owner, and manager, Midaya Ceramics Company; winner of the 1982 President's Export Award

ZAMBIA (JULY–AUGUST 1986)

J. A. Banda, Senior Economist and Senior Trade Promotion Officer, Foreign Trade Department, Ministry of Commerce and Industry

Brian S. Baynes, Director of Finance, Zambia Consolidated Copper Mines

Hellins V. Chabi, Director, Manifold Global Fund; Director, African Commercial Bank (previously with the Ministry of Local Government, the Tobacco Board, the Finance and Development Corporation, and INDECO)

Peter Chanda, Superintendent, Personnel Administration Services, Zambia Consolidated Copper Mines

Dennis Kampamba, Assistant Superintendent and Chief of the Personnel Research Division, Copper Industry Services Bureau

N. Kataya, Commercial Manager, Metals Marketing Corporation of Zambia

E. C. Kaunga, Director of Corporate Planning, Zambia Industrial and Mining Corporation (previously Head of the Department of Economics, University of Zambia; Permanent Secretary of the National Commission for Development and Planning; Permanent Secretary of the Ministry of Finance)

Samuel Lungu, Assistant Secretary General for Administration and

Organization, Zambia Congress of Trade Unions (previously served on the Livingston Municipal Council and was Shop Steward of the Livingston Fire Brigade; also General Secretary of the Municipal Workers Union; General Secretary of the Zambian United Local Authorities Workers Union; and Zambian representative to the Organization of African Trade Union Unity)

James Mazyopa, Director of Research, Zambia Congress of Trade Unions

Francis S. Mphepo, Managing Director, National Cash Register Company (Zambia), and President of the Lusaka Chamber of Commerce

James M. Mtonga, Permanent Secretary of the National Commission for Development Planning

John Mwanakatwe, Senior Partner of MMW and Company; Director of the African Commercial Bank (was the first Zambian to hold a position in the Zambian national civil service; representing the United National Independence Party, was a Member of Parliament; also Junior Minister of Labor and Mines, Minister of Education, Minister of Mines, Director of the Civil Service, Minister of Finance, and Chairman of the Commission on Salaries and Terms of Service)

Ackim Mwanza, Economist, Investment Policy Division, Public Finance Section, National Commission for Development Planning

Dominic Mwimba, Assistant Superintendent, Industrial Relations, Copper Industry Services Bureau

Nyambe Namushi, Assistant to the Chief Executive, Zambian Industrial and Commercial Association

Esau S. S. Nebwe, Permanent Secretary, Ministry of Finance (previously Permanent Secretary of both the Ministry of Commerce and Industry and the Ministry of Power, Transport, and Communications)

Bwalya E. Ng'andu, Superintendent, Human Resources, Zambia Consolidated Copper Mines

Chiselebwe Ng'andwe, Director and Chief Executive, Small Industries Development Organization (previously Head of the Department of Economics, University of Zambia)

Martin Sakala, Deputy General Manager, Economic Research, Bank of Zambia

Koshita Shengamo, Deputy General Secretary, Mineworkers Union of Zambia (previously with the Ministry of Community Development)

Simeo Benson Siame, Director, Investment Policy Division, National Commission for Development Planning

256

Max D. Sichula, Director of Human Resources, Zambia Consolidated Copper Mines

Neziah Tembo, retired, was the first President as well as Senior Trustee and Treasurer of the Zambia Congress of Trade Unions

Bernard Yamba-Yamba, Group Industrial Relations Manager, Copper Industry Services Bureau

Index

Absolute capacity, 7, 8, 13–14, 35; in Costa Rica, 204; in Korea, 119; in sectors compared, 13–14; in Sri Lanka, 155; in Zambia, 66

Accelerated Mahavelli Scheme, 177, 181

African coffee and tea producers, 151, 197

Agency, issue of, xi

Agrarian Revolution (Paige), xii, 3n.2, 246–47

Agriculture, export, 246–47; in Costa Rica, 187, 188, 189, 203–4, 219–20, 222; in Sri Lanka, 145. *See also* Coffee production; Tea industry

All-Ceylon Estates Labor Federation, 165–66

Ameringer, Charles, 184n.1, 200n.54, 201n.58, 201n.61, 207n.79, 209nn.84–85, 211n.91, 216n.107, 217n.109, 221n.122

Amsalem, Michel, 55n.24, 58n.35

Amsden, Alice, 97n.4, 97n.6, 98n.8, 101n.22, 103, 105n.39, 110n.57, 111n.62, 125, 129n.110, 131n.112, 134n.126, 136n.134, 137n.136, 139nn.146–47, 240n.19, 244, 245

Anderson, Leslie, 199n.51, 207n.79, 211n.89, 224n.134

Anglo-American Corporation (Zamanglo), 56, 77

Arias Sánchez, Oscar, 189

Asset/factor (in)flexibility, 10, 13, 23, 24, 34, 35; in coffee production, 199–200; in copper mining, 62–63, 70; in

light manufacturing, 110, 117–19; in tea production, 153–54

Athukorale, Premachandra, 144n.5, 145n.9, 146n.14, 163n.71, 176n.121, 177n.122, 177n.124, 179nn.131–34, 180n.139

Authoritarian governments, 20

Autonomous agencies, in Costa Rica, 207. *See also* Bureaucracy

Autonomy, 6–7, 14–15, 20; of state in Costa Rica, 214–17; in Korea, 129–31; in Sri Lanka, 168–74; in Zambia, 83–85

Balakrishnan, N., 146n.12, 155nn.40–41

Balassa, Bela, 112n.64, 113n.68, 240n.17

Baloyra-Herp, Enrique, 228n.5, 229n.7

Banana industry (Costa Rica), 186, 213, 214

Bandaranaike, Dias, 148n.21, 158n.51, 176n.118, 178n.127, 180n.139

Barlett, Peggy, 190n.22, 191nn.24–25, 193n.34, 199nn.51–52, 206n.77, 211n.89

Barriers to entry, 109, 114; in coffee production, 191, 193; in copper production, 51–53; in light manufacturing, 109; in tea plantations, 149–50, 151

Barriers to exit, 32–33, 34, 47; in high/high sectors compared, 37–38; in international market, 25; and tax institutions, 36

Bates, Robert, 70n.82, 73n.91, 74n.94, 75n.99, 76, 79n.110, 80n.116,

Cornell Studies in Political Economy

EDITED BY PETER J. KATZENSTEIN

Collapse of an Industry: Nuclear Power and the Contradictions of U.S. Policy, by John L. Campbell

Power, Purpose, and Collective Choice: Economic Strategy in Socialist States, edited by Ellen Comisso and Laura D'Andrea Tyson

The Political Economy of the New Asian Industrialism, edited by Frederic C. Deyo

Dislodging Multinationals: India's Strategy in Comparative Perspective, by Dennis J. Encarnation

Rivals beyond Trade: America versus Japan in Global Competition, by Dennis J. Encarnation

Democracy and Markets: The Politics of Mixed Economies, by John R. Freeman

The Misunderstood Miracle: Industrial Development and Political Change in Japan, by David Friedman

Patchwork Protectionism: Textile Trade Policy in the United States, Japan, and West Germany, by H. Richard Friman

Ideas, Interests, and American Trade Policy, by Judith Goldstein

Ideas and Foreign Policy: Beliefs, Institutions, and Political Change, edited by Judith Goldstein and Robert O. Keohane

Monetary Sovereignty: The Politics of Central Banking in Western Europe, by John B. Goodman

Politics in Hard Times: Comparative Responses to International Economic Crises, by Peter Gourevitch

Closing the Gold Window: Domestic Politics and the End of Bretton Woods, by Joanne Gowa

Cooperation among Nations: Europe, America, and Non-tariff Barriers to Trade, by Joseph M. Grieco

Pathways from the Periphery: The Politics of Growth in the Newly Industrializing Countries, by Stephan Haggard

The Politics of Finance in Developing Countries, edited by Stephan Haggard, Chung H. Lee, and Sylvia Maxfield

Rival Capitalists: International Competitiveness in the United States, Japan, and Western Europe, by Jeffrey A. Hart

The Philippine State and the Marcos Regime: The Politics of Export, by Gary Hawes

Reasons of State: Oil Politics and the Capacities of American Government, by G. John Ikenberry

The State and American Foreign Economic Policy, edited by G. John Ikenberry, David A. Lake, and Michael Mastanduno

The Paradox of Continental Production: National Investment Policies in North America, by Barbara Jenkins

Pipeline Politics: The Complex Political Economy of East-West Energy Trade, by Bruce W. Jentleson

The Politics of International Debt, edited by Miles Kahler

Corporatism and Change: Austria, Switzerland, and the Politics of Industry, by Peter J. Katzenstein

Industry and Politics in West Germany: Toward the Third Republic, edited by Peter J. Katzenstein

Small States in World Markets: Industrial Policy in Europe, by Peter J. Katzenstein